BUSH TUCKER

BUSH TUCKER

AUSTRALIA'S WILD FOOD HARVEST

TIM LOW

Angus&Robertson
An imprint of HarperCollinsPublishers

Photographs appearing on preliminary pages:

Title page: waterlily (*Nymphaea gigantea*)

Opposite Contents page: native cherry (*Exocarpos cuppressiformis*)

Contents page: (from top to bottom) long yam (*Dioscorea transversa*); cunjevoi (*Alocasia macrorrhizos*)—fruits *not* edible; lilly pilly (*Acmena smithii*); mountain kangaroo apple (*Solanum linearifolium*).

AN ANGUS & ROBERTSON BOOK
An imprint of HarperCollinsPublishers

First published in Australia by Angus & Robertson Publishers in 1989
Reprinted in 1991, 1992
CollinsAngus&Robertson Publishers Pty Limited (ACN 009 913 517)
A division of HarperCollinsPublishers (Australia) Pty Limited
25 Ryde Road, Pymble NSW 2073, Australia

HarperCollinsPublishers (New Zealand) Limited
31 View Road, Glenfield, Auckland 10, New Zealand

HarperCollinsPublishers Limited
77– 85 Fulham Palace Road, London W6 8JB, United Kingdom

National Library of Australia
Cataloguing-in-Publication data:

Low, Tim. 1956–
  Bush tucker.

  Bibliography.

  Includes index.
  ISBN 0 207 16373 1.

    1. Food, Wild — Australia. I. Title.

574.6'1'0994

Designed by Leonie Bremer-Kamp

Typeset in Australia by Midland Typesetters, Maryborough
Printed in Australia by Griffin Press

5 4 3
96 95 94 93 92

FOR MY PARENTS, DELL AND BERNARD

CONTENTS

PREFACE

Bush tucker is a very special field of natural history, for it embraces both biology and ecology, both history and anthropology. It is "natural history" in its most literal sense—a blending of nature and history. In Australia the subject is enormously rich and varied in scope, for as well as the many foods of the Aborigines, it includes the plants and animals eaten by explorers, convicts, white settlers and Chinese labourers. Significantly, the wild foods of the immigrants were often different from those eaten by Aborigines. In addition, there are hundreds of plants in Australia that are known to be edible only from overseas accounts. These plants include introduced weeds used as vegetables by peasants in Asia and Africa, and native plants that are eaten in Asia or the South Pacific where they also occur. In all, the number of edible plants in Australia runs to several thousands,

although no-one has ever tried to compile a list. The variety of edible animals is much larger, as nearly all can be eaten.

Plants, both native and introduced, are the main focus of this book. Most wild food plants are easy to identify, and can be recognised simply and safely from the photos in this book. This is not, however, a book of identification, and the reader keen to taste wild foods is referred to my field guides, *Wild Food Plants of Australia* (1988) and *Wild Herbs of Australia & New Zealand* (1985), which identify native and introduced foods respectively. Both books are published by Angus & Robertson.

This book is written for non-botanists, and I have used the words "bean" and "lily" (and a few other words) in their broadest sense. A taxonomist might argue that the matchbox bean is not a true bean and that golden stars and

Taro (*Colocasia esculenta*).

Polynesian arrowroot are not lilies, but I have grouped them under these headings because they are closely related and, in the case of the lilies, ecologically equivalent. Any reader interested in the problems of defining lilies is referred to the *Flora of Australia*, volume 45 (published by AGPS).

Many people helped make this book possible. Thanks go to the staff of the State herbaria of Queensland, New South Wales, Victoria and South Australia, and to Dr Bob Johnson and Ralph Dowling especially. Mark Savage-Morton of the Cape York Wilderness Lodge, Doug Laing and Wendy Low provided hospitality. Judith McKay, Richard Robins and Bruce Cowell helped supply information and photos. Steve Page took me into the desert, and Grace Macintyre and Lennie Duncan showed me plants. Annette Read helped in so many ways. Lastly, I thank those inspired men and women of the nineteenth century who so vividly recorded Australian colonial life, and especially those who wrote sympathetically of the Aborigines, whose traditional ways are fast disappearing.

Several of the chapters in this book are adapted from articles published previously in the magazines *Australian Natural History* and *Nature & Health*. They are: Wild Orchids, published as "Ground Orchids—Salute to Saloop" (*ANH* **22**[5]: 202–203); Pigfaces, published as "Succulents for Supper" (*ANH* **22**[5]: 262–263); Foods of the First Fleet (*ANH* **22**[7]: 292–296); On the Liru Trail (*ANH* **22**[9]: 420–422); The Yarrabah Way (*ANH* **22**[12]: 558–559); Wild Coffees (*N & H* **8**[4]: 10–13); Wild Teas (*N & H* **9**[1]: 27–31); Wild Nuts (*N & H* **9**[3]: 17–21).

Long-leaf mat-rush (*Lomandra longifolia*).

GLOSSARY

Aromatic: having a strong, almost resinous aroma that would be fragrant in smaller amounts.

Astringent: containing tannins, which produce a drying, puckering sensation in the mouth and cause the tongue and teeth to feel fuzzy. Banana skins, unripe persimmons and strong black tea are astringent.

The broad-leaved native cherry (*Exocarpos latifolius*) has an unusually developed pedicel which is red, fleshy and edible.

Berry: a juicy fruit with the seeds embedded in the pulp rather than inside a stone.

Bitter: the taste of old lettuce leaves, lemon seeds and bitter beer.

Bract: a leaf-like structure at the base of a flower.

Bulb: the base of a stem and its surrounding leaf bases, swollen with food reserves to form a storage organ.

Compound leaf: a leaf with its blade divided into separate segments, such as a palm frond, a rose leaf or a clover leaf.

Corm: a short stem base swollen with food reserves to form a discrete storage organ.

Fruit: botanically speaking, the seed-bearing structure of any plant. A botanist would call pumpkins, nuts and grass grains fruits. I use the word to refer to any fleshy edible structure containing or attached to seeds.

The bulbine lily (*Bulbine bulbosa*) bears an edible tuber, not a bulb as implied by its scientific name. Scientific names are often misleading.

Genus: A group of closely related species, all of which are given the same *generic* name (the first word of any scientific name).

Herb: any plant that does not produce a woody stem.

Leaflet: any of the segments of a compound leaf. A clover leaf has three leaflets.

Pedicel: the stalk of a single flower or fruit.

Pinnate leaf: a leaf divided into a series of smaller paired segments, like a palm frond or fern.

Potherb: old word for cooking herb or vegetable.

Rhizome: an underground stem, usually growing horizontally, and sometimes containing starch.

Stamens: the male parts of the flower, usually on stalks, containing the pollen.

Tuber: a storage organ formed by the swelling of part of an underground stem or root.

INTRODUCTION

Wild foods played a significant part in Australian history, keeping explorers alive and settlers healthy. They helped ensure Captain Cook's success, and the first colony's survival. Without bush foods Sturt would have fallen from scurvy in central Australia and Leichhardt would not have reached Port Essington.

Of Australia's foremost explorers, Cook and Leichhardt were especially dependent on wild foods. Captain Cook become the first mariner to conquer scurvy, after plying his crew with wild fruits and leaves at each landfall during his epic voyage. On returning to England Cook was awarded the Royal Society's highest honour—the Copley Gold Medal—for his paper on the prevention of scurvy. Cook had no qualms about trying unknown foods, and at Botany Bay and Endeavour River he sampled a range

of bush foods, including leaves of seashore shrubs, rainforest fruits, palm hearts and wild beans. Hardy in constitution, Cook wrote in his journal of eating taro roots "so bad that few besides myself could eat them".

The overland explorer Ludwig Leichhardt was almost obsessive about wild foods. Leichhardt may have been orally compulsive as there was little he would not place in his mouth. He was also an ardent naturalist, and his nature investigations sometimes included tasting the things he found. He more than once nibbled items found inside the innards of birds he had shot. Leichhardt made meals of fruits, tubers, gums, crows, pigeon feet, a sick dingo, lizards and emu gizzards. His flour, sugar and tea ran out many months before the expedition's end, and apart from a herd of bullocks, his men were entirely dependent on bush foods.

Of the emu, Leichhardt had this to say: ". . . the bones, heads, and necks were stewed: formerly, we threw the heads, gizzards, and feet away, but necessity had taught us economy; and, upon trial, the feet of young emus was found to be as good and tender as cow-heel." Photographed at Miles in Queensland.

Shinglebacks (*Tiliqua rugosa*) are among the few lizards that readily eat fruits and flowers, and their flesh is probably very tasty, although Ludwig Leichhardt, who ate one near the Mackenzie River in central Queensland, did not comment.

Cluster fig (*Ficus racemosa*) earns many a mention in Leichhardt's journal, sometimes as a source of alimentary distress, as in the following line: "The clustered fig-tree gave us an ample supply of fruit, which, however, was not perfectly mellow." Photographed near Townsville.

Near the Gulf of Carpentaria the daily menu was emu meat—two-and-a-half pounds (1.1 kilograms) for breakfast, the same for lunch, and another two pounds for tea. Leichhardt often pilfered supplies from Aboriginal camps, leaving trinkets in exchange. His men enjoyed much better health than the parties led by Sturt and Grey, who mostly eschewed wild foods.

Sturt almost died of scurvy in central Australia, and became so stricken he had to be carried about by cart. He endured violent headaches, painful joints, a sore mouth and spongy gums until he ate some fruits, probably wild tomatoes (*Solanum* species), on which local Aborigines were feeding. Sturt recovered quickly, and paid tribute to the small acid berries.

The convicts of the First Fleet were greatly stricken by scurvy, and wild foods provided the only cures. Native currants (*Leptomeria acida*) and the leaves of seashore plants probably saved many lives. Of those of us with convict ancestry, some would not be here except for those life-giving plants. Well into the nineteenth century outback drovers were using bush foods to stave off scurvy.

If bush foods were important to colonists, they were absolutely essential to Aborigines. The original owners of the land grew no crops, and let the bush supply all their needs. Over forty thousand years they became extraordinarily adept at locating tubers and snaring game. City Australians often assume that hunter–gathering was a life of endless toil, but the evidence suggests otherwise. Explorers often wrote of envying the Aborigines their free and easy life; and lost travellers living naked with Aborigines were sometimes reluctant to return to civilisation. The Aborigines seemed to be happier and to live more easily than nineteenth-century whites. Perceptive colonists noted that the "natives" could often supply their daily needs in only a few hours, a finding borne out by modern studies.

Tribal Aboriginal life was rich in meaning and integrity, but it could not survive the European onslaught. In south-eastern and south-western Australia, where Europeans first settled in large numbers, the Aboriginal way of life was obliterated. In the deserts and far north, black communities have survived to this day, along with much of their tribal knowledge, including bushcraft skills. To reconstruct traditional diet we can talk to living Aborigines and refer to articles by contemporary anthropologists. In the south-east and south-west we depend almost entirely upon nineteenth-century writers, whose testimony poses many problems.

Many colonial authors writing accounts of Australia talked of

Aboriginal foods, but such comments were usually superficial, second-hand and clouded by racism. Few observers were interested and competent enough to leave a record of value.

Explorers George Grey and Edward John Eyre penned extraordinarily detailed accounts of how Aborigines hunted game. Grey witnessed the hunting of possums by moonlight, the spearing of pigeons at thirty paces, and the arduous stalking of kangaroos. His prose is often picturesque, as, for example, in his account of frog catching: ". . . in summer a whole troop of native women may be seen paddling about in a swamp, slapping themselves to kill the mosquitoes and sandflies, and every now and then plunging their arms down into the mud, and dragging forth their prey. I have often seen them with ten or twelve pounds [4.5 to 5.5 kilograms] weight of frogs in their bag." Grey stressed that the Aborigines ate well, and could usually obtain, "in two or three hours, a sufficient supply of food for the day".

Colonial botanists Baron Ferdinand von Mueller and Joseph Maiden compiled long lists of plants eaten in Victoria and New South Wales. Maiden was director of the Sydney Botanic Gardens and much of his information was obtained second-hand from correspondents, which limits its value. In northern Australia, the protector of Aborigines Walter Roth supplied a remarkably comprehensive account of life in north Queensland. He listed a hundred shellfish and over two hundred food plants eaten.

The most interesting account of traditional Aboriginal life, I think, is *Tom Petrie's Reminiscences of Early Queensland*, transcribed by his daughter Constance at the turn of the century. Petrie was one of those enlightened colonists who not only acknowledged the common humanity of the Aborigines, but thought their culture in many ways superior. As a fifteen-year-old, Tom travelled with a hundred Aborigines from Brisbane to a Bunya nut feast in the Blackall Ranges, over 160 kilometres away. *Reminiscences* tells of the Aborigines gathering yams, honey and possums: "To them it was a real pleasure getting their food; they were so light-hearted and gay, nothing troubled them; they had no bills to meet or wages to pay.

Perhaps only an emergency food, the grey sedge (*Lepironia articulata*) has a woody rhizome yielding little starch. The only information we have about Aboriginal use is Walter Roth's comment "Tubers eaten" and the Yarrabah name for the plant.

Only from a list published by Baron Ferdinand von Mueller do we know that Aborigines once ate the tubers of pale vanilla lily (*Arthropodium milleflorum*). How many traditional food plants remain unrecorded? Probably dozens.

An 1840s shipwreck survivor, Barbara Thompson, probably fed upon the starchy tubers of *Ipomoea mauritiana*, a common vine on Prince of Wales Island where she lived with islanders for four years. The tubers are eaten in Asia. Photographed at Cape York.

even a mouthful of the horribly astringent starch. On the other hand, it is easy to discover edible fruits, such as flax lily berries (*Dianella* species), which appear on no-one's lists, but which must have been Aboriginal foods. Even in northern Australia the record is incomplete. I spent two months at Cape York sampling wild plants and discovered several foods that have not previously been listed. The tubers of the local *Ipomoea mauritiana* could even have served as staples. There are probably Aborigines somewhere in north Queensland who remember eating these long ago, but unless some record is made the information will soon be lost.

The wild foods of the pioneers are also very poorly known. Nineteenth-century historians showed little interest in recording the diet of squatters and outback drovers. A number of well-educated settlers left journals recounting their use of native game and fruits and leaves, but there is so little overlap among the plants they list that the record is obviously very incomplete.

The records that do survive are mainly from south-eastern Australia. As historical documents, they are sometimes difficult to interpret. What do we make of Mrs Lance Rawson's *Enquiry Book* of 1894, which provides recipes for stewed ibis, roast flying fox and small seabirds on toast? Rawson was a very adventurous woman, even for her times, and few readers may have followed her advice.

The same was perhaps true of the Reverend William Woolls, an early wild foods buff, who described a variety of "indigenous vegetables", but lamented that "there are persons who reside in the midst of plants which might be substituted for garden vegetables, and yet for the want of a little information, they never turn them to any practical account".

The Reverend Woolls and Mrs Rawson, like Cook and Leichhardt before them, were unafraid of unknown foods.

And there were no missionaries in those days to make them think how bad they were."

Using Petrie, Maiden, von Mueller and others, archaeologists have bravely tried to reconstruct the traditional diet of the south-east. The task is hopeless. The records are too fragmentary and enigmatic. Maiden lists storksbill tubers (*Pelargonium australe*) as foods, but though I have dug them at all stages of growth, and cooked them in different ways, I have never been able to swallow

Of small seabirds such as this wandering tattler, Mrs Lance Rawson noted that they "are never used as food simply because their delicacy and goodness are not known . . . All small birds are best cooked whole— that is, without being cut up at all. They can be run on a long skewer, and roasted, and laid on toast, or they can be stewed with herbs and a rich stock or gravy."

They did not harbour the belief, so widespread today, that tasting wild plants is dangerous. I find it extraordinary that most Australians hold an almost morbid fear that poison berries lurk in every forest grotto waiting to strike down the unsuspecting forager. In truth it is very difficult to be poisoned by plants. Most of the poisonous species warn of their danger by tasting bitter or acrid. Leichhardt foraged all the way from Brisbane to the Northern Territory without falling seriously ill. I have tasted many unfamiliar plants without ever being significantly poisoned. (My worst experience was a burning throat after biting a tuber.) The only really dangerous plants are those few mushrooms and fruits (see Australia's Wild Fruits chapter), and large seeds like those of cycads, which are both palatable and toxic. Also of concern are the large lilies such as cunjevoi and Polynesian arrowroot which are slow to warn of their toxicity—the stinging appears some seconds after the plant is chewed. These plants pose little risk to the forager and

should not detract from what is otherwise a safe and rewarding pastime.

Wild food foraging is certainly a fulfilling way to experience the Australian bush. By learning how to gather bush tucker, even in a token way, the forager comes to feel a special empathy for the bush, a sense that the forest is provident and friendly, that one is a part of some whole. This surely is how Aborigines and other foragers saw their world. It may be something they can help us rediscover.

The tuber of Polynesian arrowroot (*Tacca leontopetaloides*) contains a poison that will badly burn the throat. The tubers may be eaten, but only after being leached overnight in running water.

PLANTS & PEOPLE

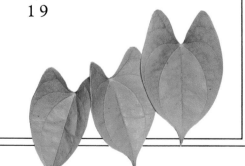

ON THE
LIRU TRAIL

Previous pages: Fields of wild grain fringe Ayers Rock. This woollybutt grassland (*Eragrostis eriopoda*) has probably fed generations of Aborigines. Few visitors to Uluru realise how rich in wild foods the surrounding desert is.

I visited Ayers Rock (Uluru) for the first time in 1987 and was so enthralled by the plant life that I didn't find time to climb the Rock. Almost five hundred plant species grow in the national park, an extraordinary number for a stretch of desert.

Near the Rock live Pitjantjatjara Aborigines, speaking their own tongue and maintaining many of their traditional ways. I hoped for some chance to make contact with these people, to learn first-hand about their desert foods.

An opportunity came in the Olgas when an Aboriginal ranger strolled by. I asked him about the sandalwood fruits (*Santalum lanceolatum*) I was photographing.

"Don't ask me!" he said. "I'm a steak and veges man. Apples and oranges are all I know about." It transpired that he was just down from Darwin on work experience. The desert was as new to him as to me.

My second encounter proved more enlightening. Two days later I contacted the ranger station, and four Pitjantjatjara women, national park rangers, led me along the famous Liru Trail which runs to the base of Ayers Rock. I was awed by these desert women. They strolled into the forty-degree heat without footwear or water, while I lumbered along behind, embarrassed by my heavy waterbottle.

These women proved extremely shy. They knew almost no English, and I was shocked by the cultural chasm dividing us. I have travelled many countries of the world, have stayed in remote villages in Borneo, but have never felt so distanced from other human beings—and in my own country. I could not fathom the body language of these people, much less the words they spoke.

To learn about their food plants was difficult. For the most part they could only point and say "bush tucker". They understood few of my questions and I

The bleak-looking mulga woodland (*Acacia aneura*) at the base of Ayers Rock is rich in wild foods. This narrow-leaf form of mulga is very different from the broad-leaf mulga of western Queensland and New South Wales.

could grasp little of what they said. Sometimes I could not decide if they were speaking Pitjantjatjara or English.

Once I pointed to a small leafy spurge (*Euphorbia* species) and asked if it was used as medicine. I knew that some desert tribes used spurge sap to remove warts. They seemed to confirm this usage, saying what sounded like "ointment, ointment", until I realised with a jolt that their actual words were "emu food, emu food"—the spurge was merely food for emus.

Our outing was only brief—before long their feet became scorched and we had to return. On the way back they drank most of my water. But I was content, for they had agreed to return the next morning.

On our second walk they showed me just how rich in wild foods a stand of mulga (*Acacia aneura*) can be. Mulga is the common outback wattle that forms vast, bleak thickets where few other plants can grow. A stand of mulga looks an unlikely place for wild foods, yet it was here the women best flaunted their skills. They beckoned me to a mulga stem covered in shiny red lumps—the sugary shells of a tiny sap-sucking bug, mulga lerp (*Austrochardia acaciae*). In the foliage they pointed out mulga "apples"—small green galls formed by wasp larvae. Most kinds of tree galls taste horribly astringent, but these were slightly sweet and very reminiscent of dried apple. On the lower mulga twigs the women found lumps of glistening gum, candy-hard outside, syrupy sweet within. These precious sticky treats ooze from mulga branches following insect attack.

The mulga trees were not in seed, or no doubt I would have been shown another important food. The small but highly nutritious mulga seeds were traditionally pounded into flour and baked as cakes. Dried mulga seeds comprise twenty per cent protein and almost ten per cent fat. At a different time of year I would also have seen the

To outback bushmen the mulga apple was "a great dainty", according to colonial botanist Joseph Maiden. The "apple" is actually a gall surrounding a small wasp grub.

Red lerp (*Austrochardia acaciae*) is eaten straight from mulga stems as a sweet treat, nowadays mainly by Aboriginal children. In times past large amounts were sometimes brought back to camp for leisurely eating.

Compared to most gums, mulga gum is good eating, having a distinctly sweet taste. Many gums are almost tasteless but make a pleasant jelly when soaked in water. Nineteenth-century descriptions suggest the sweetest gums came from south-western Australia.

Forgotten food: the Pitjantjatjara at Ayers Rock have largely forgotten that tar vine roots (*Boerhavia* species) were a traditional food. A pretty-coloured caterpillar that feeds on the leaves was also eaten.

edible fruits of the pale-leaf mistletoe (*Amyema maidenii*), which hangs limply from mulga boughs. In all, five different foods, four of them sweet, on one species of tree!

But this was not the end of the lesson. In open spaces between the stands of mulga I was directed to clumps of woollybutt grass (*Eragrostis eriopoda*) and pigweed (*Portulaca oleracea*), two of the desert's most important foods. After rain these small plants produce copious seed which Aboriginal women ground into flour and baked as loaves.

While photographing the pigweed I was reminded of a comment by colonial botanist Joseph Maiden, who wrote in 1889, "One would suppose that so small a seed would scarcely repay the labour of collecting", although he conceded that the Aborigines "get in splendid condition on it".

Nutrition tests by Sydney University show why. Pigweed seeds outscore wheat and rice on almost every nutrient. They yield 18.5 per cent protein, compared with 11.5 per cent for wholemeal bread and only 6.9 per cent for brown rice. Woollybutt seeds are just as impressive,

One of several trees known as sandalwood, *Santalum lanceolatum* has aromatic wood which was once exported to China. The sandalwoods of Asia are related species of *Santalum*, with a similar aroma.

with 17.4 per cent protein and an iron content of thirty-one milligrams per hundred grams, compared with a mere 3.2 milligrams in wholemeal flour. By any reckoning, these are impressive foods.

Growing alongside the pigweed were wild tomatoes (*Solanum* species), a very important desert food, and tar vines (*Boerhavia* species), small herbs with triangular leaves. I know from Aboriginal food lists that tar vine taproots were widely eaten, so I was surprised that the oldest woman shook her head dismissively when I pointed out one of these. But a disagreement later broke out, and one of the other women approached and said that tar vines *were*

used as foods, "in olden times". This was a salutory lesson, for it showed that despite the obvious expertise of these women, some of their traditional knowledge has been lost.

The Liru Trail winds to a close at a bitumen road close to Ayers Rock. We walked through stands of woollybutt grass to the base of the Rock where stands of sandalwood shrubs grew, their blue-grey drooping leaves shimmering in the heat. These shrubs produce tasty purple fruits, relished by the Pitjantjatjara (and by white rangers), although emus take most of the crop. These shrubs had lost most of their fruit from a violent hailstorm a few weeks previously. Sandalwood seems to need the extra runoff from the Rock, for I didn't see shrubs in the surrounding countryside, although they were common in the Olgas along gully lines.

One other fruiting shrub grows at the base of Ayers Rock or, rather, on the Rock itself. This is the small-leaved rock fig (*Ficus platypoda*), a scrawny shrub or sprawling tree that produces hundreds of sweet gritty figs. Aborigines in some areas stored the dried figs for future use, but we gladly ate all we could find.

My tour of the Liru Trail was specially arranged, but public walks are run almost every week. Thousands of Australians and overseas visitors have now been introduced to Pitjantjatjara foods. For me it was an exceptional experience, and I hope one day to return for an extended desert walk. I hope the women have forgiven me for my clumsy and no doubt offensive attempts at communication. Next time I shall make sure I have mastered some Pitjantjatjara words, and especially their rules of social etiquette. I owe them that much, at least.

Around caves and boulders at the base of Ayers Rock, the small-leaved rock fig (*Ficus platypoda*) bears its small juicy figs. The plants grow as sprawling shrubs, their sinuous roots twining among the rock crevices.

THE
YARRABAH WAY

The dainty flowers of *Fenzlia obtusa* fade with age, adding to the charm of this small shrub of north Queensland shores. The flowers are followed in autumn and winter by tiny, sweet, egg-shaped fruits.

In cultivation for hundreds of years, the red yam (*Dioscorea alata*) is now found throughout the tropics of the world. It was introduced by islanders into Australia and now runs wild both in north Queensland and in Torres Strait, where it is called "dob".

Across the harbour from the Esplanade at Cairns stands a rugged, heavily forested mountain range. It is Cape Grafton, once the home of the Kungganji Aborigines and now incorporated into Yarrabah Aboriginal Reserve.

Yarrabah township was set up under odious circumstances. It was a Church of England "orphanage" for half-caste children seized from Aboriginal camps around Cairns. These children were denied all traditional knowledge and were segregated from the eighty or so tribal Aborigines still living on the Cape. The latter became "rice Christians", sitting in on Yarrabah church services in exchange for food.

Given its sorry history, Yarrabah seemed an unlikely place to learn about traditional Aboriginal foods. When I visited the reserve last year I was warned not to expect much. My guide for the day was Darryl Pollard, the groundsman at Yarrabah school. He drove me along a sandy road to a weedy patch of open forest on the edge of town.

I was astonished by the first plant he showed me. It was a vigorous vine with bright green heart-shaped leaves, trailing over a dead fallen tree. I recognised it as an Asian yam, *Dioscorea alata*; Darryl called it "red yam" after the colour of its big edible tuber.

Darryl said he had recently bought land and was planting out red yam "seeds" (actually aerial tubers, or bulbils). His grandfather had advised planting a flat stone under each yam to ensure it grew outwards and not deep into the soil. Darryl was surprised to learn that the yam was not a traditional Aboriginal food. There were more surprises in store for both of us.

The next plant he showed me was the flowering shrub "gungjinarra" (*Fenzlia obtusa*). Its beautiful pink flowers are followed by tiny sweet fruits.

We then came across two plants unknown to Darryl, but which I knew from historical accounts to be old Aboriginal foods. One was wombat berry (*Eustrephus latifolius*), with small sugary tubers; the other was painted orchid (*Geodorum neocaledonicum*), which has tuberous rhizomes. I felt strange, showing an Aborigine traditional Aboriginal foods, but Darryl didn't seem to mind. He liked the taste of the orchid.

We then came upon another yam, this time the native long yam (*Dioscorea transversa*), Darryl's favourite. With his grandfather and cousin, Darryl takes turns digging a deep angular hole with a shovel to extract the long starchy tuber. Even with the three of them it can take more than half an hour to dig up one tuber, which is then cleaned and boiled. The top of the yam is replanted to ensure a future, although smaller, tuber.

Darryl gave the name of this tuber as gungjinarra. When I protested that this was the name of the fruiting shrub we

saw earlier, he became confused, and said he wasn't sure about the old yam names.

We then came upon a sweet sandpaper fig (*Ficus opposita*), one of my favourite bush fruit trees. But Darryl surprised me by saying the fruits were never eaten, they were "parrot food".

We looked at a few more plants, then drove back to town where Darryl introduced me to his grandfather, Mervyn Smith. Mervyn at least knew the red yam was introduced—"by South Sea Islanders". But he puzzled me by talking about "New Zealand apples", white fruits of the rainforest that supposedly came from New Zealand.

Later on, a local schoolteacher, Rob Hinxman, was able to clear up much of my confusion. Rob has studied the local food plants and maintains a native foods garden in the schoolyard. He hopes to foster interest among schoolchildren in their traditional culture, and believes the way to do this is through their stomachs.

Rob said that knowledge of many food plants, such as the figs, had been lost over the years, and that names of other plants had been transposed. The shrub *Fenzlia obtusa*, originally called gungunyu, has taken on the name of the long yam,

Framed by lush foliage, Darryl shows me a vine of the red yam, one of his favourite bush foods. The yams grow to enormous sizes.

Most tuberous plants, such as this long yam (*Dioscorea transversa*), replace their tuber each year. The new tuber is crisp, white and much tastier than the old.

The long yam of northern Australia produces strings of tiny white buds towards the end of the wet season, followed by insignificant flowers, then by characteristic winged seed pods, the shape of which is important for identification.

Sweet and tangy when ripe, the fruit of the yellow plum (*Ximenia americana*) contains deadly cyanide while still green. In India the leaves have been cooked as a vegetable; they were not used by Aborigines.

which grows in the same sandy soils. Similarly, the traditional name of what I call yellow plum (*Ximenia americana*) is now applied to the lollyberry (*Salacia chinensis*). Both plants grow together in the same strand vegetation, and lollyberry, a creeper, often twines through the branches of the yellow plum. The latter, having forfeited its traditional name, is now called "wild apricot".

Rob could not explain why the native white apple (*Syzygium forte*) is called New Zealand apple. As for the Asian yam, he suggested it came in with island labour imported to build mission houses long ago.

Yarrabah is a strong community and locals talk with pride of the "Yarrabah way". I can see that where wild foods are concerned, the Yarrabah way is about practicalities, not the preservation of tradition. Darryl eats red yams because he likes the taste, not because it's the traditional thing to do. Indeed, he could teach me next to nothing about Aboriginal tradition.

Even so, I greatly enjoyed my outing with Darryl. It was a real pleasure to go foraging with a kindred spirit. I suppose I should feel sad that so much of Yarrabah's traditional knowledge has been lost. But I prefer to dwell on the richness of the culture as it exists now, and to marvel at its hybrid origins.

Among the food plants Rob Hinxman has planted is the wongi tree (*Manilkara kauki*), a species not native to Yarrabah and unknown to Darryl's forebears. If ever there is a renaissance of Aboriginal culture in Australia, as seems likely, I can imagine a twenty-first-century anthropologist visiting Yarrabah, and being solemnly shown a wongi plum as a traditional food, with a traditional Yarrabah name. In such ways are traditions made.

Aptly named lollyberries (*Salacia chinensis*) look like jaffas and taste sublime; they are found on a vine that twines through shrubbery on tropical beaches. As the scientific name indicates, this plant also grows in China.

FOODS OF THE
FIRST FLEET

Two hundred years ago Captain Arthur Phillip landed at Port Jackson and founded the colony of New South Wales. His settlement devastated the local Aboriginal tribe, despite his friendly overtures. Phillip hoped to bestow upon the "natives" the gift of agriculture, confiding in his journal that "to put into the hands of men, ready to perish for one half of the year with hunger, the means of procuring constant and abundant provisions, must be to confer upon them benefits of the highest value and importance".

But Phillip was wrong. The Aborigines were not starving; his own men were. Agriculture, that "means of procuring constant and abundant provisions", failed dismally on Sydney's infertile soils. English supply ships came late, and ravenous convicts and soldiers were forced to forage like Aborigines, plucking

at leaves and berries to supplement dwindling rations.

The wild foods eaten by the colonists are recorded in journals written by several of the First Fleet officers. These lists make fascinating reading, for they mention many plants that were not Aboriginal foods. The colonists had no appreciation for the Aboriginal way of life and showed no interest in their foods—of which fern starch was probably the most important. Instead, they sought out foods in the image of English vegetables, and the discoveries they made were largely their own.

First Fleet officers saw Sydney Aborigines eating "fern root", possibly that of bungwall (*Blechnum indicum*). This fern was probably common in Sydney's swamps, but as the swamps have vanished it's impossible to be sure of this. Photographed at Childers, Queensland.

Left: "Chicken claws" and "sausage plant" are country names for samphire (*Sarcocornia quinqueflora*), a leafless plant that photosynthesises through its fleshy stems. Photographed at Lota, Queensland.

A plant of many guises, sea celery (*Apium prostratum*) convinced First Fleet officers it was two species of plant, a celery and a parsley. This broad-leaved variety of sunny beaches scarcely resembles the narrow-leaved form of inlets (at right), but intermediate plants show that they are the same species. Photographed in South Australia.

Right: This slender-leaved form of sea celery is much tastier than the broad-leaved form of coastal dunes. Herbs that grow in the shade, as this plant does, are usually less fibrous and bitter than their sun-loving kin. Photographed by the Brisbane River.

David Collins, judge advocate of the colony, recorded that "wild celery, spinach and parsley fortunately grew in abundance about the settlement: those who were in health, as well as the sick, were very glad to introduce them into their messes". Lieutenant William Bradley listed "wild spinage, samphire & parsley & small quantity of sorel and wild celery, all of which with the leaves of several kinds of bushes were eaten by us for want of better vegetables which were not yet supplied from the Gardens". Another (anonymous) officer wrote that "Parsley, balm, a sort of sage, and other European herbs, were found of natural growth". And the surgeon George B. Worgan listed "Balm, Parsley, Samphire, Sorrel, & a kind of Spinnage, but all indifferent in kind".

These lists make intriguing reading, for with a knowledge of the present Sydney flora it is possible to identify most of the plants. The "samphire" of Bradley and Worgan is the easiest to ascertain. It is Australian samphire (*Sarcocornia quinqueflora*), a small saltmarsh herb very similar to European samphire (*S. stricta*), which the English used at that time as a pickle. Fifty years later, explorer George Grey ate this plant on the Gascoyne River in Western Australia and pronounced it "a fair article of food for hungry men".

The "parsley" and "celery" of Collins and Bradley are two varieties of sea celery (*Apium prostratum*)—one a wispy

form from shady swamp margins, the other a broad-leaved form of open dunes. This herb was first eaten by Captain Cook at Botany Bay as a scurvy cure and later settlers cooked it in soups.

The "spinach" was New Zealand spinach (*Tetragonia tetragonoides*), another of Cook's scurvy cures and a plant made famous by Joseph Banks, who took seed to England where it was grown as a summer spinach (see Colonial greens chapter). It was first encountered by Cook in New Zealand, hence its name. The "sort of sage" can only be grey saltbush (*Atriplex cinerea*), a seashore shrub with edible leaves the same colour, shape and size as English sage, although it is unrelated. Grey saltbush, known as "Botany Bay greens", helped sustain Tasmania's first colonists during a famine in 1807.

I cannot guess the identity of the "balm", but the sorrel of Bradley is probably one of the wood sorrels (*Oxalis* species), small herbs of woodlands and dunes with lemony clover-like leaves. These were gathered as vegetables and salad plants by later colonists, and in Tasmania were even baked in tarts in place of fruit.

The striking feature of this list is that nearly all these vegetables are seashore plants. Only the wood sorrel can be considered a true forest herb, although it, too, often grows by the sea.

Captain Phillip's colony had over a thousand hungry mouths to feed, and stocks of these vegetables soon grew scarce. Foraging parties roamed as far as Botany Bay, where they risked death from the Aborigines. Yet the wild greens were not especially popular with the officers, judging from the comments in their journals. Captain Watkin Tench condemned them as "too contemptible to deserve notice". The convicts were no doubt less fussy, and perhaps sometimes overindulgent, as suggested by a line in Collins's journal: "One poor [convict] woman about this time killed herself by over-loading her stomach with flour and greens which she had made into a mess."

But to the Aborigines, these plants were probably not foods at all. They do not appear on recent or historical food lists from eastern and southern Australia. Indeed, the historian Daniel Mann could write in 1811 that Botany Bay greens were "esteemed a very good dish by the Europeans, but despised by the natives".

I think I know why. The wild greens eaten by the English (except the sorrel and celery) were halophytes—plants that store salt in their tissues. This salt leaches out during boiling, producing a tender and succulent vegetable. But traditional Aborigines had no cooking pots and no way to boil foods. They

The "sage" of First Fleet officers was grey saltbush (*Atriplex cinerea*), a plant now rare around Sydney. Shrubs are either male or female; the brown spike identifies this plant as a male. Photographed at Gippsland Lakes.

Saviour of the scurvy-stricken, the remarkable New Zealand spinach (*Tetragonia tetragonoides*) deserves a book all of its own. Called by colonists "spinach, spinage, or spinnage", it was the first Australian food plant to be grown in Europe. Photographed at Bass Point near Kiama.

would have avoided the halophytes, which are too salty to eat raw.

Halophytes thrive on saline soils, where they absorb enough salt to render them distasteful to most herbivores. Plants of other habitats use other means to deter plant eaters—they produce distasteful tannins, essential oils, or poisonous alkaloids. Substances like these are not removed by boiling and the leaves of forest-growing plants are rarely edible. For this reason the plants of the seashore were disproportionately important to the founding colony.

Wild leaves are the foods most mentioned in the journals, but there are references to other bush foods, especially "sweet tea" and wild currants (*Leptomeria acida*).

Scurvy was rampant during the first year of convict settlement and various bush plants were tried as cures. Two that became very popular were native sarsaparilla (*Smilax glyciphylla*), the leaves of which were made into sweet tea, and the small acid fruits of native currants. Recent nutrition tests show that native currants are a modest source of vitamin C, containing about twenty milligrams per hundred grams (compared with fifty milligrams in oranges), but that sweet tea was probably almost useless.

The fruits of native currants, plucked from a broom-like shrub on the ridges around Sydney, were very sour eating, and taken more as medicine than food. Later settlers put them to good use in jellies. Mann lauded the jelly as "uncommonly fine", and colonial botanist Joseph Maiden was unusually generous in praise: "The jelly is of a pale colour, and has a delicate flavour when the acidity has been masked by a sufficiency of sugar. It is an excellent substitute for red-currant jelly, as I can testify."

Other fruits eaten by the First Fleeters are difficult to identify. Governor Phillip mentions "a small wild fig, and several cherries", and surgeon Worgan records a fig and berries (plus the inner shoot of the cabbage palm, *Livistona australis*). The fig is probably Port Jackson fig (*Ficus rubiginosa*) or perhaps sandpaper fig (*F. coronata*), and the "cherries" of Phillip are probably native cherry (*Exocarpos cupressiformis*), and magenta lilly pilly (*Syzygium paniculatum*), first discovered by Captain Cook at Botany Bay. A "small purple apple" described by Captain Tench may be the magenta lilly pilly; he also refers to edible orchid roots. Worgan mentions a "shrub bearing a fruit like a sloe"—probably the native plum (*Podocarpus spinulosus*).

Common appleberry or dumpling (*Billardiera scandens*) was certainly among the first of the berries to be used, for it is

First Fleet surgeon general, John White, declared currant bush fruits (*Leptomeria acida*) "a good antiscorbutic; but I am sorry to add, that the quantity to be met with is far from sufficient to remove the scurvy". Photographed at Waterfall near Sydney.

Of common appleberry (*Billardiera scandens*), colonial botanist Joseph Maiden claimed, "It has been eaten by children ever since the foundation of the Colony, and is one of the earliest known food-plants of the blacks." Photographed on Black Mountain, Canberra.

mentioned as edible in James Smith's *A Specimen of the Botany of New Holland* published in 1793, only five years after the colony's founding.

Sampling wild plants is not as risky as most people think, and mishaps among the Europeans were few. One convict was poisoned by cycad seeds (*Macrozamia* species), which were eaten by Aborigines only after careful preparation. And Governor Phillip and Surgeon General John White were stricken by the beach bean (*Canavalia rosea*), as White's journal of 1790 recalls: "As we proceeded along a sandy beach, we gathered some beans, which grew on a small creeping substance not unlike a vine. They were well tasted, and very similar to the English long-pod bean. At the place where we halted, we had them boiled and we all eat very heartily of them. Half an hour after, the governor and I were seized with a violent vomiting."

Phillip and White probably nibbled on these beans before boiling them, for the cooked beans are known to be edible. Captain Cook ate them at Endeavour River and I have tried them a number of times without mishap.

Two hundred years have passed since the founding of Sydney and botanically much has changed. Gone are the beaches and forests of the inner suburbs; coasts have become infested with weeds; and Botany Bay has become an industrial wasteland.

But hardy forests still linger in the outer suburbs, where the food plants of the convicts can still be found. Native sarsaparilla vines twine along shaded gullies, currant bushes bear fruit along the ridges in autumn, and New Zealand spinach thrives on coastal cliffs beneath runoff from houses and drains. These plants are our heritage, no less than Cadman's Cottage or Fort Denison. In their cycles of growth and fruiting a part of our convict past lives on.

After being made ill by beach beans (*Canavalia rosea*), Surgeon General White and Governor Phillip drank warm water which, according to White, "carrying the load freely from our stomachs, gave us immediate relief". Photographed at Burleigh Heads on the Gold Coast.

BEVERAGES

WILD
COFFEES

Coffee is the world's most popular hot drink, though nowadays many people are turning to caffeine-free alternatives. Unfortunately these are expensive to buy, but it is easy to make your own. Coffee alternatives are a delight to prepare and the choice of ingredients is limitless. Kitchen vegetables, Aboriginal food plants, even garden weeds can be used.

The blue-flowered herb called chicory (*Cichorium intybus*) is the most famous coffee substitute. Grown commercially in New Zealand and on Phillip Island near Melbourne, it is an ingredient in most coffee substitutes. In nineteenth-century Europe chicory was enormously popular as a drink and adulterant, and even chicory itself was adulterated. Food regulations were not then as they are now, and there are horrendous tales of

chicory in England being mixed with ground roast beans, dog biscuits and bread, sawdust, baked livers of horses and bullocks, parsnips, cockroaches, oak bark, acorns and even iron rust.

Chicory drinks are still adulterated today, but the modern additives are more mundane (and listed on the label!). Most popular are rye, barley, carrots and beetroot. These crops are easier to grow than chicory and their starchy seeds or roots can be ground to an excellent coffee-like powder. Among native plants there are hundreds with starchy seeds or roots, and the potential for wild coffees is almost unlimited. But Australians are unadventurous with their foods and few of these have been tried.

That most eccentric of Australian explorers, Ludwig Leichhardt, was one of the first to dabble with native coffees.

Leichhardt's supplies gave out long before he staggered into Port Essington in the Northern Territory and for almost six months his men scavenged off the land. Leichhardt's convict companion, Mr Phillips, was especially partial to coffee, and he roasted and ground the seeds of several plants.

One of those used was Mackenzie bean (*Canavalia papuana*), a common creeper of river banks with pink flowers and pods like broad beans. Phillips pounded the seeds, and Leichhardt found they made "an excellent substitute for coffee, which I preferred to our tea, which, at that time, was not very remarkable for its strength".

Leichhardt also made satisfactory coffees from seeds of the sacred lotus (*Nelumbo nucifera*) and kurrajong (*Brachychiton* species), the latter producing a "good beverage with an agreeable flavour".

But not all of Leichhardt's brews were successful. Phillips downed a whole pint of wattle seed brew, despite Leichhardt's warning about its peculiar bitter taste. Phillips suffered "violent vomiting and purging during the whole afternoon and night".

And on Leichhardt's second expedition, Mackenzie bean coffee was again tried, with disastrous results. Expedition botanist, Daniel Bunce, exclaimed that "one dose of this beverage was sufficient, as it created violent vomiting and diarrhoea".

The quest for wild coffees is not so hazardous as these anecdotes might suggest. It is dangerous only where poisonous seeds or roots are used. Over the years I've prepared delicious coffees from all manner of native plants, and from garden weeds and vegetables, without ever falling ill.

Among native plants my favourites are the seeds of kurrajongs, prickly moses and beach bean. The kurrajong (*Brachychiton populneus*) is a majestic tree of eastern woodlands, especially common on inland plains, where it is well known to farmers. The leathery pods crack when ripe to expose rows of starchy seeds encased in irritating yellow hairs. These seeds were an important Aboriginal food, and the roots of the saplings were also eaten.

Prickly moses, or mimosa bush, (*Acacia farnesiana*) is a common shrub on roadsides and grazing lands in the northern half of Australia. Aborigines once sucked the pods and ate the seeds, and I have made these into a delicious coffee drink. Prickly mimosa is one of the wattles, easily recognised by its zigzag

The highly nutritious seeds of the kurrajong (*Brachychiton populneus*) yield eighteen per cent protein and twenty-five per cent fat. Aborigines ate the seeds as well as the sappy roots of young kurrajong trees.

Sticky-sweet pods of prickly moses (*Acacia farnesiana*) are browsed by cattle, which spread the seeds, and vast thickets of this native shrub have spread over grazing lands in Queensland and New South Wales.

stems and tiny pinnate leaves. The flowers have a strong sweet scent, and in France this plant is cultivated by the perfume industry.

Roasted seeds of various other wattles can be made into drinks, and some are now being marketed by the emerging native foods industry as coffee substitutes and ice-cream flavourings. The exact species used are trade secrets.

The coffee-making technique is much the same for all seeds and roots. After oven-roasting for about forty minutes, or dry-frying in a heavy pan, the seeds and roots are ground to a fine powder with a mortar and pestle. Roots should be scrubbed clean and coarsely grated before roasting, and must be watched closely, for they easily burn. The pieces are ready for grinding when brown, brittle and easily crumbled; they should not be allowed to turn black. The coffee should be stored in a plastic bag inside a small airtight container to prevent the aromatic flavouring oils from escaping.

My favourite wild coffee plants are those I can gather from my own suburb,

where they grow as weeds. Dandelions, catsears, salsify, chicory and swamp dock are all suitable.

Dandelion coffee is famous in its own right for its tasty flavour and mild diuretic effects. It's sold through health food stores but tends to be expensive, as the small roots yield only two or three cups of brew. Dandelion (*Taraxacum officinale*) is a common lawn weed in south-eastern and south-western Australia, easily recognised by its sunny yellow flowers on hollow unbranched stalks, and by its saw-toothed hairless leaves. It is sometimes confused with the common catsear (*Hypochoeris radicata*), which has wiry branching stalks and furry leaves.

Catsear also makes fine coffee, but the tiny roots yield only a single cupful, a poor return for the labour of digging, scrubbing, grating, roasting and grinding. Catsears are a very common garden weed—there are dozens in my garden. Like the dandelion, they have edible leaves, ideal for soups and quiches.

Few people are aware that chicory is a

One of our prettiest weeds, the salsify plant (*Tragopogon porrifolius*) sprouts showy violet flowers from clumps of grass-like foliage. A native of the Mediterranean region, it grows along road verges and rail embankments. Photographed near Warwick.

Since the 1500s the stout taproots of salsify have served as a vegetable. English herbalist John Gerard in 1597 declared it "a most pleasant and wholesome meate, in delicate taste far surpassing either Parsenip or Carrot".

common Australian weed. Although rarely seen about cities, it thrives in colonies along farm roads. It has metre-tall wiry flower stalks covered in pale blue flowers; these open only during the morning and paint a beautiful display along country lanes. Chicory is closely related to the dandelion, catsear and salsify, and all have edible leaves and roots and attractive flowers with strap-like petals. Chicory is the most popular for coffee, perhaps because its roots are so large, yielding up to fifteen cups each. They should be harvested while young, before flowering has advanced, or a woody unusable core develops inside. Chicory is often cultivated as a salad plant—its crisp inner leaves are relished for their bitterness—and the seeds can be bought from specialty stores.

Sunflowers (*Helianthus annus*) spring up along roadsides wherever passing trucks drop the seeds, as here at Roma in Queensland. First-generation weeds have a single stalk with an enormous flower, but subsequent generations revert to taller shrubby weeds with multiple stalks and smaller flowers.

An eerie weed, cleavers (*Galium aparine*) has bristle-covered leaves with a distinctly sticky feel. The seeds can be ground for coffee, and the young leaves cooked and eaten. Photographed near Adelaide.

Salsify (*Tragopogon porrifolius*), a wispy weed of roadsides in southern Australia, yields the most unusual wild brew. Salsify looks like a clump of grass, with two striking differences—the sap is milky, and the flowers are violet daisies. Salsify sports enormous taproots from which a dozen or more drinks can be made. What is unusual about salsify brew is its rich, sweet, chocolate taste. This comes from the breakdown of starch-like inulin into sugars and caramel, and the brew is too sweet to be passed off as coffee. Salsify "chocolate" is an excellent natural drink for children, and I like to sprinkle it over ice-cream as a flavouring. The roots also make an excellent vegetable, having a subtle seafood flavour. (The fishy aroma is said to fool cats, but mine remains unimpressed.) Salsify seeds can be bought from specialty stores, for this herb is sometimes cultivated.

Swamp dock is a common garden weed from which a tasty yellow coffee can be made. This plant is described in the Weeds chapter. Two other weeds make passable coffee—cleavers and sunflower. Cleavers (*Galium aparine*) is a bristly, sticky, twining, trailing weed with tiny paired seed pods. Cleavers coffee is made, not from the roots, but from the tiny seeds. Although much smaller than peas, these were a traditional coffee source in Europe. (The young leaves were also eaten.)

Sunflowers (*Helianthus annuus*) are grown widely for their oily seeds, used mainly in margarine. In farming districts the seeds fall from trucks and sprout along roadsides, brightening the verges with great golden blooms. The seeds crowded in the centre of each flower produce a delicious coffee, once used by North American Indians. Pawnee and Dakota Indians boiled the flower heads to extract an oil which they used to polish their hair.

To make wild coffee, one need not wander as far as the roadside or the bush. Fine coffees can be made from kitchen vegetables. Carrots, parsnips and beetroot are ideal; each produces a distinctive aroma-laden brew. Potatoes, however, should be avoided at all costs. I shudder to recall an experimental coffee I once prepared from grated roasted potatoes. It tasted like . . . potato chip soup!

WILD
TEAS

Tea was a valued commodity among Australia's explorers and colonists. Ludwig Leichhardt, ill-fated explorer of the north, declared in his journal that "Tea is unquestionably one of the most important provisions of such an expedition; sugar is of very little consequence, and I believe that one does even better without it. We have not felt the slightest inconvenience from the want of flour." Strong words, from one who was not even an Englishman!

Early bushmen and travellers coped with dwindling tea stocks by substituting native plants. Old journals and almanacs speak of many such alternatives for tea, often made from obscure forest plants. With renewed interest in tea substitutes inspired by the natural food movement, these indigenous brews deserve new scrutiny. They include some delightful drinks, rich and aromatic in flavour, caffeine-free, and costing nothing to harvest and prepare. Native teas grow in bushland everywhere, even close to major cities. Gathering them is fascinating and fun, for not only are they flavoursome, but they provide a living link to our pioneering past.

The very first and most famous Australian bush tea was the "tea tree" of Captain Cook. This was probably manuka (*Leptospermum scoparium*), a shrub or small tree found in south-eastern Australia and New Zealand (the name is Maori). In New Zealand Cook harvested this plant as a scurvy preventive, and even brewed beer from the branches and leaves. Early settlers found that many kinds of *Leptospermum* made satisfying teas, and these plants became known as "tea-trees". ("Ti-tree" is an alternative, but nonsensical, spelling.)

Opinions on these teas varied. One visitor to Van Diemen's Land (Tasmania) in 1832 exclaimed that "the leaves infused make a pleasant beverage, and with a little sugar form a most excellent substitute for tea". But J. O. Balfour, writing in 1845, complained that "its leaves I have seen made into a beverage called tea. It, however, was loathsome and had not the slightest resemblance to any known Chinese tea."

I have tried several native tea-tree teas and, apart from some with an awful turpentine taint, most were very pleasant, although more like lemon grass tea than Chinese brew. The best are manuka and lemon-scented tea-trees like *L. petersonii*. These are easily identified

Widely grown as an ornamental shrub, the lemon-scented tea-tree (*Leptospermum petersonii*) furnishes an excellent lemon-flavoured tea. The aromatic oils in the leaves consist mainly of citral and citronellal.

Dainty white flowers and blunt-tipped blue-green leaves identify the coast tea-tree (*Leptospermum laevigatum*), a very common tree of south-eastern beaches. A passable lemony tea can be made from the young leaves. Photographed in Sydney.

Aromatic tea can be made from the leaves of the paperbark tea-tree (*Melaleuca quinquenervia*). Aborigines stripped off sheets of the paperbark to roof their huts, and the women were often obliged to carry the sheets for long distances.

by the strong lemony scent of their leaves. In fact, the scent of crushed leaves is the best guide to most bush teas; and any that smell good will be safe to try.

The easiest place to find lemon-scented tea-trees is not in the bush, but growing on footpaths and in city parks, where they are widely cultivated.

The woolly tea-tree (*L. lanigerum*) was used by Tasmanian colonists in the 1830s. The coast tea-tree (*L. laevigatum*) is also worth trying. It is a common shrub or small tree forming dense thickets behind beaches in Victoria and New

South Wales. It grows wild at La Perouse, and behind Melbourne beaches in eastern Port Phillip Bay. The leaves are bluish green, with blunt tips and a lemony odour.

Tea-trees are shrubs or small trees with fibrous or papery bark and pretty cream, pink or white flowers with five rounded petals. They grow commonly in heathlands and along streams in south-eastern Australia.

Trees of the genus *Melaleuca* are also called "tea-trees", and were occasionally used for tea. The paperbark tea-tree (*Melaleuca quinquenervia*) makes a reasonable lemon-flavoured brew, although not of the standard of *Leptospermum* tea. Aborigines made drinks from nectar-laden melaleuca blossoms by steeping them in troughs of water.

Tea-tree (*Leptospermum*) tea became the most popular of colonial brews, but the first to be widely used was made from a little-known vine now known as native sarsaparilla (*Smilax glyciphylla*). In eighteenth-century New South Wales this plant, known as "sweet tea", was considered a precious medicinal product, and leaves were even exported to China.

The first convicts arriving in Sydney Town ailed badly from scurvy, and the surgeons of the fledgling colony looked to forest plants for cures. An infusion of sweet tea was deemed especially efficacious, and desperate men risked the spears of Aborigines to obtain it. Yet recent tests suggest the plant was probably useless.

In the 1800s sweet tea fell into disuse, although as late as 1860 the naturalist George Bennett was claiming it "would form an excellent beverage for the labouring class during the sultry summer months, and well-suited to the climate". I do not find the tea at all tasty, and when scurvy declined this "cure" evidently faded into obscurity.

As Australian settlement unfolded, an increasing variety of plants was tried as tea. Most of these, like the tea-trees, were very aromatic, but a few actually tasted like Chinese tea. The native tea (*Verticordia pennigera*) of Western Australia was one of these; bidgee widgee (*Acaena anserinifolia*) another.

Bidgee widgee is a dainty herb with shiny toothed leaves and bristly seed pods, found creeping across sand dunes and forest clearings in south-eastern Australia. A drink brewed from the leaves tastes quite tea-like, and almost certainly contains some tannin. Quaker missionary James Backhouse recorded in

1843 that "The leaves of this plant are said to be an excellent substitute for tea. It is common every where, and well known from the annoyance caused by its seeds hooking to the stockings, and other parts of the dress of pedestrians."

Another colonist, P. Cunningham, claimed that burnet (bidgee widgee) tea was so similar in "taste and qualities to the bohea [low-grade Chinese tea], that one individual actually mixed a chest of bohea with dried burnet, and the difference between them could not be detected".

An even better tea was made from the leaves of white correa, known also as Cape Barren tea (*Correa alba*). Nineteenth-century sealers in Bass Strait made a delicately fragrant brew from the mildly aromatic leaves. I once greatly impressed a Japanese friend by serving her white correa tea. Correa is a wind-sheared shrub of coastal dunes in south-eastern Australia. Identifying features are the grey-green, furry leaves with whitish undersides, borne in pairs, and the pretty flowers with only four curly white petals. I strongly recommend the tea made from this plant.

Australia has other correas, all with fragrant leaves, and some are probably usable as tea, although ones I have tried had a turpentine taint.

The turpentine taint is probably due

One of the best wild tea sources is white correa (*Correa alba*), a common shrub of southern shores with delicately fragrant leaves. Look for it at La Perouse, along Woollongong beaches (where this plant was flowering) and at Wilsons Promontory.

Left: A pretty herb with a dainty name, bidgee widgee (*Acaena anserinifolia*) makes a good substitute for Chinese tea. This plant was growing on a coastal sand dune at Lakes Entrance, Victoria.

Aromas can deceive: the crushed leaves of thyme myrtle (*Melaleuca thymifolia*) have a fragrant smell like thyme, but produce a tea with an awful resinous taint. Most of Australia's aromatic flora is rendered unsuitable for flavouring by unpalatable oils such as cineole.

It runs along the ground sprouting flowers that are postbox red, hence the name "running postman" (*Kennedia prostrata*). Settlers brewed tea from the leaves, and Aborigines reportedly sucked nectar from the flowers. Photographed in the Grampians.

to the aromatic oil cineole. All aromatic leaves take their flavours from aromatic oils (also called essential oils—see Wild Herbs and Spices chapter). Examples include menthol in peppermint, anethole in aniseed and fennel, and citral in lemon and lemon grass. Whether a bush tea is enjoyable or not depends on the combination of oils. Eucalyptus leaves nearly always contain distasteful oils such as cineole and pinene, and even where the predominant flavour is peppermint or lemon, the leaves are unsuitable for tea. Another example: I once flavoured a cheese dish with the leaves of the thyme myrtle (*Melaleuca thymifolia*), a small shrub with a pleasant thyme-like smell, but the dish was ruined by a turpentine taste. So despite Australia's rich flora of aromatic plants, the prospects for tea making are limited. The experience of the Aborigines is of no use here: traditional Aborigines did not boil water and never made teas.

Settlers discovered their teas by trial and error, brewing up any leaves with a promising aroma. In Tasmania, the *Hobart Town Almanac* of 1834 listed the popular tea plants as Cape Barren tea, hoary tea-tree, black wattle (*Acacia decurrens*) and sassafras (*Atherosperma moschatum*). The use of wattle leaves is unusual, for of eight hundred or so Australian species only one other has been used as tea—the sweet wattle (*A. suaveolens*) of eastern Australia.

In southern Australia the creeper called running postman (*Kennedia prostrata*) was brewed into a bland tea. The plant has pea flowers coloured post-box red, and rounded leaflets in threes.

Alpine heaths yielded two tea substitutes—the lemon-flavoured alpine baeckea (*Baeckea gunniana*), and yellow kunzea (*Kunzea ericifolia*), known also as native tea, once regarded as a tonic. Bushmen in the coastal scrubs used the bark of yellow sassafras (*Doryphora sassafras*) and the spicy leaves of scrub ironwood (*Austromyrtus acmenoides*).

Other teas were made from native mints and wild basil (see Wild Herbs and Spices chapter).

Bushmen in Australia are still experimenting with wild teas. At Cape York I met a Bavarian, Albert Auer, who had ridden a horse from the Darling Downs to Cape York, partly retracing the steps of fellow German Ludwig Leichhardt. Albert showed me a wild "mint" from which he had often made fragrant tea during his trek. The "mint" was hyptis (*Hyptis suaveolens*), an aromatic weed from South America, widely used as a flavouring overseas.

Sometimes plants were used, not as substitutes for Chinese tea, but as additives to enhance the aroma. Fruit-salad plant (*Pterocaulon sphacelatum*), with its curious smell of apples or fruit salad, was used to enrich teas in South Australia. Drynan's House Australia presently market an Old Bush brand eucalyptus tea, "a blend of finest black teas and the oil from the broad-leaved and narrow-leaved peppermint eucalyptus trees, combining a mild aromatic minty flavour with a fresh invigorating note".

For those interested in sampling alternative teas, there is no need to venture into the bush. Tea substitutes grow all about in the form of common

Hyptis (*Hyptis suaveolens*), an invidious weed of tropical forests, has one redeeming feature—its leaves make a fragrant, wholesome tea. Photographed during the wet season at Cape York.

garden plants. For instance, maidenhair fern leaves (*Adiantum* species) produce an excellent substitute for Chinese tea; they have been used in this way in Ireland. Use a large handful for a small pot of tea, but don't overdo it or the brew will taste like seaweed. (Incidentally, tea has been made from seaweed—in Korea dried sponge weed [*Codium* species] is used.)

The maidenhair ferns of Australian gardens are native plants, growing also in our damp coastal forests. Common maidenhair (*Adiantum aethiopicum*) frequents every State of Australia and New Zealand, and also grows in Africa, as its name indicates.

Other garden plants plucked overseas as teas include honeysuckle (*Lonicera japonica*—flowers as well as leaves), tulip tree (*Liriodendron tulipifera*) and Oswego tea or bee balm (*Monarda didyma*). The tea plant is itself a species of Camellia but I have not heard of garden camellias being used.

Japanese Buddhists supposedly make a sweet tea from hydrangea shoots (*Hydrangea* species), but a tea I prepared was anything but sweet. The raw buds are poisonous, causing diarrhoea and nausea. Photographed at Marrickville in Sydney.

Below: An unwelcome intruder in native forests is Japanese honeysuckle (*Lonicera japonica*), which sprouts along creeks in damp eucalypt forests, usually near human disturbance. In Asia the leaves and petals are dried for tea, which can be bought from Vietnamese stores in Australia.

One Japanese book I consulted claimed that new leaves of garden hydrangeas (*Hydrangea macrophylla*) contain a natural sweetener called phelloductin. Japanese Buddhists brew a sweet tea from the leaves for ceremonies. I made a tea but was disappointed to find it was not sweet.

Another tea I tried was a brew of pine needles (*Pinus radiata*). American backwoodsmen make teas from several conifers, and some are rich in vitamin C. My first pot of pine needle tea had an appalling resinous taste and smelt like toilet cleanser. I tried a second time using only the new, yellow-green, innermost needles, and the tea proved a pleasant surprise, having a mild lemony taste.

The hybrid bottlebrushes (*Callistemon* species) grown for ornament in Australian gardens also produce pleasant lemony tea. Although they are native shrubs, there appears to be no record of settlers using them.

If you would like to try dabbling in native teas, keep in mind the following:

Most bush teas are weaker than

Chinese tea and larger amounts are needed. Crush the leaves in a teapot or cup and simply pour on boiling water. Most teas improve when left to brew, but some deteriorate markedly, becoming too astringent, bitter or aromatic. Experiment freely with doses and brewing times. Also, some teas taste better when made from fresh leaves, although most do not. Bush teas can also be mixed with Chinese tea for interesting blends. Try blends using any of the following: tea-tree leaves, bottlebrush leaves, white correa leaves, dried jasmine flowers, apple blossoms.

Brewing bush teas is a fascinating pastime for there is still much to discover. I once read in a musty old book that Jamaicans make tea from jequirity bean (*Abrus precatorius*) leaves. This vine grows near my home but I had never dared touch it because the red-and-black

seeds contain one of the most potent toxins known. I bravely nibbled a leaf and was delighted to discover it had a sweet liquorice flavour (colonists called the plant "wild liquorice"). I prepared a tea, expecting a rich aniseed brew, but was rewarded instead with a dull liquid tasting like grass clippings. I have tried making this tea several times since, using both fresh and dried leaves, but cannot capture that liquorice taste. I shall keep trying, however, for that is the challenge of bush teas—to capture new and special flavours, using only boiling water and a handful of wild leaves. Perhaps one day we will justify the optimism of Australian botanist–explorer A. Meston, who in 1904 declared: "There is good reason to believe we possess plants which would take the place of tea, and berries which would make a beverage superior to coffee."

So many different bottlebrushes (*Callistemon* species) and their hybrids are grown in gardens that it is difficult to identify specimens such as this one, planted in a park in Brisbane. All varieties seem suitable for tea making.

FRUITS

AUSTRALIA'S
WILD FRUITS

Previous pages: One of the many lilly pillies, the white apple (*Syzygium cormiflorum*) of northern rainforests produces its watery fruits from along its trunk and branches, as food for fruit bats. Photographed at Cape Tribulation.

Fruits are the glamour foods of the Australian bush. No other foods are more tasty and refreshing, nor more alluring to the eye. So appealingly are fruits packaged that they make tubers, leaves and seeds look dull and stodgy.

Fruits look good because they are meant to be eaten. They are a parcel of food offered to a bird or fruit bat in return for dispersal of the seeds. Fruits (and nectars) are the only parts of plants designed expressly to be eaten, and this accounts for their superior flavours, bright colours and attractive presentation.

If some bush fruits taste bitter or distasteful (or are poisonous), this is only because they are designed to feed birds, not people. The tastier fruits, like the large jungle figs and plums, are often those targeted at fruit bats, whose palates seem much like our own.

Aborigines ate literally hundreds of different kinds of fruits and berries,

ranging from tiny mistletoe fruits to the hefty great morinda, which smells like rotten cheese dunked in sewage. The everchanging calendar of ripening bush fruits must have done much to enliven a sometimes narrow diet. Bush fruits were also valued by early settlers, who made jams and preserves from wild heaths, raspberries and other forest dainties.

Many urban Australians, trying wild fruits for the first time, are repelled by the odd flavours. Fruits that taste salty, aromatic or bitter can take some getting used to. The range of flavours far exceeds that found in tubers, seeds or leaves, or, for that matter, cultivated fruits.

Nonetheless, the wild food forager will find much that is familiar. Common appleberry (*Billardiera scandens*), a widespread forest vine, has berries that taste like stewed Granny Smiths, and the fruits of muntari, or crab apple, (*Kunzea pomifera*) have a dried apple texture and taste. Pigfaces (*Carpobrotus*) taste of salty

A delightful aniseed flavour distinguishes sweet appleberry (*Billardiera cymosa*), one of South Australia's tastiest fruits. The berries turn soft and transluscent when ripe. Photographed at Beachport, South Australia.

represented by no fewer than forty-five species, mostly found in jungles, although only a few can compare in flavour with the commercial fruit, which has thousands of years of cultivation and improvement behind it. Australia also has native persimmons (*Diospyros* species), a native cucumber (*Cucumis melo*), and fruits in the same genus as the eggplant, tamarillo and potato (*Solanum* species). We even have a Queensland rainforest fruit (*Prunus turnerana*) closely related to the prune.

Anyone who tries foraging for native fruits soon discovers that some habitats yield much more than others. In rainforest in season every second tree seems to drop fruit. Seashore vegetation is also rich. Eucalypt forests offer poor returns, except in tropical woodlands where bat fruits like cocky apple (*Planchonia careya*) and nonda (*Parinari nonda*) are common.

The differences are easily explained. Many fruit-bearing plants are opportunists—plants that grow in new clearings created by tree falls, floods or fires. In the holes rent in rainforests by huge fallen trees, nearly all the shrubs and vines that sprout are fruit bearers. Presumably the best way to get seeds to such clearings is to coat them with food for birds. Seashore scrubs are rich in fruits because stormy winds striking the soft dunes create new clearings, and plants carrying fruits (and wind-borne seeds) are the first to colonise. In the outback, fruiting plants regenerate burnt ground in the same way.

Rainforest is a special case because many of the tall forest trees, as well as the opportunists, bear fruit. Ecologists believe that seed-eating beetles and rats are a special problem, and that here again the best way to scatter seeds is via animal vectors. Australia's rainforests have plenty of these, ranging from bowerbirds and pigeons to cassowaries and bats.

Fruit bats are most numerous in

strawberries and nitre fruits (*Nitraria billardieri*) of salted grapes. Sweet appleberry (*B. cymosa*) smacks of aniseed.

Some wild fruits taste like the kitchen equivalents because they are closely related. Our native limes, of which there are five species in rainforests (genus *Microcitrus*) and one out west (*Eremocitrus glauca*), are true members of the citrus family. In our rainforests grow three native passionfruits (*Passiflora* species) and three wild bananas (*Musa* species). (One of the latter has been collected only once, on the Daintree River in the 1870s, and is feared extinct.) Australia has six native raspberries (*Rubus* species), four in rainforest, one in open woodland and one in Tasmania's Alps. They are closely related to the raspberry of Europe, and the pink-flowered native raspberry (*R. parvifolius*) tastes much the same. Figs (*Ficus*) are

Pink-flowered native raspberry (*Rubus parvifolius*) is close kin to the cultivated raspberry. The plant has an odd distribution, occurring also in Japan, where wine has been fermented from the juicy berries. Photographed at Cunninghams Gap west of Brisbane.

In Australia the ulcardo melon, or native cucumber, (*Cucumis melo* subspecies *agrestis*) is just one of many outback fruits. But in Asia and Europe, where this plant also grows, it has been bred into all manner of melons and cucumbers, including the cantaloupe.

Closely related to the tamarillo and looking much the same, the mountain kangaroo apple (*Solanum linearifolium*) grows in cool woodlands in south-eastern Australia. The fruit has a tangy, almost sickly taste and bursts when ripe. Photographed on Black Mountain near Canberra.

The tall groundberry (*Acrotriche aggregata*) is one of the many heaths found in eastern Australia, usually on hillsides. The tiny flowers and pea-sized sour fruits are borne on the undersides of the stems.

Top right: The minute fruit of the peach heath (*Lissanthe strigosa*) is difficult to pluck from the prickly foliage. Colonial botanist Joseph Maiden was exaggerating when he said, "They are the size of small peas, white and sweet." Photographed in the Adelaide Hills.

Below: The dazzling flowers of the flame heath (*Astroloma conostephioides*) are followed by small apple-flavoured fruits which develop within the flower calyx. Emus eat both the flowers and fruit. Photographed in the Grampians.

northern Australia, where many fruits dispersed by them can be found. These are usually big, soft and smelly, and usually lack the bright colours of bird fruits (bats are colourblind). Most of our cultivated tropical fruits, including mangoes, bananas and pawpaws, were originally bat-dispersed.

In the chapters that follow I describe the typical fruits of Australia's rainforests, seashores and deserts. There is one other habitat where fruits are common, and which is worth considering here in detail—heath.

Heaths are the low scrubs found on infertile sandy soils in eastern and south-western Australia. It is difficult to explain why, but these coarse scrubs are rich in fruit-bearing plants. Where the soil is slightly better, as in the forests around Sydney, heath plants grow beneath a canopy of eucalypts. Although of small size, heath fruits were popular foods of early colonists, who gathered them for jams and pies. On Kangaroo Island, heath fruits are still used in this way.

Heath takes its name from the heathers, the small shrubs of English heaths. Heathers are not native to Australia (although one species grows as a bushland weed), but Australia has its counterparts in the Australian heath family (Epacridaceae). Australian heaths are small shrubs with small, hard, often spiny-tipped leaves, and dainty flowers. A majority of species bear small edible fruits, and these were popular snack foods of Aborigines and settlers.

Around Sydney the popular heaths were the native cranberry or wild apple (*Lissanthe sapida*), five corners (*Styphelia triflora*), and native cranberry (*Astroloma humifusum*), which botanist Joseph Maiden said in 1898 was "the delight of small boys to this day". The cranberry was said to make an excellent preserve when mixed with native raspberry.

Another famous group of heathland plants are the geebungs (*Persoonia*

In the Royal National Park just south of Sydney, strings of ripening pine-leaf geebungs (*Persoonia pinifolia*) attract hungry foxes, whose scent can be detected near the trees.

Colonial botanist Joseph Maiden said of the cranberry heath (*Astroloma humifusum*): "The fruits of these dwarf shrubs are much appreciated by school-boys and aborigines. They have a viscid sweetish pulp, with a relatively large stone." Photographed in the Grampians.

species). The green fruits of these are unusual in being designed for dispersal by kangaroos and other mammals, having chewy flesh and very hard stones. Geebungs were important foods of Aborigines but were little appreciated by white settlers because of their cotton-wool texture. The Brisbane suburb of Geebung is named after this fruit, although the word itself apparently comes from a New South Wales tribe.

The native cherries (*Exocarpos* species) are probably the best-known of heathland fruits; many people have seen pictures of the unusual double-jointed

As tart as lemon juice are the small green fruits of the leafless currant-bush (*Leptomeria aphylla*), here growing on an ancient sand dune at Flinders Chase National Park on Kangaroo Island. The small shrub has stems ending in spines.

Typical of the geebungs, the broad-leafed geebung (*Persoonia cornifolia*) has greenish egg-shaped fruits with a persistent spike-like style. The flesh is stringy and sweet and surrounds a large woody stone. Photographed in Girraween National Park near Stanthorpe.

fruits, although few have actually tasted them. These fruits are discussed in the Native Cherry chapter.

Devil's twines (*Cassytha* species) are eery leafless vines that twine about heathland shrubs. The small fruits are edible but resinous.

Fruits of the common currant-bush (*Leptomeria acida*) were an important food of the First Fleet, and probably saved the lives of scurvy-stricken convicts, thanks to their modest content of vitamin C (see Foods of the First Fleet chapter). In Victoria and South Australia the spiny currant-bush (*L. aphylla*) of mallee heaths supplies a similar sour fruit, which colonial botanist Baron von Mueller described as "succulent, pleasantly acidulous and harmless".

In alpine heaths there grow several fruiting heaths, as well as the alpine ballart (*Exocarpos nanus*) and mountain plum pine (*Podocarpus lawrencei*). The interesting feature of alpine fruits is that nearly all are red. I believe this to be an evolutionary response by the plants to the shortage of fruit-eating birds at such altitudes. By evolving fruits of uniform size and colour the plants maximise the chance of these being found and the seeds inside dispersed. There are many

Tiny edible fruits can be plucked from the shrub of the mountain plum (*Podocarpus lawrencei*), a plant closely related to the brown pine, although the former's two-segmented fruit is much, much smaller. Photographed near Cooma, where it was growing alongside colonies of edible murnong.

more fruits found in Australia's heathlands, and hundreds more edible fruits in Australia overall.

Foraging upon such fruits has been one of my greatest pleasures. Contrary to popular wisdom, it is not especially dangerous to sample wild fruits, although the serious forager should be wary of the finger cherry (*Rhodomyrtus macrocarpa*) and tie bush (*Wikstroemia indica*), two species that are palatable but dangerous. (They are described in detail in my field guide *Wild Food Plants of Australia*. Finger cherry, found in north Queensland rainforests, has reddish, egg-shaped fruits containing several kidney-shaped seeds. Tie bush is a small coastal shrub with orange-red fruits five to fifteen millimetres long, and soft glossy green leaves two to four centimetres long.)

Over the years I have sampled more than a hundred different kinds of forest berries and fruits without ever being poisoned, even mildly. The experience of new flavours still excites my palate. But not all my pleasures have been gastronomic. I find myself continually

intrigued by the mysteries of seed dispersal of some of our fruits. Why are there so many fruits in the heathlands? Why do the berries of kangaroo apples always burst when ripe? And what kind of animal disperses the green, well-hidden fruits of the cranberry heath? With questions like these to be answered, and new flavours to be discovered, wild fruits are a naturalist's perpetual delight.

Probably poisonous, the fruit of the tie bush (*Wikstroemia indica*) turns tomato red when ripe. In South-East Asia, where this shrub is common, the fibrous bark has been spun into string. Photographed at Dee Why, Sydney.

NATIVE CHERRY

To nineteenth-century Englishmen Australia was a topsy turvy land where "dogs" hopped on hind legs and "water moles" sported duck's bills and laid eggs. Early historians believed this freakishness extended to the plant kingdom. W. C. Wentworth in 1819 exclaimed: "Such is the climate of Botany Bay; and, in this remote part of the earth, Nature (having made horses, oxen, ducks, geese, oaks, elms, and all regular and useful productions, for the rest of the world) seems determined to have a bit of play, and to amuse herself as she pleases. Accordingly, she makes cherries with the stone outside."

In the *History of New South Wales* (1801) a writer commented: "Of native fruits, a cherry, insipid in comparison of the European sorts, was found true to the singularity which characterizes every New South Wales production, the stone being on the outside of the fruit."

The "cherry" in question is the native cherry (*Exocarpos cupressiformis*), a well-known forest fruit, known also as wild cherry, forest cherry and cherry ballart. The fruits grow on a small leafless tree of open forests and heaths that has drooping foliage made up of pendulous, cypress-like stems. Despite its name, this small forest fruit is no relation to the European cherry (one of the stone fruits), but has affinities with the primitive mistletoes and the desert quandong. By the late nineteenth century, Australian colonial botanists were coming to the defence of the maligned native cherry. Joseph Maiden in 1889 wrote sadly of "the poor little fruit of which so much has been written in English descriptions of the peculiarities of the Australian flora. It has been likened to a cherry with the stone outside (hence the vernacular name) by some imaginative person."

Colonial traveller Mrs Charles Meredith thought poorly of the native cherry, and of Australian fruits generally: "The fruit, so celebrated among Antipodean contrarieties for having the 'stone outside,' is like a small yew-berry, but still less pleasant in flavour, with a hard seed growing from its end, fancifully termed the stone. Of all countries or climates, I think that Australia must be the most barren of useful natural products of the vegetable kingdom; for this miserable 'cherry' is the best specimen of its indigenous fruits, if not the only one."

Victorian botanist Baron Ferdinand von Mueller in 1877 explained the true structure of the fruit: "It . . . has been mentioned so often in popular works as a cherry-tree, bearing its stone outside of the pulp. That this crude notion of the structure of the fruit is erroneous, must be apparent on thoughtful contemplation, for it is evident at the first glance, that the red edible part of our ordinary Exocarpus constitutes merely an enlarged and succulent fruit-stalklet (pedicel), and that the hard dry and greenish portion, strongly compared to a cherry-stone, forms the real fruit, containing the seed."

A clearer explanation is provided by nature writer Edith Coleman in the *Victorian Naturalist* in 1934: " . . . that which is erroneously called the stone is really a one-seeded nut, hard and inedible. It is the fleshy stalk which we eat. What is commonly called the fruit, then, is really a swollen stalk, juicy and sweet to taste, while the so-called stone is the fruit."

Native cherry became one of the best-known of antipodean fruits, not only because it looked odd, but because most colonists liked the taste. R. Dawson in 1830 proclaimed the fruit to be "similar in colour to the Mayduke-cherry, but of a sweet and somewhat better quality, and slightly astringent to the palate; possessing on the whole an agreeable flavour. This, so far as I know, is the only natural production in Australia worthy the name of fruit, and the only one which a traveller would turn out of his road to pluck."

But some comments were derogatory. G. C. Mundy in 1852 spoke of the "cherry-tree . . . bearing a worthless little berry", and the surgeon P. Cunningham complained of cherries "destitute both of pleasant taste and flavour". D. D. Mann complained the fruit was nauseous and "nearly unfit to eat".

The journal of Governor Phillip mentions "cherries" eaten by the convicts and officers of the First Fleet, and these were probably the native cherry (although they may also have been lilly pillies [*Syzygium paniculatum* and *S. australe*]).

Labillardière, the French naturalist accompanying D'Entrecasteaux on his voyage in search of missing French mariner La Pérouse, was the first to scientifically describe the native cherry. He was on the coast of Van Diemen's Land (Tasmania) on 9 May 1792 when he recorded in his diary finding "an evergreen tree, which has its nut situated, like that of the acajou [cashew], upon a fleshy receptacle much larger than itself. I therefore name this new genus *exocarpos*."

Labillardière's excitement at his discovery was overshadowed by his fears that a leopard was stalking their camp that night. His journal recalls: "The cold had obliged us to kindle a large fire. Some of us were scarcely beginning to fall asleep, when we suddenly heard the cry of a beast of prey at a few paces distance. Our fire had probably been of greater service to us, in preventing this animal, which from the sound of its voice we believed to be a leopard, from approaching nearer, than we should have expected when we kindled it."

Labillardière thought the native cherry

Suckering from its parasitic roots, the native cherry (*Exocarpos cupressiformis*) forms groves of small trees, which are easily mistaken for forest oaks (*Allocasuarina* species). Settlers used the wood for turning and carving. Photographed at Spicers Peak south of Brisbane.

impediment to dispersal by birds. Writing in 1887 he mused: "Had the stone which grows outside been at the reverse end of the fruit the birds might have eaten the latter without interfering with the seed, but actually the stone first presents itself, and it is so small as to make it a matter of no moment to the bird whether it eats it or not."

If native cherries were popular with early settlers, we can be certain that Aborigines also ate them. Early writers confirm this, including Joseph Maiden, who noted that native cherries "afforded small, toothsome portions to the hungry blacks". Maiden was here referring to several kinds of native cherry, for there are another eight members of the genus *Exocarpos* in Australia, all with edible "fruits". (There are twenty-six *Exocarpos* species all told, found also in South-East Asia, New Caledonia, New Zealand and Hawaii. One species is even restricted to Lord Howe Island.)

Native cherry plants are typically shrubs with broom-like foliage and minute greenish yellow flowers. The leaves are either very slender, or small and scaly and soon fall away, presenting foliage like that of a she-oak or cypress. The green stems do the photosynthesis. Only the broad-leaved native cherry (*E. latifolius*) of northern and eastern Australia has leaves of typical shape. All the cherries have edible pedicels, although these may be red to pink, white, mauve or yellow.

What marks these plants as especially interesting is not their odd fruit, but their parasitic habit. They are root parasites, tapping the root systems of adjacent plants to draw off nutrients. This makes them difficult to grow and they are rarely seen in gardens.

The common native cherry (*E. cupressiformis*) is the best-known member of the group. It grows in hilly areas with open eucalypt forests, and on consolidated coastal sands, throughout eastern and southern Australia, and west

Bush medicine: the broad-leaved native cherry (*Exocarpos latifolius*) is used by many northern Aboriginal tribes as a medicine. On Groote Eylandt the bark was taken as an abortifacient, and in Dampier Land it was used to heal sores and cuts and to repel mosquitoes.

to be closely related to the cashew, an understandable association, as the latter also produces its seed at the end of a swollen stalk. Cashew "fruits" are much larger, the size of peaches, and have a sour pineapple-like flavour. They are sold in markets in Asia.

The seed of the cashew is dispersed by fruit bats which carry the fruits off in their teeth; by comparison the native cherry seed is spread by honeyeaters and other small birds who swallow the whole fruits. Nineteenth-century naturalist Donald MacDonald appreciated that this arrangement was not freakish, and no

Buffeted by desert winds, a broom ballart shrub (*Exocarpos sparteus*) grows in oak woodland close to Ayers Rock. The edible fruits of this species are red or pink.

Pale ballart (*Exocarpos strictus*) is the only native cherry, apart from the common native cherry, found in the Sydney region, where it grows on sandstone ridges. Photographed at Comfort Hill on the Sydney–Canberra road.

to Eyre Peninsula. From afar it looks remarkably like one of the forest oaks (*Allocasuarina*), but the foliage is more yellowish and drooping, and the plant forms clumps which are suckers from one tree. They grow to about eight metres.

The broad-leaved native cherry (*E. latifolius*), also called broad-leaved ballart, or mistletoe tree, grows in rainforests and coastal scrubs in northern and eastern Australia, as far south as Evans Head. Explorer Ludwig Leichhardt ate the fruits in north Queensland, and found they had a "very agreeable taste". Aborigines in northern Australia eat them to this day. The broom ballart (*E. sparteus*) and leafless ballart (*E. aphyllus*) are broom-like shrubs found in scattered colonies in woodland and coastal dunes in the southern half of Australia. One of these, called "chuck", was made into jam by early settler Ethell Hassell in Western Australia in the 1880s: "It is a very graceful tree of weeping willow habit, with narrow pale green leaves. The fruit grows all along the stems between the leaves, and is like a small red currant . . . The fruit is sub-acid, very like a currant. The [Aboriginal] women used to collect

The pale pink fruits of coast ballart (*Exocarpos syrticola*) have the astringent aftertaste so characteristic of the native cherries. The fleshy portion of the fruit is the size of a small pea.

Shifting sands serve as a harsh substrate for the coast ballart, which suckers from its parasitic roots to avoid submersion. Photographed at Beachport, South Australia.

and made a clear red jam, in flavour and looks very like red currant."

Pale ballart (*E. strictus*) is a leafless shrub with a tiny fruiting pedicel that can be mauve or red but is usually white. With the common native cherry, this is the only *Exocarpos* around Sydney, where it grows on the sandstone ridges. It also occurs in Victoria and Tasmania.

Along southern coasts on dunes grows the coast ballart (*E. syrticola*), a leafless shrub with a pinkish white fruit. This is sweet and juicy, but has that slight astringency typical of the native cherries. The other native cherries are the alpine ballart (*E. nanus*), a dwarf alpine shrub with red fruits, *E. odoratus* of coastal woodlands in Western Australia, and *E. humifusus* of rocky subalpine slopes in Tasmania. "Ballart", by the way, comes from a Victorian Aboriginal word for the native cherry. Truly, the ballarts are interesting plants!

great quantities of this fruit for the trees bear very freely, and look very beautiful when in full fruit. Their method was to spread their *baarks* round the tree, and shake them well. The fruit fell easily on to the *baarks* beneath, then the women would gather round, eat what they wanted and bring the rest to the camp. I made the jam like currant jam, skimming the seeds off as they came to the top,

SEASHORE
FRUITS

Aborigines who lived by the sea enjoyed the best of both worlds. Not only did they have an abundant supply of fish, shellfish and crabs, but the fringing forests yielded a bounty of plant foods, especially fruits. Seashore scrubs are second only to rainforests for their variety of fruits and berries. Some of the fruits even served as staple foods.

Along the coasts of South Australia and western Victoria, the creeper called muntari (*Kunzea pomifera*) was a treasured resource. Late each summer tribes trooped to the coasts to feast on the flavoursome fruits. Whole creepers were torn up and carried to camp for leisurely picking. Surplus fruit was pounded into cakes and stored, or traded to other tribes.

According to early settler James Dawson, the berries were gathered by

At Vivienne Bay on Kangaroo Island, muntari (*Kunzea pomifera*) carpets a dune crest with its small curly leaves and fluffy blossoms. Muntari has an unusually small distribution, occurring only from Yorke Peninsula to the Glenelg River, and north into the mallee deserts of Victoria.

white people to make "excellent jam and tarts". During a visit to Millicent, South Australia, a few years ago I was delighted to discover that local fetes still sell the jam. The fruit, which tastes remarkably like dried apple, is known as muntaberry, crab apple or cranberry. An old-time resident of nearby Beachport, Dela Cameron, told me the dunes near that town smell like apple orchards when the

One of only two fruits on southern shores that can be conveniently dried (quandong is the other), muntari was an enormously important food of coastal Aborigines. The delicious fruits could be stored, or traded for axe heads.

A member of the eucalypt family, muntari has flowers with the small white petals and large stamens typical of eucalypts and tea-trees. It is finding a place in horticulture for its attractive flowers and fruits. Photographed in the Adelaide Botanic Gardens.

Top right: Like so many of Australia's seashore plants, the coastal saltbush (*Rhagodia candolleana*) has saline leaves that may be cooked like spinach, a plant to which it is related.

muntaberry is fruiting. Further west, on Kangaroo Island, snacking schoolchildren gather the fruits.

Muntari is a woody creeper of dunes and mallee woodlands, and even grows on road verges and unkempt footpaths. In spring and early summer it explodes into fluffy white blossoms, followed in late summer and autumn by the small furry fruits. It is both a beautiful and a useful plant, and has been brought into cultivation as a ground cover.

Three other fruit-bearing creepers grow on southern coastal dunes. Karkalla, with its delicious strawberry-flavoured fruits, is described in the Pigfaces chapter. Bower spinach

(*Tetragonia implexicoma*), one of the most common seashore creepers in the south, bears juicy red fruits with a salty sweet taste (and edible leaves). Seagulls feast greedily on the fruits and help spread the seeds. Sweet fan flower (*Scaevola calendulacea*) is a creeper with beautiful sky blue flowers, forming large mats on sheltered dunes in southern and eastern Australia. The purplish fruits taste salty-sweet. I can find no record that Aborigines (or settlers) ever ate bower spinach or fan flower fruits, which indicates the gaps in our knowledge, for both fruits must have been used.

The fleshy-leaved coastal saltbush (*Rhagodia candolleana*) has small leaves

No-one seems to know that the fruit of the sweet fan flower (*Scaevola calendulacea*) is good to eat. This sprawling beach creeper is found right around Australia's southern and eastern coasts. Photographed at Dee Why, Sydney.

that can be eaten like spinach and red fruits that look like tiny buttons. *Rhagodia* berries are recorded as Aboriginal foods, but those of coastal saltbush, although edible, taste intensely bitter. Dela Cameron remembers crushing the berries in the late 1940s to make ink used at school. The shrub was known as "red ink bush".

Behind beaches there are other climbing vines with edible fruits. Sweet appleberry (*Billardiera cymosa*) of southern shores produces aniseed-flavoured berries, the tropical lolly berry (*Salacia chinensis*) has fruits looking like jaffas, and the devil's twines (*Cassytha* species), also known as devil's guts because of their wiry leafless stems, bear sticky-sweet fruits. South Australia's coast lignum (*Muehlenbeckia gunnii*) sports orange fruits only millimetres in length, among Australia's smallest; although minute, they are pleasant eating.

If shrubs and trees are included, the choice of edible fruits becomes endless. Midyim (*Austromyrtus dulcis*), a small coastal shrub, produces one of the

tastiest wild fruits. Quaker missionary James Backhouse, an early bush tucker expert, rated it "the most agreeable, native fruit, I have tasted in Australia". The soft aromatic fruit, which all but melts in the mouth, was a favourite of Aborigines, and it was said that "even the elders will join with gusto in its eating".

Midyim grows in open forests by the sea between Grafton and Fraser Island, a very small range for a native plant. In sunny spots it forms a neat, bright green shrub up to a metre high; in shady gullies the foliage is darker and the slender branches scramble up to twice this height. The white speckled berries, about one centimetre wide, ripen profusely in summer and autumn. In recent years midyim has become a very popular ornamental shrub around Brisbane, where it is often featured in ornamental gardens outside banks and other public buildings.

A shrub that is unlikely to find favour with gardeners is the fleshy-leaved nitre bush (*Nitraria billardieri*) of southern beaches and inland plains, known also as

Stradbroke Island pioneer Thomas Welsby said of the delectable fruit called midyim (*Austromyrtus dulcis*): ". . . one can go through acres of the shrub with its white, sweet-tasting berry until stopped by lagoon or salt water. It is the most sought-for berry or fruit on the island."

Left: One of Australia's tiniest fruits is the coast lignum (*Muehlenbeckia gunnii*) of South Australian beaches. This creeper also grows in Tasmania, but the fruits there are large and green; early settlers called them Macquarie grapes.

Nitre bushes (*Nitraria billardieri*) "yield fruits really relishable", according to colonial botanist Baron von Mueller, writing in the *Picturesque Atlas of Australasia* in 1886. Photographed at Port Augusta.

Top right: Staple of seagulls and fairy wrens, the tiny fruits of coast beard heath (*Leucopogon parviflorus*) have a lemony or grape-like taste, although the great English botanist J. D. Hooker dismissed them as "insignificant and barely edible".

On wind-scoured headlands in southern Australia, the hardy coast beard heath is often the only shrub. Its coarse leaves are well designed to resist salt spray and sand. The plants are found as far north as Fraser Island. Photographed south of Millicent, South Australia.

dillon bush and wild grape. The shrubs form spiky impenetrable clumps up to three metres high and five times as wide, providing refuge for rabbits and other vermin. In summer these shrubs sprout bright red fruits one or two centimetres long, tasting much like grapes dunked in salt water. Nitre bushes grow on suburban Adelaide beaches but few people realise the fruits can be eaten.

At the base of nitre bushes one often finds the small fleshy shrubs of ruby saltbush (*Enchylaena tomentosa*) and wallaby bush (*Threlkeldia diffusa*). Both have tiny edible red fruits and edible leaves. Fruits of ruby saltbush look like buttons, those of wallaby bush like barrels.

Boobialla (*Myoporum insulare*) is a coastal shrub or tree with pretty purple fruits and a pleasant-sounding name. But the fruits fail to meet expectations and, though listed as edible, are bitterly aromatic and salty-sweet in taste. The tree, common on southern shores, is sometimes cultivated as an ornamental.

The proliferation of fruits on Australia's southern beaches can be appreciated when one stands on a foreshore and peruses a thicket of boobiallas and nitre bushes festooned by fruiting bower spinach and coastal lignum, with coastal saltbush, ruby saltbush, wallaby bush, karkalla and muntari growing below. Two other

fruiting plants, both shrubs, grow in the same, extraordinarily rich, coastal scrubs.

Coast ballart (*Exocarpos syrticola*) is a leafless, broom-like shrub producing small pinkish white fruits with an external seed. Its roots parasitise other plants.

Coast beard heath (*Leucopogon parviflorus*) is a very common shrub bearing small creamy fruits with a lemony flavour. This is the most numerous coastal shrub along the Great Ocean Road around Port Campbell in Victoria,

and along coasts and roadsides in South Australia. It actually behaves as a native weed, sprouting on road verges and in cleared paddocks. Seagulls, silvereyes, fairy wrens, emus and even rabbits feast upon the sweet fruits and help spread the seeds.

Australia's northern coasts do not yield the range of fruits found in the south, but the fruits that do occur are usually bigger and more significant. Three such fruits are especially interesting.

Great morinda (*Morinda citrifolia*) is Australia's answer to the infamous durian of Asia. The fruits are big, white, bumpy, and unappealing to the eye. But what gives them away is the sledgehammer smell—like rotten cheese in a urinal. Keep a peg over your nose to avoid feeling bilious. If you can muster the courage the fruit is almost palatable, like mushy over-ripe custard apple blended with blue vein cheese.

The pandanus "palm" (*Pandanus* species—not a true palm) bears enormous fruits the size of human heads, which crumble when ripe into wedge-shaped segments, the inner bases of which may be sucked, but only after roasting in the fire. The pulp tastes of apricot or custard apple.

Lady apple (*Syzygium suborbiculare*) is a scrawny tree of tropical woodlands and coastal dunes with big leathery leaves and red fruits resembling small apples. Like Australia's other native "apples" these are no relation to the greengrocer's Delicious or Granny Smith. The fruits are an important food for Aborigines, having a juicy, sweet, refreshing taste and containing a reasonable store of vitamin C.

Along the coasts of Queensland and the Northern Territory Aborigines bring big hoards of lady apples to their campsites, and great thickets of lady apple seedlings later sprout in the soil around the camp. Such campsites are often bounded by older thickets, attesting to much earlier feasts. These thickets can probably serve as valuable archaeological markers by signposting the locations of ancient Aboriginal camps.

A coast pandanus (*Pandanus tectorius*) stands sentinel on a headland on Moreton Island. In Aboriginal middens in nearby dunes the woody pods of this fruit lie alongside old seashells and flakes of stone, attesting to its importance as food in times past.

Very shiny leaves give mirror plant (*Coprosma repens*) its name. The fruits are salty-sweet and not bad to eat. Photographed at Bondi Beach.

A feral shrub of mirror plant near Bondi Beach. This is surely the only New Zealand shrub to have become a weed in Australia. Although common in south-eastern Australia on headlands close to towns, it never penetrates native bushland.

Like every other environment, Australia's seashore scrubs have been hard hit by European impact. Real estate developments, four-wheel drive cars, goats and brumbies have left their mark. One measure of this disturbance is the rate of invasion by exotic weeds. The beaches in temperate Australia are horribly infested. Fruiting weeds from South Africa and Latin America have thrived, especially bitou bush, prickly pear, boxthorn and stinking passionfruit. These fruits are featured in the Feral Fruits chapter.

Around Sydney and Melbourne there is an additional fruiting weed, albeit a benign one. It is mirror plant (*Coprosma repens*), an attractive shrub with shiny leaves that hails from New Zealand. You can see it on the path running south from Bondi Beach. The orange fruits have a salty-sweet taste and starlings love them. I know this not only from watching the birds eat the fruits, but from spying an unusual sight at St Kilda. The towering date palms in the park there have mirror bushes sprouting from their crowns. How did the shrubs get up there? Ask the squabbling starlings that roost among the fronds, treating the tree as their toilet.

PIGFACES

There is something of the animal in succulent plants. Those fleshy leaves and succulent stems recall the textures and shapes of fingers and limbs. So *fleshy* are such plants they make other plants look flat and two-dimensional. No wonder whole clubs and societies are sworn to cacti and their kind.

But to botanists succulent plants are a professional nuisance. Often too bulky to squeeze into botanical plant presses, the turgid leaves are also too watery to be easily dried. They are apt to sprout and grow within their folders, weeks or even months after collection. Even when successfully dried they shrivel and shrink into a pitiful mockery of the original plant.

Australia's botanists are luckier than most; our succulent plants have small leaves. American botanists fare much worse—imagine devoting a field trip to drying and pressing agaves and cacti (ouch!).

But even in Australia lazy botanists may skirt the larger fleshy plants, leaving these under-represented in Australian herbaria. Botanists in Adelaide told me how they put in a special effort to collect an agave (*Agave americana*), an introduced feral plant now common in South Australia but scarcely recorded in the State herbarium. With its fleshy spike-edged leaves a metre or two long and stout flower spikes ten metres tall, it's no wonder most botanists look the other way.

Yet succulent plants often bear edible parts and, in America, Indians harvested the leaves, seeds and fruits of cacti, as well as juicy agave leaf bases. In Australia, explorers and settlers made vegetables of the saltbushes, and Aborigines harvested the fruits of succulent pigfaces.

Pigfaces are attractive plants. From

Sand-binder par excellence, eastern pigface (*Carpobrotus glaucescens*) has thick heavy leaves and long trailing stems. Photographed on Fraser Island.

creeping stems they sprout forth showy mauve flowers, followed by purple or red fruits with two horns. The juicy pulp, sucked from the base of the fruit, tastes delightfully like salty strawberries or soft figs, and pigfaces can be rated among the best of native fruits.

Pigfaces were important to Aborigines, as early observers attest. The Reverend C. W. Schurmann in 1879 wrote rapturously of the fruit, in a style suggesting the Garden of Eden: "The size of the fruit is rather less than that of a walnut, and it has a thick skin of a pale reddish colour, by compressing which, the glutinous sweet substance inside slips into the mouth. When it is in season, which is from January to the end of summer, a comparatively glorious life begins for the Aborigines; hunger can never assail them, as this fruit is abundant all over the grassy part of the country, and they never tire of it; the men gather only as much as they want to eat at the time, but the women bring great quantities of it home to the camp, to be eaten at night."

Pigface was also a favourite of Aborigines in Tasmania, as Labillardière noted in 1793: "This fruit is a delicacy of

Karkalla (*Carpobrotus rossii*) wends its way across a cushion bush (*Callocephalus brownii*) at Beachport, South Australia. Cushion bush leaves look exceptionally pale because of a covering of white hairs that reduces water loss on the wind-swept beaches.

Karkalla was known to many settlers as "Hottentot fig", after a South African species of pigface which looks much the same. The pulp of these delectable fruits tastes similar to figs. Photographed near Millicent, South Australia.

New Hollanders, who seek it with care, and eat it as soon as they find it."

Europeans often feasted on the fruits. Explorer Edward John Eyre ate it in southern Australia: "All our party partook of it freely, and found it both a wholesome and agreeable addition to their fare. When ripe, the fruit is rich, juicy, and sweet, and about the size of a gooseberry. In hot weather it was most grateful and refreshing. I had often tasted this fruit before, but never until now liked it."

During an expedition to central Victoria in the 1840s the colonist E. M. Curr overindulged: "On this trip it was exceedingly hot during the day, though not at night, and the pigs'-faces were covered with ripe fruit, so, naturally, as we had been living on mutton and damper for months, we indulged in them

rather more than we should have done, and suffered in consequence a smart indisposition of a few hours."

The vast inland plains of pigface in southern Australia have long vanished under the hard hooves and sharp teeth of introduced cattle and sheep. Curr's journal provides a valuable eyewitness record of the devastating change: "The plain, for the thirty miles [50 kilometres] we followed it, from the Campaspe to Mount Hope, was one bed of ripe fruit, some juicy and some dried like raisins. As often, however, as I crossed the same country afterwards, I never again saw the pigs'-faces ripe, so that I fancy they only came to maturity in exceptional years. The plant is now nearly, if not quite, extinct in that locality."

Australia has six native pigfaces, although some of these are difficult to distinguish and the species definitions are open to dispute. The problem lies partly in their succulence: botanists collect pigfaces rarely, so the pool of specimens for study is small. There are three species of *Carpobrotus* on coastal dunes: *C. glaucescens* in eastern Australia, karkalla (*C. rossii*) in the south, and *C. virescens* in Western Australia. Inland pigface (*C. modestus*) and karkalla are found on inland plains in southern South Australia and Victoria. These species are sometimes confused with *Sarcozona*

praecox and *S. bicarinata* of southern deserts and plains, although the latter are more upright plants and their flowers have fewer petals (actually modified stamens, called by botanists "staminodes"). Some botanists believe *S. bicarinata* to be a natural hybrid between *S. praecox* and *C. modestus* and in old reports of Aboriginal use it is sometimes

difficult to know which plant is referred to.

These true pigfaces are easily confused with round-leaved pigface, or rounded noon-flower, (*Disphyma crassifolium*) of southern beaches and inland plains. It has smaller, less angular leaves, and small capsules on tall stalks in place of fleshy fruits. The flowers are slightly smaller, with fewer staminodes, and the latter are white at the base.

The leaves of round-leaved pigface are juicy and edible, and were probably a food of Aborigines in southern Australia, although no record of this survives. They can be used to advantage in salads or as a substitute for spinach in spanakopita.

Leaves of the common pigfaces (*Carpobrotus*) are also edible, although there is sometimes an irritating aftertaste. Eyre found that Aborigines throughout southern Australia ate the leaves "as a sort of relish with almost every other kind of food".

Pigfaces must not be confused with garden pigweed (*Portulaca oleracea*), an edible weed with tiny yellow flowers. Pigweed is so named because pigs eat its leaves; pigfaces, on the other hand, just look like pigs—they have something of the animal in them.

When explorers talked of Aborigines eating pigface leaves, they were probably referring in part to the foliage of round-leaved pigface (*Disphyma crassifolium*), the leaves of which taste crisp and refreshing (and salty!). Photographed at Hallets Cove, Adelaide.

Pigs are fond of pigweed (*Portulaca oleracea*), hence its name. This plant is unrelated to the pigfaces, which probably take their name from the Afrikaans term "big vys", which is applied to African pigfaces.

RAINFOREST
FRUITS

One of dozens of obscure edible rainforest fruits, red-jacket (*Alectryon tomentosus*) has astringent pulp which is probably best left to the birds. The tree is found in light rainforests north of Newcastle and is sometimes cultivated in gardens and parks.

Wander into a rainforest in summer or autumn and you will find the forest floor littered with fruits and berries of every hue—with cobalt blue quandongs (*Elaeocarpus grandis*), orange tamarinds (*Diploglottis australis*), purple grapes (*Cissus hypoglauca*) and translucent white native mulberries (*Pipturus argenteus*). Such fruits are foods of the many rainforest birds and bats, which in exchange for a free meal unwittingly disperse the seeds, in an ancient symbiotic relationship that has fostered much of the richness of the Australian rainforest.

Traditional Aborigines followed winding trails through rainforests to small clearings where yams and cunjevoi could be dug, and fruits and berries gathered. Fruits were eaten raw, or sometimes kneaded with water into sweet edible paste.

We know much about the rainforest fruits eaten in north Queensland, thanks to the testimony of living Aborigines, and the detailed accounts of colonial ethnographer Walter Roth. But this cannot compensate for our abysmal ignorance about southern Queensland and New South Wales, where some of the richest rainforests grew. Aboriginal life in these areas went largely unnoticed and was soon obliterated. It is much to our shame that almost nothing survives from this era. Anthropological records are so incomplete that we cannot even confirm that Aborigines ate such common fruits as native tamarind and walking stick palm (*Linospadix monostachya*), although they must surely have done so. Many of the fruits they would have used were gathered by settlers for jam, and notes on this can be found in old books, especially Frederick Bailey's *The Queensland Flora* (1899–1902).

Finger lime (*Microcitrus australasica*) is a rainforest citrus, of which Australia has five delicious species, found mainly in Queensland. One form of finger lime, found only on Mount Tambourine, has blood-red fruit with pink pulp.

Of the rainforest fruits used by colonists, one of the most noteworthy is the delectable finger lime (*Microcitrus australasica*). This is borne on a spiny shrub or small tree found only in rainforests between Ballina, in far northern New South Wales, and Mount Tamborine in Queensland, a total range of just over a hundred kilometres. A true member of the citrus family, this fruit makes excellent jam. Settlers in the Canungra Valley have been gathering the fruit for generations, and when scrub was felled the shrubs were left standing. The slender fruits, up to seven centimetres long, are red, yellow, purplish black or green when ripe—probably the widest range of colours found on any native fruit. Finger lime is sometimes cultivated, and seeds have been collected by South African horticulturists for cross-breeding with commercial citrus.

Some of the most widespread rainforest fruits are surprisingly little known. Hairy psychotria (*Psychotria loniceroides*) is found in light rainforests throughout eastern Australia, from southern New South Wales to Cape York, but although the small yellow fruits are edible, there seems to be no record of Aborigines or settlers eating them. The fruits are not very tasty, so this is perhaps unsurprising.

Much better known are the various large tropical fruits called "plums" (no relation). Of the black plum (*Planchonella australis*), colonial botanist Joseph Maiden noted, "The rich milky

sap resembles cream in taste; the fruit is nearly black, and like a very large plum, but somewhat astringent to the taste. The large seeds and the frequent occurrence of maggots in the fruit are drawbacks, but it yields a very fair jelly or preserve, frequently made in the country districts, where it is a prolific bearer."

The Burdekin plum (*Pleiogynium timorense*) is noteworthy as a species collected by Joseph Banks when the *Endeavour* was under repair in north Queensland. The fruits are much liked by Aborigines, and make a truly excellent tangy jam, but the raw pulp is very

Hairy psychotria (*Psychotria loniceroides*) is aptly named, for the whole surface of this plant is furry, even down to the tiny bland-tasting fruits. Photographed in a rainforest clearing on the steep slopes of Mount Keira west of Woollongong.

Below: No fruit is more susceptible to maggots than the rainforest black plum (*Planchonella australis*). Even the colonial botanists drew attention to its extra ingredients. The brownish pulp, with or without the grubs, has a bland but pleasant taste.

Joseph Banks wrote scornfully of Burdekin plums (*Pleiogynium timorense*), which he gathered at Endeavour River, complaining that the fruits were "so full of a large stone that eating them was but an unprofitable business".

Brown pine (*Podocarpus elatus*) is yet another rainforest tree with fruits compared to plums. According to Maiden, writing in 1898, the fruits "are known to our small boys as plums or damsons". The recent boom in wild foods has put brown pine on the menu of Australian restaurants. A sauce made from the fruits is served with meats in several native foods eateries.

The fruits of lilly pillies (*Syzygium* species) are also appearing in restaurants, in the form of fragrant sauces and preserves. The name "lilly pilly" used to apply to the rainforest tree called *Acmena smithii*, the fruit of which is brightly coloured but by no means tasty. In the May Gibbs stories Lilly Pilly is an actress who performs with her pet bulldog ant. The name is now applied to related plants of genus *Syzygium* and the fruits of some of these are now served as sauces in delicatessens and restaurants.

astringent. Banks compared the fruits to "indifferent damsons".

The queen of Australian rainforest "plums" is undoubtedly Davidson's plum (*Davidsonia pruriens*), a rare tree of rainforests in far northern New South Wales and north Queensland. The soft juicy pulp tastes exquisitely sour, and makes what is probably the best Australian bush jam. The tree is sometimes sold by nurseries (the large fronds and dangling plum clusters are very ornamental), and there is talk of cultivating it as a crop.

The magenta lilly pilly (*S. paniculatum*) is an uncommon tree restricted to seashore rainforests in New South Wales, where most of its habitat has been destroyed by resort development. The dark red fruit is noteworthy as probably

Like the native cherry, the brown pine (*Podocarpus elatus*) has a false fruit consisting of a fleshy sweet stalk attached to a big stone. Although somewhat resinous in taste, the fruit was popular among Aborigines and settlers in New South Wales.

the first ever eaten in Australia by a European. Joseph Banks's diary of 3 May 1770 records that Captain Cook and Dr Solander found "several trees which bore fruit of the Jambosa [an Asian lilly pilly] kind, much in colour and shape resembling cherries; of these they eat plentifully and brought home also abundance, which we eat with much pleasure tho they had little to recommend them but a slight acid."

Australia has more than sixty different lilly pillies, and all appear to have edible fruit, ranging in colour from white to pink, red, purple, blue or black, and tasting sour, fragrant, watery and often astringent. It is likely that all were eaten by Aborigines, for we know that settlers often gathered the fruits for jam. Colonial cookery writer Mrs Lance Rawson wrote in 1894 that "While rather acid to eat raw, they have a very pleasant sharpness when properly preserved." She commended them as making "a good preserve" and "a good summer drink".

Like the lilly pillies, wild figs are a group well represented in Australian rainforests, where about forty species grow. Native figs can be white, pink, red, yellow, purple or black; as small as grapes or bigger than plums. Some of the smaller figs taste dry and gritty, but the large strangler and cluster figs have a rich sweet pulp. Settlers made them into jam.

Like many Australian rainforest trees, the creek lilly pilly (*Syzygium australe*) is known to timbermen by trade names, such as creek satinash and native myrtle. It is often planted by gardeners as a decorative shade tree.

Top left: The famous lilly pilly (*Acmena smithii*) has a reputation it simply cannot live up to. The meagre layer of pulp surrounding the stone is dry, astringent and tasteless. The tree is often cultivated as an ornamental in Victoria and New South Wales.

Below right: The most widely grown of all Australian rainforest trees is probably the cherry alder, or riberry, (*Syzygium luehmanii*) which can be seen in parks and gardens ad nauseum. Sweet pittosporum and the flame tree are the other candidates for this dubious honour.

Explorer Ludwig Leichhardt was very fond of cluster figs (*Ficus racemosa*), although the rich fruits seldom agreed with his constitution. His journal speaks of severe attacks of indigestion, and of figs that were "not perfectly mellow". He first saw the trees along the Burdekin River, where he noted they were "fifty to sixty feet high, with a rich shady foliage; and covered with bunches of fruit. The figs were of the size of a small apple, of

Bunches of sweet, watery, semi-fermented cluster figs (*Ficus* species) hang from a tree trunk in the Lockerbie Scrub near Cape York. Fruit bats attracted by the smell carry the figs to new clearings where they drop the seeds, allowing new trees to grow.

Right: Aborigines ate Moreton Bay figs (*Ficus macrophylla*) and made fishing nets from the durable bark. Fig birds and fruit bats dote on the succulent figs, and accidentally drop the seeds in stumps where new trees grow.

an agreeable flavour when ripe, but were full of small flies and ants. These trees were numerous, and their situation was readily detected by the paths of the natives leading to them: a proof that the fruit forms one of their favourite articles of food."

The Moreton Bay fig (*F. macrophylla*), one of the largest of the fig trees, was a shade tree of colonists and a symbol of the grandeur of Moreton Bay. Visitors to the Australian colonies were often disappointed by the scrawny eucalypts around Sydney, but greatly impressed by the tall rainforests lining the Brisbane River. Three Brisbane rainforest trees greatly impressed the colonists—the Moreton Bay fig, Moreton Bay chestnut (*Castanospermum australe*) and Moreton Bay pine (*Araucaria cunninghamii*), now

called hoop pine. These majestic trees were planted in parks all over Australia where they may be seen to this day. Moreton Bay figs were also left as shade trees for cattle when scrubs were cleared. The Brisbane suburb of Fig Tree Pocket is named after a tree so enormous that a horse and dray could hide between its buttressed roots. The figs make fine eating apart from the gritty seeds.

Just east of Brisbane, convicts endured horror at the penal settlement of St Helena Island. Nowadays the ruins are overgrown by small-leaved rock figs (*F. platypoda*) which yield crops of sweet red figs. This tree spans an extraordinary range of habitats, from rainforests to deserts, even growing on the base of Ayers Rock.

Other fig trees of interest include the strangler fig (*F. watkinsiana*), a towering jungle giant, and the sandpaper fig (*F. coronata*), with leaves that Aborigines used as sandpaper, and sweet edible fruit.

The list of edible rainforest fruits can be extended on and on. In clearings grow the various native raspberries (*Rubus* species), native elderberries (*Sambucus* species) and kangaroo apples (*Solanum aviculare*). Native tamarinds drop sour orange fruits onto the leaf litter, from which colonists made a jelly "with a pleasant tang of the wild about it", according to one writer. Native grapes (*Cissus, Cayratia* and *Tetrastigma* species) twine through the branches, yielding

Towering above the forest floor is this huge strangler fig (*Ficus obliqua*) at Cape Tribulation, a magnet for the many birds and mammals that feast upon the figs. Animals feeding amongst the foliage of these trees often create a cacophany of wing-flapping and calls.

bunches of fruits which look and taste like grapes, but leave an irritant aftertaste. This irritant survives boiling, and the grapes can be made into a jam that also stings. The adventurous forager might even try the fruits of the various stinging trees (*Dendrocnide* species) which, if a few stinging hairs are left attached, provide a truly unforgettable taste sensation.

Left: After gently touching these fruits of the mulberry-leaved stinging tree (*Dendrocnide photinophylla*), my finger stung slightly for several hours. The sting is produced by tiny hairs scattered over the surface of the fruits—which are very tasty.

Convict ruins on St Helena Island provide the habitat for a small-leaved rock fig (*Ficus platypoda*), which helps contribute to their decay. This versatile tree is the same species that appears in the chapter on Outback Fruits.

OUTBACK
FRUITS

No matter where you are, wild fruits provide a sweet succulent snack. But in the desert, in the heat of the day, the wet taste of a fruit is especially refreshing. Not surprisingly, wild fruits were treasured foods of inland Aborigines, and in the past they formed an important part of desert diet.

Of the many outback fruits eaten, none were more important than the wild tomatoes. These are members of the remarkable genus *Solanum*, that enormous group of 1500 species that includes the potato, the eggplant, kangaroo apples and blackberry nightshades. Wild tomatoes are small shrubs with purple flowers, furry leaves, and fruits like small unripe tomatoes. In the scorching desert sun the fruits sometimes shrivel on the shrub, producing sweet "raisins". These were exceptionally precious foods.

Anthropologist Donald Thomson once found a deserted Pintupi camp laden with raisins (*S. centrale*): "On top of some of the brushwood shelters . . . reserves of prepared vegetable foods had been left. Some of this had been desiccated and was carefully stored. One of these foods was brown in colour, with the appearance and texture of a mass of pulverized preserved figs . . . It had a half-sweet, half-tart or acid flavour, but it proved palatable and satisfying, as it was evidently obtained in large quantities even in this drought year, it was probably an important staple food."

Aborigines elsewhere gathered enormous amounts of the raisins and ground them with water to a thick paste, which was rolled into balls, covered with red ochre, and sun-dried. These big soccer balls of fruit, weighing over a kilogram, could be stored for a year or two in tree forks or shelters.

Some kinds of bush tomato are

Springing up on desert flats after rain, the wild tomato (*Solanum centrale*) produces a tomato-like fruit containing about one-third of the vitamin C of oranges. Some kinds of wild tomato contain more of this vitamin than do oranges.

Right: The marble-sized fruit of the wild tomato (*Solanum ellipticum*) is carried beneath the plant. Anthropologists Cleland and Tindale noted that "The prickles are not very aggressive so that one can handle the bush without being severely punished". Photographed at Broken Hill.

The pretty flowers of this wild tomato (*Solanum orbiculatum*) are characteristic of the group, featuring yellow stamens and five joined mauve petals. Some Aboriginal tribes ate the fruit of this species, others did not. Photographed at Ayers Rock.

intensely poisonous, and at Uluru the Pitjantjatjara claim that lookalike edible and poisonous varieties grow side by side, as if to confuse the forager. The edible *S. ellipticum* has *S. quadriloculatum* as its toxic twin. The Pitjantjatjara eat a variety of wild tomatoes but avoid the bitter *S. orbiculatum*, even though this is taken by other tribes.

The fruits of some wild tomatoes are rich in vitamin C, containing up to twice that of oranges. The "acid berry" that cured the scurvy of desert explorer Charles Sturt was probably one of these. In western New South Wales one of the wild tomatoes (*S. esuriale*) was cooked by drovers with their mutton chops.

Another treasured fruit of outback Aborigines was the rock fig (*Ficus platypoda*). The sweet gritty figs were eaten raw, or gathered when dry and rolled into balls for storage. So important was this fruit that Aborigines performed ceremonies to increase the supply. Some fig bushes were deemed sacred and anyone damaging them could be killed. Outback settlers cooked the fruits in jams.

The figs of the small-leaved rock fig (*Ficus platypoda*) contain up to 4000 milligrams of calcium per hundred grams, far more than any Western food. Milk contains one-twentieth of this amount.

A small-leaved rock fig sprawls untidily across a saddle of the Olgas. On mountain ranges throughout the arid tropics, rock figs sprout in crevices and among boulders. The trees never survive on open ground, where fires soon kill them.

Sandalwood (*Santalum lanceolatum*) was one of those versatile plants that Aborigines turned to for a variety of services. The fruit was eaten, the leaves and bark were applied medicinally for various ailments, and the foliage was burned to repel mosquitoes.

Gracie Macintyre inspects a sandalwood shrub growing on a creek flat at Kamaran Downs Station in south-western Queensland. Sandalwood shrubs in this part of Queensland bear much smaller fruits and thinner leaves than the shrubs to the east and west.

Yet another important desert fruit was the quandong (*Santalum acuminatum*), the favourite wild food of outback Australians to this day. Even among white settlers the pulp was dried, mainly as an ingredient for tarts and pies. The scarlet pulp has a delectable sour flavour, and the oily seeds are also edible (see Wild Nuts chapter). Botanist Joseph Maiden suggested at the turn of the century that this tree be cultivated, an idea taken up recently by the CSIRO in Adelaide. Quandong trees are dying out in central Australia, evidently from the depredations of browsing camels.

Emu apple (*Owenia acidula*) looks rather like the quandong, except its fruit is not shiny and the leaves are pinnate. The fruits ripen only after falling to the ground, where they are greedily gobbled by emus. The Reverend Tenison-Woods, travelling in central Queensland last century, proclaimed the fruit "grateful to the taste of a thirsty traveller in these hot arid regions".

Sandalwood (*Santalum lanceolatum*) is one of a number of tall shrubs with fragrant woods used by the Chinese to make incense. The blue-black fruits are fair eating. Aborigines sometimes gathered the dried fruits' from beneath the trees to reconstitute them with water. Juice squeezed from the fruits provided a handy dye.

Native capers (*Capparis* species) of various kinds grow on inland plains alongside sandalwood. Country people make drinks from the seed-filled pulp. The most popular caper is the so-called wild orange or bumble tree (*C. mitchellii*), named after Major Mitchell, the first

Overgrazed and rabbit-infested, this paddock at Broken Hill has been smothered by nitre bush (*Nitraria billardieri*) to the exclusion of nearly all other plants. Nitre bush is one of Australia's many native weeds—plants that benefit from human disturbance, thriving on degraded land.

Top left: Major Mitchell first saw wild oranges (*Capparis mitchellii*) at Aboriginal camp fires, and his journal describes the fruit: ". . . with a rind like an orange, and the inside, which appeared to have been eaten, resembled a pomegranate." Photographed north of Birdsville.

Below: If you can overlook the saltiness, the fruit of nitre bush tastes much like a grape. Although widespread in southern Australia, these juicy fruits are not often eaten. Photographed at Broken Hill.

white man to see the tree. He declared the fruit had "an agreeable perfume".

Nitre bush fruits (*Nitraria billardieri*) were the favoured fare of Aborigines in southern Australia. Explorer Edward John Eyre thought the fruit "juicy and saline, though not disagreeable in taste", and noted that it was "a staple article of food in season, among the natives of these districts where it abounds, and is eaten by them raw, stone and all".

CSIRO researcher J. C. Noble suggested that the nitre plant might serve as a food crop for arid areas. But sample fruits that he canned tasted bitter and astringent and scored low in vitamin C.

On soils disturbed by human activity nitre bush behaves like a weed, forming prickly thickets on abandoned wheat

farms, overgrazed pastures, stock routes and river flats. It is probably more common today, especially on soils ruined by rising salt, than in precolonial times.

In central Queensland the desert lime (*Eremocitrus glauca*) is also behaving like a weed. It proliferates on black-soil plains wherever soil is disturbed by clearing and grazing. Farmers collect the grape-sized citrus fruits to make delicious drinks and jams. Explorer Ludwig Leichhardt was lucky to find this fruit during his northern expedition: "Yesterday in coming through the scrub, we had collected a large quantity of ripe native lemons, of which, it being Sunday, we intended to make a tart; but, as my companions were absent, the treat was deferred until their return, which was on Monday morning, when we made them into a dish very like gooseberry-fool; they had a very pleasant acid taste."

As well as the foregoing, there are many smaller desert fruits on which

Tiny desert morsels, the fruits of ruby saltbush (*Enchylaena tomentosa*) are eaten by honeyeaters, foxes and pigs. Country people sometimes call them "plum puddings". Photographed near Oakey, southern Queensland.

Sweet and colourful boobialla fruits (*Myoporum acuminatum*) are a food of desert birds. The shrub is becoming more common on outback plains in places disturbed by grazing. Photographed at Broken Hill beside groves of nitre bush.

Aborigines snacked. Boobialla (*Myoporum acuminatum*) bears pretty purplish fruits with a salty-sweet taste; ruby saltbush (*Enchylaena tomentosa*) has button-shaped fruits that can be soaked in water to make a drink. Other small fruits include native currants (*Canthium* species) and prickly fan flower (*Scaevola spinescens*).

Since Europeans settled the land, a couple of introduced fruit plants have spread inland. Prickly pear cacti (*Opuntia* species) from Latin America bear heavy crops of sticky-sweet red fruits which are not bad eating, apart from the irritating bristles. In the Riverina there even grow wild melons (probably feral watermelons [*Citrullus lanatus*]), although Melbourne journalist Donald Macdonald, writing in 1887, gave them the thumbs down: "The taste for these melons is hard to acquire, no doubt. Ancient shepherds and boundary-riders, who have lived for a quarter of a century on the plains, pretend to like the fruit, but their palates have been ruined by an ever-lasting diet of mutton and dyspeptic damper, and they have long since forgotten the flavour of a genuine melon."

The prickly pear cactus (*Opuntia stricta*) takes its name from the shape of its "leaves", for the fruits neither look nor taste like pears. If anything, their taste can be likened to that of very sticky plums. Photographed north of Augathella in central Queensland.

FERAL
FRUITS

One of the most pervasive urban myths is the idea that blackberry nightshade berries are poisonous. Australians of all ages and from all walks regard the glossy black berries with an almost mortal dread. I have even been reprimanded by a small boy for plucking the berries from a footpath bush. Curiously, everyone confuses the blackberry nightshades (*Solanum nigrum, S. americanum*)—both common garden weeds with sweet edible fruit—with the deadly nightshade (*Atropa belladonna*) of Europe, a plant not found in Australia.

Only last century Australian pioneers gathered nightshade berries for food. Norfolk Island convicts in the 1830s boiled the berries, and they were also eaten by settlers near Lismore. Queenslander Mrs Lance Rawson's

Australian Enquiry Book of 1894 explained how to make jam from the tiny shiny fruit: "Night Shade or Blackberry.—Every one is acquainted with the little bushes covered with glossy black-berries that come up all over scrub land when it is first cleared. It is, I believe, correctly speaking, a nightshade, but certainly it is not deadly; on the contrary, it makes one of the nicest jams I know. Pick the berries when they are just ripe, throwing out all stalks. Ten ounces of sugar to the lb. is sufficient if the jam is not required to be kept long." And so on.

Not only are berries of nightshades not poisonous, but their soft green leaves may be boiled and eaten. These are harvested in Timor and New Guinea and by the Kanaks of New Caledonia.

Definitely not poisonous, the berries of glossy nightshade (*Solanum americanum*) have a sweet mulberry flavour. Some forms of common nightshade have bitter fruit, which may explain the fear felt towards these berries. Baron von Mueller in 1877 typified the confusion: "The small black berries are poisonous; therefore children cannot be sufficiently warned to abstain from them, though at times the poison-principle (an alkaloid called Solanin) seems little or not developed."

Right: A provider of food and medicine, the blackberry (*Rubus fruticosus*) is unfortunately also an invidious weed. The leaves have been used since the time of Pliny to treat sores and dysentery. Photographed at Tenterfield.

The *raw* leaves of nightshades are poisonous, and the green berries, but the same is true of most plants, including cultivated fruits. The ill-effects are merely diarrhoea and stomach cramps.

Nightshades are but one of many fruiting weeds, originally from overseas, that now run wild in Australia. Blackberries, sweet briar, prickly pear, boxthorn, hawthorn and the like make up a highly visible component of our rural flora. These plants thrive near cities and towns, and offer a major source of sustenance for the adventurous forager.

The infamous blackberry (*Rubus fruticosus*) is the most prolific of these weeds. Throughout the damp belt of temperate Australia this bramble prospers along roadsides and gullies. In Victoria alone, more than 663 000 hectares are ensnared. Colonial botanist Baron Ferdinand von Mueller deserves some blame for the spread of this weed: he wrote in 1879 that blackberry "deserves to be naturalised on the rivulets of any ranges", and is thought to have spread the seeds during expeditions to remote regions. The bramble is now Victoria's worst weed. Early this century, enormous loads of wild blackberries were sent to Sydney factories to make jam. Eighty to one hundred tons of fruit were sent annually from Bulli alone.

Apart from the blackberry, two other English hedgerow shrubs run wild in Australia—hawthorn and dogrose. Hawthorn (*Crataegus monogyna*) is a tall deciduous shrub (or small tree) bearing thorny branches and lobed leaves. During spring the plant explodes into cascades of pink or white blossoms, followed in summer by sprays of shiny red fruits. These have a dry yellowish flesh and closely resemble the garden cotoneaster (the fruits of which are also edible). Although the fruits are unpleasant to eat raw, English peasants gathered them for jellies and sauces. Old legends say that Christ's thorny crown was woven from the stems. In Australia, hawthorn hedges

were planted on farms in Victoria, Tasmania, the Adelaide Hills and the New England Tableland, where the shrubs now run wild on paddocks and verges.

Dogrose (*Rosa canina*) is a wild rose with prickly stems and showy pink flowers (which like all wild roses have only five petals). In Australia it is outnumbered by the sweet briar (*R. rubiginosa*), a similar wild rose from western Asia. Both roses produce red hips (fruits) which are rich sources of ascorbic acid, containing up to fifteen times the vitamin C of oranges. The raw hips taste dry and unappetising, but a nutritious syrup can be made by coarsely

The dazzling berries of hawthorn (*Crataegus monogyna*) were gathered by European peasants to make haw sauce and haw jelly. Hedges of the tall spiky shrubs served as fences to contain cattle and sheep. Photographed east of Tenterfield.

Below: Reverend William Woolls noted that the sweet briar (*Rosa rubiginosa*) "is complained of by some settlers, but I think that most English people will be pleasingly reminded of the old country . . . and the fruit, which in some countries is made into a conserve, furnishes food for small birds". Photographed in the Warrumbungles.

A towering prickly pear cactus (*Opuntia stricta*) stands beside a road north of Augathella in central Queensland. Careful handling is required when harvesting the fruits in order to avoid being injured by the irritating hairs that arm the plant.

Although they are considered inedible, I have found that African boxthorn berries (*Lycium ferocissimum*) make good fillings for tarts and pies. Birds spread the seeds widely, and seedlings can often be seen beneath trees and fence posts. Photographed at Broken Hill.

chopping the hips, stripping them of seeds, and simmering them in water and sugar until a rich dark syrup can be siphoned off.

Wild roses grow in paddocks over much of south-eastern Australia from the Mount Lofty Ranges to Stanthorpe. Wild emus dote on the fruits (and help spread the seeds of these noxious weeds). The hips are egg-shaped, about as big as sparrow eggs, and spiny (sweet briar) or smooth (dogrose).

Two other fruiting shrubs were popular as hedges in temperate Australia: African boxthorn and prickly pear. Boxthorn (*Lycium ferocissimum*) is a spiny shrub with shiny berries like tiny tomatoes. I have used them to make tasty jams and tarts but they are widely

considered to be poisonous. The raw berries, although sweet, often impart a bitter aftertaste, which may indicate traces of toxic alkaloids.

Boxthorn has become an insidious spiky weed of farmlands, roadsides and wastelands in southern and eastern Australia. It is especially common on black soils, and on coastal sand dunes, where it is said to favour the enriched soil of old Aboriginal middens, thereby serving as a marker for archaeologists.

Prickly pear (*Opuntia vulgaris*) came to Australia with the First Fleet as a source of cochineal for soldiers' uniforms. The red dye is produced by sap-sucking bug larvae which can sometimes be found on wild cacti: they stain the fingers red if squeezed. Nowadays, informed as we are by jungle warfare, we would not imagine dressing soldiers in fire-engine red, but soldiering in the 1780s was more ritualised, and England feared a hostile Spain would sever the cochineal supply lines. Australia was seen as an alternative producer, and Governor Phillip brought out cacti to Sydney in pots. Others came in as hedge plants and garden oddities, and more than twenty species now run wild in Australia, where they are invasive pests. Most have edible fruit.

The common prickly pear (*Opuntia stricta*) has purplish fruits with sticky sweet pulp and hard black seeds. The

fruits are armed with tufts of irritating hairs and should be held in gloves, sliced into halves, and the pulp scooped out with a spoon. The fruits make a very sticky jam, and the upper leaf pads can be boiled as a lacklustre vegetable. The spines have been used as gramophone needles.

There is one other prickly shrub worth mentioning—the Indian jujube or chinee apple (*Zizyphus mauritiana*). Around Townsville dense groves of these shrubs (or small trees) crowd the roadsides and cow paddocks. They are especially common near old mining camps, and this provides the clue, for they were introduced last century by miners and labourers from China. The fruit of the jujube is a tasty plum-sized "apple" with a large woody stone. Fruits often dry on the twigs and then taste much like the Chinese dates sold in health food stores, which is exactly what they are. Although common in Queensland they are little used as food.

Another very interesting tree in northern Australia is the African tamarind (*Tamarindus indica*). Old tamarind trees standing on isolated headlands along the Northern Territory coast hark back a century or two to when Macassan fishermen plied the northern Australian coast. Macassar was a major trading port on the Indonesian island of Celebes (now Sulawesi), and doughty Macassan fishermen came each year to harvest trepang (the sea-cucumber, also known as bêche-de-mer), an item much esteemed in Chinese cuisine. On the Arnhem Land coast the Macassans set up stone hearths and bamboo and lawyer-vine sheds for boiling and smoke-drying the sea-cucumbers. Around the abandoned campsites old tamarind trees still throw their shade, and the sour fruits have become a popular food of Aborigines. On Groote Eylandt the fruit is so important it has an Aboriginal name—Angkayunwaya. Locals say the fruits ripen in spring when the stringybarks stop flowering. The sticky pulp is rubbed on the forehead to cure headache.

Tamarind trees are grown in parks south to Brisbane. The leaves are finely pinnate and the fruits are dangling pods. The sticky brown pulp, like sour apricot, is used in Asian curries, much in the manner of lemon juice. It can be bought from Asian stores. The tamarind, along with the African boxthorn and Indian jujube, provides an interesting example of how plants can serve as historical markers.

The tamarind was undoubtedly introduced into Australia, but with some fruiting plants we cannot be sure. The so-called native gooseberry (*Physalis minima*) may really be an introduced weed. This small plant bearing sweet edible berries is widespread in northern Australia, and occurs throughout the tropics of the world. Northern Aborigines eat the fruits, but some tribes have no traditional name for the plant. Is it native to Australia, an introduction of

Furry leaves, stems and fruits distinguish the Cape gooseberry (*Physalis peruviana*) from its native kin. This weed often sprouts in rainforest clearings, its seeds carried in by birds, as here at Mount Keira near Woollongong.

Right: Native or introduced? Where the native gooseberry (*Physalis minima*) is concerned, it is difficult to say for sure. This weedy herb usually grows at sites of human disturbance, as here on Prince of Wales Island in Torres Strait.

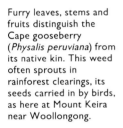

early Europeans, or an import of Macassans or other seafarers?

The closely related Cape gooseberry (*P. peruviana*) is definitely introduced. A native of South America (*peruviana* means "of Peru"), it was introduced into Australia via South Africa, hence its colloquial name (after Cape Town). This gooseberry was perhaps brought in by the First Fleet, for we know from an old journal that its bitter leaves were used in beer brewing as early as 1796. The plant soon became a weed, and the fruits a popular food of settlers. Lieutenant Breton in 1833 was able to say of the colony of New South Wales that "The native fruits of the country are the cherry, raspberry, currant and gooseberry: they are chiefly used for preserves". The Queensland colonial botanist F. M. Bailey recorded in 1888 that the weed "Springs up at almost every clearing, and from these plants rather than from cultivated plants the fruit is gathered for sale".

Cape gooseberry even became a weed on Norfolk Island. Quaker missionary James Backhouse noted in 1835 that "Many old roads, formerly used for bringing timber out of the woods, are grown up with the Cape Gooseberry, *Physalis* [*peruviana*], which produces

abundance of pleasant, small, round fruit, in a bladder-like calyx. This is eaten by the prisoners, who also collect and cook the berries of the Black Nightshade, *Solanum nigrum*."

Cape gooseberry and native gooseberry are unrelated to the gooseberries of Europe; they are members of the ubiquitous nightshade family. The sweet, tangy, marble-sized berries are concealed inside the straw capsules, which do not deter birds and caterpillars from taking most of the crop. Cape gooseberry is a small shrub of gullies and rainforest edges, often grown around homesteads for its juicy fruit, which is used mainly in jams.

Another fruit that may be an early introduction into Australia is stinking passionfruit vine (*Passiflora foetida*). Although this plant is certainly of South American origin, a couple of tribes in northern Australia have their own names for it. The Gunwinggu of Arnhem Land know it as "djalamartawk", and the Enindilyakwa of Groote Eylandt call it "kiriba"—although this is merely a corruption of the English "creeper".

Stinking passionfruit, better known as "wild passionfruit", is much liked by white children, and most Australians, Aborigines included, believe it to be a native plant. The cherry-sized fruits have a papery yellow skin wrapped in lichen-like bracts. They ripen prolifically in summer, but birds steal most of the crop.

The common cultivated passionfruit (*P. edulis*) is also a weed in eastern Australia. Vigorous feral vines trail through bushland near Sydney, Brisbane and coastal country towns. The vines prosper along national park trails deep inside mountain rainforests, the seeds presumably carried in by birds and picnickers. The wild vines produce excellent fruit.

In Queensland wild passionfruit vines can sometimes be found growing beside groves of wild guavas (*Psidium guajava*), another import from South America. The wild trees produce fruits aplenty which are packed full of vitamin C and fruit-fly maggots. Guavas were one of the first trees grown at the convict colony of Brisbane, and they have spread into paddocks where rainforest once grew, in both Queensland and northern New South Wales, and on Lord Howe Island. (In Hawaii they are a serious pest of native forests.) Unfortunately, Australians have little appreciation for the fruit, and most crops are left to rot. They make an excellent red jelly.

Feral olive trees (*Olea europaea*) thrive in South Australia, growing even on sandy beaches. This fine specimen stands in dunes at Normanville on the Fleurieux Peninsula, near the last remaining coastal scrubs of the eastern Gulf of St Vincent.

Olives taken from wild trees are small but oily, and well suited for pickling. The wild trees bear enormous crops, which often ferment on the ground below. Photographed at Normanville.

In South Australia a very conspicuous wild fruit tree is the European olive (*Olea europaea*). Olives obviously enjoy the climate and soils of the Adelaide region, for they are prolific on the hot ridges and nearby plains, and even sprout on coastal sand dunes and beach shingle. The wild trees bear heavy crops of passable black olives, which are evidently spread by birds, creating problems in nature reserves and native forests, where the trees are most unwelcome. Former Premier Don Dunstan's cookery book included recipes for the oil-rich fruits. There is an ancient grove of olives on St Helena Island off Brisbane, the legacy of convict plantings.

Wild strawberries grow in the damp

Most Australians think the stinking passionfruit (*Passiflora foetida*) is a native plant, which shows how well established this South American weed has become. The fruit has an excellent flavour, and the young leaves can be boiled and eaten.

Lantana (*Lantana camara*) is a weed even on the outer islands of Torres Strait, as here on Murray Island, where it grows alongside huge groves of feral bamboo. Most people wrongly think the fruits are poisonous.

Wild tobacco (*Solanum mauritianum*) is a weed so widespread in Australia that many people believe it to be a native plant, although its scientific name indicates otherwise.

forests of eastern Australia and these, too, are introduced plants. They are Indian strawberry (*Duchesnea indica*), a small yellow-flowered herb cultivated, not for its fruit, which tastes insipid, but as an ornamental garden edging. The seeds are spread by birds. Around Nimbin wild strawberries grow in paddocks and along roads forged into rainforest.

The list of fruit-bearing weeds runs on and on. Few people realise that the fruits of lantana (*Lantana camara*) are edible (though not very tasty). Nowhere can I

A bitou bush (*Chrysanthemoides monilifera*), one of our prettiest noxious weeds, sprawls over a sand dune north of Woollongong. A scatter of shells can be seen on the sand at left, indicating an Aboriginal midden.

find written records to suggest that berries of the rainforest wild tobacco (*Solanum mauritianum*) are edible, though I have found them palatable. (The furry yellow fruits are favourites of pigeons and possums, and bushmen use the soft durable leaves as toilet paper. The plant has no use as tobacco.) Bitou bush (*Chrysanthemoides monilifera*), that insidious South African invader of coastal sand dunes, also has edible fruits, although again I can find no record of anyone eating them. They taste like dried dates.

The rich variety of fruiting weeds found in Australia makes for splendid foraging, but it bespeaks disaster for the Australian bush, which is becoming ever more infested with exotic plants. Fruit-bearing weeds enjoy a special advantage, for their seeds are spread by native birds. During the height of the great prickly pear plague in Queensland, angry farmers slaughtered thousands of emus accused of spreading about the seeds. Fruit pigeons have been blamed for spreading camphor

laurel (*Cinnamomum camphora*) in New South Wales. (The black berries are not edible by people.)

There is little we can do to contain the problem. Gardeners living near native forests should be wary of growing fruiting plants, and foragers should avoid spreading about the seeds. I always spit the stones back into the bush they came from. If there was less disturbance to native forests there would be fewer opportunities for exotic weeds to invade, and herein lies the crux of the problem.

Bane of our beaches, bitou bush is replacing groves of native coast wattle along the coasts of New South Wales and Victoria. The sweet fruits, tasting like dates, are spread by birds.

SEEDS

WILD
SEEDS

Of all the different kinds of plant foods, seeds are by far the most nutritious. In one dense package they provide everything a baby plant needs for growth—vitamins, minerals, and a store of starch (and often fat) for energy. So sustaining are seeds that they provide the staple diet of nearly all human cultures. Without grass seeds there would be no bread, pasta, rice or breakfast cereals.

Australia's Aborigines made good use of wild seeds. In the outback, tiny seeds of grasses, pigweed and wattles were staple foods, and a great many other seeds were eaten. In the tropics large starchy cycad seeds, stripped of their toxins, sustained huge social gatherings of hundreds of Aborigines for weeks at a time. In the Atherton rainforests, Aborigines lived largely on oily rainforest nuts, using special stones to grind the seeds. And in the Bunya Mountains and Blackall Ranges, three-yearly bunya nut feasts attracted parties of Aborigines from hundreds of kilometres around.

The larger seeds with hard shells, especially those containing oil, are usually referred to as nuts. The next chapter (Wild Nuts) considers these in detail. The seeds of leguminous plants (families Fabaceae, Caesalpiniaceae, Mimosaceae) are especially high in protein, and we call them beans and peas; they too earn a chapter of their own (Native Beans and Peas), except for the wattles, considered below. The other seeds are described here.

The largest wild seed in Australia is the coconut (*Cocos nucifera*). Botanists dispute whether coconut palms grew in Australia in pre-European times. Early explorers never reported the palms during their journeys along our coasts, but much of their time was spent out at

sea. We can be sure that coconuts did not grow on mainland beaches, but there may have been a few groves growing naturally on remote islands. They were widely cultivated by islanders in Torres Strait long ago. Wild coconuts have a narrower nut than the cultivar which now infests north Queensland coasts. It is distressing that alternative lifestyle practitioners are spreading the palm along the beaches north of Daintree, for there this tree is an exotic weed, and no more belongs in the wilderness than lantana or prickly pear.

The other tropical "palms" with edible seeds are the so-called "pandanus palms" (*Pandanus* species), also called screwpines and breadfruit, although they are no relation to palms, pines or breadfruit. Along Northern Territory coasts the big orange or red "nuts" are split to extract the seeds, which, although small, are rich in oil. Aborigines in parts of Arnhem Land used a special steel tool to extract the white seeds. In centuries past the steel was traded from Indonesian fishermen.

Pandanus "palms" are often the characteristic trees on beaches and headlands along tropical coasts. But wherever white sand gives way to estuarine mud they are replaced by mangroves. Mangrove swamps can be intimidating places, infested with sandflies, box jellyfish and crocodiles. But two of the common trees in these swamps furnished Aborigines with a staple source of starch.

The grey mangrove (*Avicennia marina*) and the orange mangrove (*Bruguiera gymnorhiza*) produce large "seed pods" which were eaten after lengthy preparation, involving pounding, soaking, sifting and baking, to remove astringent tannins. The pods were a staple food of Barbara Thompson, the shipwreck survivor who lived an astonishing four years with islanders on Prince of Wales Island in the 1840s. Orange mangrove pods were soaked in basin-shaped holes in the beach sand, and such holes were a characteristic sight along the coasts of Cape York Peninsula last century.

In sunny open woodlands behind the mangroves and beaches, stands of

Symbol of the tropics, the remarkable coconut palm (*Cocos nucifera*) supplies humankind with food, oil and building materials. On Murray Island in Torres Strait, where these trees were growing, the fronds are thatched into houses as part of a revival of tradition.

Grey mangrove pods (*Avicennia marina*) are actually germinated seeds, and when peeled open are found to consist largely of thickened seedling leaves. Seedling establishment in mangrove mud is so difficult that most mangroves produce highly specialised seedlings.

Joseph Banks's journal told how *Endeavour* crewmen sampled seeds of the cycad *Cycas media*, "but were deterrd from a second experiment by a hearty fit of vomiting which was the consequence of the first". Photographed near Cairns.

Right: Packaged to attract emus? The brightly coloured pith surrounding burrawang seeds (*Macrozamia communis*) probably entices emus to swallow the fruit and disperse the seeds. Both pith and seeds are poisonous to people. Photographed on the south coast of New South Wales.

ancient cycads supplied Aborigines with one of their major staple foods. Cycad seeds look the perfect food: big and starchy and borne in abundance. The problem is, they are extremely poisonous. Aboriginal women removed the toxins by laboriously cracking, soaking, grinding and baking the seeds. Early explorers found the husks at Aboriginal camps and, assuming the seeds were safe to eat, proceeded to poison themselves. Captain Cook, La Pérouse, Matthew Flinders, George Grey, Ludwig Leichhardt, John Stuart, all were witness to the retchings and other agonies of their men, although, curiously, none of the leaders themselves was poisoned. The first cycad poisoning dates back to the Dutchman de Vlamingh in 1696, whose men vomited so violently "there was hardly any difference between us and death"; it was said of them that "The sailors who ate these nuts crawled all over the earth and made ungovernable movements". Cook's crewmen were poisoned at Endeavour River, and Joseph Banks noted that men who ate just one or two seeds "were violently affected by them both upwards and downwards". It has been said that explorers were too proud to read each other's journals, and so the poisonings continued over the next century.

Cycads caused so many problems, not simply because they are poisonous, but because there is no warning smell or

taste. I once boiled up some burrawang seeds (*Macrozamia communis*) and was delighted by the sweet chestnut taste, though I would have been severely purged had I swallowed any.

Cycads are ancient plants, with a fossil record reaching back at least 200 million years: they are the palm-like plants in dinosaur dioramas. In northern Australia Aborigines used cycads of the genus *Cycas*; in the east various *Macrozamia* and *Lepidozamia* species were used, and in the south-west, the pulp around the seeds of *M. riedlei* was prepared and eaten.

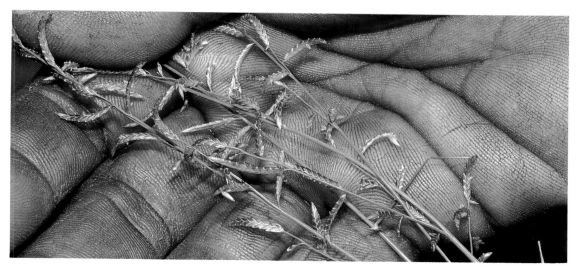

Premium grain of outback Aborigines, woollybutt (*Eragrostis eriopoda*) is exceptionally nutritious, containing thirteen to seventeen per cent protein and very large amounts of iron and zinc. Wholemeal wheat is 11.5 per cent protein and brown rice only 6.9 per cent.

The other large seeds of importance to Aborigines were the bunya nuts (*Araucaria bidwillii*). These were gathered by clambering to the crowns of towering bunya pines, those majestic trees of rainforests in the ranges of southern Queensland. A relictual colony of these trees persists in north Queensland, showing that in prehistoric times these pines were widespread. Bunya nuts (and coconuts) are the only large seeds in Australia that may be eaten raw (all the others are poisonous unless leached). They are described in the Wild Nuts chapter.

The staple seeds of coastal Aborigines—cycads, mangroves, rainforest beans and the like—are all large. Smaller seeds, like those of Polynesian arrowroot (*Tacca leontopetaloides*), were eaten as snack foods, but coastal Aborigines did not make much use of the tiny grains of grasses. But in the outback, where foods are fewer, small seeds of grasses, wattles and pigweed, and nardoo spores, were major staples. More than seventy different outback seeds were eaten.

The seeds of desert grasses were ground and baked as damper. Especially important were wild panicums (*Panicum* species) and woollybutt (*Eragrostis eriopoda*) and, in the Gulf of Carpentaria, wild rice (*Oryza meridionalis*). Woollybutt seeds are the size of sand grains and seem

Delectable damper was made by Aborigines from the protein-rich seeds of native millet (*Panicum decompositum*), a close relative of Italian millet and an outback staple food. Graziers value this grass, for it fattens cattle and sheep.

an unlikely food, but four characteristics render them valuable: they are soft and easy to grind, they husk easily, they are carried on the plant for months after ripening, and they are produced in abundance on outback plains. They are also extremely nutritious, easily outscoring wheat and wholemeal rice in protein and minerals.

The seeds of at least thirty different wattles (*Acacia* species) were eaten in the

Groves of mulga trees (*Acacia aneura*) supplied desert Aborigines with one of their most nutritious seeds, the protein content of which exceeds twenty-five per cent. The hard wood of the tree was rendered into spears, boomerangs and digging sticks of great strength.

Pods of desert wattle (*Acacia dictyophleba*) yield exceptionally nutritious seeds, containing up to twenty-six per cent protein and eleven per cent fat. Wholemeal wheat contains only 11.5 per cent protein and 2.5 per cent fat. Photographed at Uluru.

Aborigines warred over the pods of coast wattle (*Acacia sophorae*). The feared Kukata tribe of South Australia used to burn the wattle groves of their adversaries as an act of provocation. Photographed at Beachport, South Australia.

outback, and these are also extraordinarily nutritious foods, containing several times the protein content of wheat. Dried wattle seeds were ground between stones and baked as damper; green seeds were eaten like peas. Some wattles bear prolifically. Anthropologist Peter Latz estimates a yearly yield of mulga seed (*A. aneura*) of at least a hundred kilograms per hectare. So abundant is mulga in the Northern Territory that the seed produced in an average year could feed a quarter of a million people.

Although wattles grow Australia-wide, it appears that only desert dwellers used them as food—with one notable exception, the coast wattle (*A. sophorae*) of southern seashores. In South Australia and Tasmania its pods were roasted and the "peas" eaten.

Pigweed (*Portulaca oleracea*) grows throughout much of Australia, but it too was a seed crop only in the outback, where dense colonies sprout on flood plains after rain. The fleshy plants were heaped onto bare ground, or onto bark sheets or hides, and left to dry till the seed capsules burst. So oily are the seeds that they stained the grinding stones used by the Aborigines, and these can be

Slowly dying on a diet of nardoo (*Marsilea drummondii*), W. J. Wills lamented: "Starvation on nardoo is by no means very unpleasant, but for the weakness one feels and the utter inability to move oneself, for, as far as the appetite is concerned, it gives me the greatest satisfaction."

recognised even today by their oily sheen.

The infamous nardoo (*Marsilea drummondii*), upon which Burke and Wills "starved" to death, is one of the more unlikely outback foods. Despite its clover-like appearance, it is a fern, one adapted to growing on the edges of claypans and billabongs. Aboriginal women swept up the tiny brown spore capsules and made a gritty nardoo spore damper. Burke and Wills at first thought nardoo grew on a tree, and by the time they learned how to harvest the flour they were close to death. Because nardoo did not restore their health it has been thought to be low in nutrients but, surprisingly, this has never been tested.

Somewhat larger than most outback seeds are the seeds of the kurrajongs (*Brachychiton* species). A single desert kurrajong tree (*B. gregorii*) yields about a

One of Australia's most significant food plants, pigweed (*Portulaca oleracea*) served as a vegetable for both settlers and Aborigines, and as a source of oily grain for Aborigines. The seeds contain up to twenty per cent protein and sixteen per cent fat.

thousand pods per season, each containing four to eight nutritious nutty seeds. In the Mann Ranges of South Australia the Pitjantjatjara gathered kilograms of the seeds from the dung of crows around waterholes. After pounding the seeds they made a tasty damper with them. Seeds of the common kurrajong (*B. populneus*) are particularly nutritious, comprising about eighteen per cent protein and twenty-five per cent fat.

Numerous other kinds of desert seeds

This majestic desert oak (*Allocasuarina decaisneana*) standing near Ayers Rock provided the local Pitjantjatjara with cones containing tiny edible seeds, a minor food that is nowadays rarely harvested.

were harvested as food, ranging from the tiny grains of sedges and desert samphire (*Tecticornia verrucosa*), to the large oil-rich seeds of quandongs (see Wild Nuts chapter) and the cones of the desert oak (*Allocasuarina decaisneana*).

Before finishing with the seeds, it is worth noting that a number of our roadside weeds carry edible grain. Seeds of urena burr (*Urena lobata*), onion weed (*Romulea rosea*) and fennel (see Wild Herbs and Spices chapter) have been eaten overseas. Wild oats (*Avena fatua*), a common weedy grass of vacant allotments and railway embankments, is the ancestor of the oat, and its seed is certainly edible. The grains of crowsfoot grass (*Eleusine indica*), summer grass (*Digitaria sanguinalis*) and Indian millet (*Setaria italica*) have been harvested in Asia. From these and other roadside grasses it is possible to prepare a tasty and nutritious wild foods bread.

South African children nibble half-ripe pods of onion grass (*Romulea rosea*), calling them "knikkertjies". This plant has become a significant weed in temperate Australia. Photographed on a roadside south of Wagga Wagga.

WILD
NUTS

Imagine walking into a native foods shop, picking up a packet of mixed nuts, and perusing the label: "Contains Australian rainforest monkey nuts, candlenuts, native cashews, quandong kernels, macadamias."

This scenario is not as far-fetched as it might seem. Australian native nuts are serious business. Macadamias are marketed worldwide, and premium bunya nuts can be bought from select Australian supermarkets. Two other native nuts—the rainforest monkey nut and the outback quandong—are candidates for commercial cultivation.

The significance of this can be measured against the failure of any other of Australia's plants to be commercially cultivated. None of our native fruits, vegetables, roots or grains is grown commercially.

Australia has good nuts because of our rich rainforests. Most of our nut-bearing trees come from subtropical rainforests in Queensland and New South Wales.

So little light reaches the rainforest floor that many trees produce very large seeds to give their seedlings a better chance. Such seeds are packed with nutritious starch and oil as food for the baby tree. To guard against hungry rats and beetles the seeds usually have hard shells. These seeds we call "nuts", and those rich in oil can be very, very tasty.

In general, the oilier the seed the thicker the shell needs to be to discourage rats. This explains why macadamia kernels (and candlenuts) lie protected within such incredibly hard, woody shells.

The macadamia is world-famous, but Australia's other native nuts are generally unknown. To remedy this sad situation, I present here an account of

the main edible species. Also included is a description of native flax, which, though not a nut, has an oily, nutty taste.

Australia's proud contribution to international cuisine, the exquisite macadamia, was actually developed into a crop, not by Australians, but by American farmers in Hawaii. Seeds were shipped to Hawaii early this century, spawning what is now a multimillion-dollar industry. Australia did not follow suit until 1963, when CSR began commercial production. Many of the varieties grown in southern Queensland, where the industry is based, bear Hawaiian names.

However, macadamias have always been popular garden trees in Queensland, and most Brisbanites have fond childhood memories of laying the nuts on concrete paths and whacking them with bricks. A measured blow was needed to crack the shells without mashing their contents.

A large macadamia tree, known also as

Australia's famous nut, the macadamia (*Macadamia integrifolia*), is becoming popular in North America, although the market there is supplied from Hawaii. The species shown here is the smooth macadamia; the closely related rough-shelled macadamia has a rougher nut.

The dazzling scarlet rind of the red bopple nut (*Hicksbeachia pinnatifolia*) is difficult to explain as an evolutionary attribute. What animal is it designed to attract? Perhaps cassowaries, although these no longer live in the rainforests where the nut grows.

Right: Eerie flower spikes of the red bopple nut hang from a small tree growing at the edge of a rainforest at Tomewin near Murwillumbah. This tree was probably common in the Big Scrub of northern New South Wales, a huge block of rainforest that was completely felled for farming.

the Queensland nut tree, may bear a hundred kilograms of nuts in a season. The creamy white kernels are so oily that, like candlenuts, they will burn with a bright flame for five or ten minutes.

There are actually two very similar macadamias, the smooth macadamia (*Macadamia integrifolia*), with most leaves grouped in threes, and the rough-shelled macadamia (*M. tetraphylla*), with leaves in fours. These trees are rare and grow in rainforests in southern Queensland.

Related to the macadamia is the beautiful monkey nut, known also as red bopple nut (*Hicksbeachia pinnatifolia*). This is a another rare tree of dense rainforest in far northern New South Wales and southern Queensland. It is becoming popular as a garden subject for its large frond-like leaves and strings of brilliant scarlet fruits. Each fruit has a leathery inedible rind surrounding a large edible seed. Although bland when raw, this seed tastes delicious after roasting or frying. At Macquarie University this

poor man's macadamia has been studied as a possible commercial crop. The tree's anatomy and histology were investigated. The fresh nuts would certainly look attractive on supermarket shelves—the rinds are a dazzling glossy red.

Candlenuts (*Aleurites moluccana*) are so rich in oil that Pacific Islanders skewered them on sticks as candles, hence the name. The nuts were an important food in the South Pacific, and Polynesian seafarers spread the seeds from Asia to Hawaii, where candlenut is now the state tree. In Australia candlenut grows in north Queensland rainforests, where it is presumed to be native but was possibly introduced by early travellers.

Nutrition tests by the Commonwealth Department of Defence Support show candlenuts to be an extremely rich food. The seeds contain fifty per cent fat and more than 4200 micrograms per hundred grams of thiamine—an amount far in excess of any unprocessed commercial food. (Only Vegemite, Marmite and other yeast products contain more.)

Candlenut trees are often grown in parks in Queensland and northern New South Wales. They have white flowers and maple-like leaves on long stalks. The oily kernels are borne inside round pods of golfball size, which turn brown and leathery and fall to the ground when ripe. The seeds are good eating, with the texture of macadamia nuts (but only half the flavour). They should be roasted before eating or they may cause stomach upset.

In the Philippines, candlenut oil, known as lumbang oil, is extracted commercially as lamp oil, and for paint mixes, varnishes and soap. Aborigines in north Queensland mixed it with ochre to make paint for spears.

Among the strange fruits sold in markets in Asia are those of the cashew tree. These are peach-sized, with a juicy, pineapple-like flesh, and with the curly cashew seed encased in a shell at the lower end—on the outside of the fruit. The seed, and the sticky latex that oozes from the fruit, are poisonous unless roasted.

A related tree, the Australian cashew or marking nut tree (*Semecarpus australiensis*), grows in the forests of northern Australia and has yellow or red fruits with the same structure. Aborigines roasted the fruits and ate both the sweet flesh and the nutty seeds. Explorer Ludwig Leichhardt sampled the fruits during his northern expedition and found them "extremely refreshing". I have not tasted the seeds and have heard no suggestion that the tree may be worth cultivating.

Incidentally, the poisonous sap of the cashew was used in India last century to fake bruises in court cases alleging assault. It produces excruciating blisters and lumps. The Australian cashew has similar irritating sap, and before handling the fruits Aboriginal women smeared their hands with protective clay.

North Queensland Aborigines squeezed the oil from candlenuts (*Aleurites moluccana*) and mixed it with pigments to make a simple paint for their spears. The oil is widely used in the Philippines and China.

Below: Although both fruit and nut are edible, the Australian cashew (*Semecarpus australiensis*) is a tree to beware of, for the sap produces fierce blisters and intense pain. Leichhardt was poisoned in the Northern Territory, experiencing "deep and painful ulceration".

The quandong (*Santalum acuminatum*) is a famous outback tree. Each spring its branches bow under heavy crops of scarlet fruits, a favourite food of emus (see Outback Fruits chapter). Inside the fruits lie knobbly rounded seeds, which early colonists made into necklace beads, stud buttons, and marbles for Chinese checkers. Within each nut is a rich oily kernel, a food the Aborigines gathered during droughts, when fallen seeds could be found beneath the trees.

So popular is the quandong in inland Australia that CSIRO scientists in Adelaide hope to turn it into a commercial crop. It may prove suitable for semiarid farms where over-clearing and other land abuse have raised soil salinity. The fruit is rich in vitamin C, and the kernels are very high in protein (twenty-five per cent) and oil (seventy per cent). According to the CSIRO the fruits meet with "a high degree of

consumer acceptance", but the kernels are unacceptable because of a pungent aromatic oil, methyl benzoate. I am munching quandong kernels as I write, and find them quite tasty; the methyl benzoate is noticeable only as a slight aftertaste. However, some crops are quite bitter, and CSIRO scientists who have tried treating the kernels by heating and cooking consider it a "major obstacle to their commercial exploitation as a nut crop". (Another major obstacle is the quandong tree's parasitic habit—its roots must attach themselves to those of other plants, from which it draws off nutrients.) Nonetheless, the CSIRO maintains quandong plots near Adelaide, where plants are grafted and selected; and an enterprising farmer has established a quandong farm at Broken Hill, where the wild tree is common.

Seeds of the peanut tree (*Sterculia quadrifida*) taste surprisingly like commercial peanuts. The tree is found in rainforests from northern New South Wales to the Northern Territory, and is well known to country people in places where it grows. In summer it sprouts leathery pods which split to reveal two rows of delicious "peanuts" framed by the scarlet insides of the pod.

Closely related to the peanut tree are the kurrajongs (*Brachychiton* species), all of which have nutty edible seeds inside leathery pods. The flame tree (*B. acerifolius*), often planted in gardens, is a member of this group, and it is easy to gather seeds from roadside trees to roast as treats.

The sea almond (*Terminalia catappa*) is aptly named, for this tropical seashore tree has white kernels with a strong almond taste. In northern Australia the trees grow around Aboriginal and Islander camps, and there are always a few rocks for smashing open the purple fruits. Despite the size of each fruit, the kernel inside is tiny. The purple pulp is also edible, and both fruit and nut are popular snack foods on the Torres Strait

Islands, where this tree has probably been spread by island travellers.

The European flax plant (*Linum usitatissimum*), a pretty herb with sky blue flowers, is a significant crop, harvested both for its fibrous stems, which are woven into linen, and for its oily seeds, the source of linseed oil. Australia has a native flax (*L. marginale*) which can be used in the same way. Aborigines ate the crunchy seeds and spun the stems into string for fishing nets and lines.

Native flax is a herb of dry eucalypt forests and woodlands in southern Australia, growing north as far as Stanthorpe. It is common in the hills behind Adelaide. The flat brown seeds can be gathered in summer and autumn and used like sesame seeds. They taste delightfully nutty.

The sweet purple flesh of the sea almond encloses a tiny seed exactly like an almond. On Stephens Island in Torres Strait, where I took this photo, the island headman was chewing the fruits while he prepared a soup of turtle intestines.

The delicate blue flowers of native flax (*Linum marginale*) are followed in time by tiny oily seeds tasting like sesame seeds. This herb, found in south-eastern Australia, closely resembles cultivated flax, which is the source of linseed. Photographed in the Adelaide Hills.

Bunya nut bounty:
Aborigines feasted upon
the big starchy seeds of
the bunya pine (*Araucaria
bidwillii*), which were
gathered in the
mountains west of
Gympie where the tall
trees grew. Steps were
cut into the trunks to
allow the men to climb
the trees and chop down
the nut-bearing cones.

Apart from the macadamia, the only native nut likely to be found in a store in Australia is the delicious bunya nut (*Araucaria bidwillii*). More and more supermarkets in Sydney and Melbourne are selling the big starchy seeds, which are gathered from the towering bunya pine, a magnificent rainforest tree of mountains in southern Queensland. Bunya pines are often grown in parks, where they are sometimes confused with the similar hoop pine and Norfolk Island pine. In autumn the trees drop huge cones full of large starchy seeds, delicious when boiled or baked. The flavour compares with a young waxy potato, but the seeds are much denser and very, very

filling. They were a very important Aboriginal food. Unfortunately the bunya pine supplies an excellent timber and most wild stands of this magnificent tree were felled last century. The seeds sold occasionally in supermarkets are presumably taken from street trees.

Other nuts found in north Queensland rainforests may prove promising as future crops. CSIRO scientists at Atherton speak highly of the Kuranda quandong (*Elaeocarpus bancroftii*), an excellent nut said to be equal to the macadamia. But the tree is virtually unknown in cultivation and few white people have ever tasted its precious seed.

NATIVE
BEANS AND PEAS

The remarkable bean family (Fabaceae) has contributed enormously to the human diet. The list of edible beans and peas seems endless: consider french beans, jack beans, broad beans, haricots, lima beans, mung beans, soya beans, lentils, split peas, chick peas, peanuts and snow peas, to name but a few. Processed bean products range from pea soup, baked beans and peanut paste (butter), to dhal, tofu and falafel.

Wild beans and peas grow prolifically in Australia, with more than eight hundred native species ranging from tiny creepers to giant jungle trees. One might expect that Aborigines would have harvested many of these as foods, for the seeds are highly nutritious. In fact the reverse was true—only a handful of legumes were eaten. The great majority were never used.

The problem is, nearly all of Australia's peas and beans are toxic. Some are frightfully dangerous. Even the species harvested by Aborigines were mostly poisonous, but were of such size, and so filled with starch, they were worth the bother of the leaching and special preparation that preceded each meal. Had Aborigines had cooking pots they would probably have used more of the smaller native beans, for the toxins in some of these are destroyed by cooking.

Jequirity bean, or gidee-gidee, (*Abrus precatorius*) is an example of a bean that Aborigines did *not* eat. It grows on a small twiner found worldwide in tropical and subtropical woodlands. In Egypt the cooked seeds are eaten, despite being "very hard and indigestible". According to my poisons book, the seeds contain abrin, "one of the most powerful poisons known. One seed contains more than enough toxin to kill an adult man but if it remains unbroken the poison is not released."

Cooking evidently destroys the poison.

The bead-like seeds of jequirity bean (*Abrus precatorius*) were gathered by Aborigines and glued to their tools. By trading these tools, Aborigines probably helped to spread about the seeds of this widespread plant.

A bean of giant proportions, the matchbox bean (*Entada phaseoloides*) hangs heavily from a jungle liana, carrying seeds as big as biscuits. Photographed at Cape Tribulation.

Matchbox beans were a food of nineteenth-century shipwreck survivor James Murrell, who lived for seventeen years with Aborigines near Townsville. Murrell returned reluctantly to civilisation, vowing to devote his life to the welfare of his adopted tribe, a role the colonists would not accept.

But considering the risk, and the diminutive size of the seeds, it is not surprising Aborigines left them out of their dinner. (They did string the seeds together as beads and glue them to firesticks, and the seeds were used as beads in the Old World, hence their other name, rosary pea. Also, the leaves of this vine are edible (see Wild Teas chapter).

Of the few beans that were eaten by Aborigines, one of the largest was the matchbox bean (*Entada phaseoloides*) of northern jungles. The big "beans" look like chocolate biscuits, and hang in enormous pods a metre or more long, on a giant liana. Inventive colonists hollowed and carved the beans into ornamental boxes for wax matches. The vines thrive in strand rainforest behind tropical beaches, and ocean currents disperse the seeds. Anyone who has ever walked along a north Queensland beach has found one of these curious seeds and they now gather dust on mantelpieces throughout Australia. Tourist shops paint the seeds in garish colours to sell as kitsch curios.

Within each bean is a store of white starch impregnated with toxins. Ethnographer Walter Roth, writing at the turn of the century, said this was eaten only when there was nothing better: "The seed is first baked in the ashes, then cracked up, and, inside a dilly-bag, left in running water all night." At Cape York I tried to follow this procedure but the seeds always exploded in the fire.

The largest and starchiest of the beans eaten by Aborigines were those of the Moreton Bay chestnut, or black bean (*Castanospermum australe*). This handsome tree of rainforest riverbanks north of Coffs Harbour is often grown in gardens. One of Australia's largest legumes, it has striking orange-red pea flowers attractive to lorikeets and fruit bats. In autumn the trees bear enormous seeds, which despite being poisonous

were widely used as food. Colonial botanist Joseph Maiden recorded that "The large seed was scraped by means of jagged mussel-shells, into a vermicelli like substance, prior to soaking it in water. The coarse meal was then made into a thin cake and eaten." Soaking removed the toxin.

Another method of preparation was recorded by early Brisbane settler Tom Petrie, who gave the Aboriginal name of the bean as "mai": "The nuts were cracked and soaked, then pounded, and made into cakes, and roasted. The blacks called the white man's bread 'mai' after this, when they first got into the habit of using it."

I have never tried preparing these beans—it is risky—but once tasted a boiled seed, and found it had a delightful chestnut taste, though I was careful not to swallow any. Cattle die after eating the seeds.

Another wild bean used by Aborigines

Alluring to lorikeets, the large nectar-laden flowers of the Moreton Bay chestnut (*Castanospermum australe*) justify a place for this tree in the home garden. The pea-like flowers show that this tree is a member of the bean family (Fabaceae).

A cure for cancer? The seeds of Moreton Bay chestnuts contain an alkaloid which scientists in Canada and the United States hope will treat some forms of cancer, and perhaps even AIDS.

Amongst vegetation fringing a Gold Coast beach, a beach bean (*Canavalia rosea*) sprouts flowers and beans. The vine is easily identified by its pinkish flowers and leaflets in threes.

was the rainforest velvet bean, or burney bean, (*Mucuna gigantea*) found along our northern coasts. The hard woody seeds lie protected inside a dangling pod armed with irritating hairs. Explorer Ludwig Leichhardt noted Aborigines using the seeds, and followed suit: "I gathered the large vine-bean, with green blossoms, which had thick pods containing from

Staple food of desert Aborigines, the maloga bean (*Vigna lanceolata*) has a slender edible root, and small beans which can be eaten raw. Descriptions of "yams" from the outback often refer to this creeper. Photographed near Bedourie.

one to five seeds. Its hard covering, by roasting, became very brittle; and I pounded the cotyledons, and boiled them for several hours. This softened them, and made a sort of porridge, which, at all events, was very satisfying. Judging by the appearance of the large stones which were frequently found, in the camps of the natives, still covered with the mealy particles of some seed which had been pounded upon them, it would seem that the natives used the same bean; but I could not ascertain how they were able to soften them."

Another bean used by Aborigines, the coastal beach bean (*Canavalia rosea*), is of great interest because it was eaten by Captain Cook. While repairing the *Endeavour* in north Queensland the navigator cooked up and tried the beans, which he said were "not to be dispised". Joseph Banks was derogatory, dismissing them as "a kind of Beans, very bad".

Like nearly all Australian beans, raw beach beans are toxic. They poisoned shipwrecked sailors in north-western Australia last century, and Governor Phillip was left vomiting after tasting the beans near Sydney. Luckily, the toxin is easily destroyed by heat, and the seeds need only be boiled or baked before eating. They taste remarkably like broad beans. Young pods, still flat and green, can be boiled and eaten whole; larger pods should be shelled and only the seeds used. Eventually the beans ripen into rock-hard seeds, the pods go brittle and snap, and the seeds are flung across the dunes, some of them reaching the sea where they are swept away. Accordingly, beach bean is found worldwide on tropical dunes, and it has been eaten in Malaysia, the flowers as a flavouring and the cooked beans as porridge.

In northern Australia there is a bean vine that produces "peanuts". This is maloga bean (*Vigna lanceolata*), a creeper of woodlands and desert watercourses, the white taproot of which was important Aboriginal tucker. Maloga vines produce beans of two kinds— slender green beans that sprout among foliage, and shorter beans that sprout underground. Both kinds of bean were nibbled raw by Aboriginal children, and on Groote Eylandt in the Northern Territory the latter are known as "toy peanuts".

Maloga bean has yellow pea flowers and leaflets in threes. It is one of a group of tropical bean vines with slender roots that were harvested by Aborigines. Others were cow pea (*Vigna vexillata*), coastal bean (*V. marina*) and wild mung bean (*V. radiata*).

The last of these is a curious plant, for it is the native wild form of the cultivated mung bean. Its natural distribution extends from China to India and south into Australia, as far as northern New South Wales (where it is rare). Aborigines apparently made no use of the seeds, which are small and black, and less than half the size of their cultivated counterparts. Nevertheless, the wild plants are finding a place in modern agriculture for the breeding of mung bean hybrids suited to Australia's climate and soils.

Wild mung beans grow in grassy

Australia's native mung bean (*Vigna radiata*) has slender green pods that blacken upon ripening, splitting violently to eject the tiny seeds. The mung bean of Asia is the same species. Photographed on Murray Island in Torres Strait.

Australian native mung beans are dwarfed by their cultivated counterparts, the products of hundreds of years of selective breeding. Cultivated seeds can be green or black; wild seeds are always greyish or black.

clearings in open forests. The indigenous plants are untidy wiry creepers; the cultivars have neat upright stems.

If Australia's native mung beans are proving of interest, so too are our wild relatives of the soya bean (*Glycine max*). The ancestral soya bean (*G. sojo*) hails from China and Japan, but distantly related members of the genus grow in

Although horribly astringent when raw, the taproot of *Austrodolichus errabundus* can be cooked to make a reasonable vegetable, although the rind is inedible and the core is fibrous.

forests in Australia. These native creepers are resistant to soya bean rust, a disease that so devastates soya beans that sometimes whole crops are abandoned, as happened in northern New South Wales in the 1970s. The disease has been largely ignored in the past, for it is unknown in America, where most soya beans are grown. But during the last decade Australian scientists have tried to cross native *Glycine* species with cultivated soya beans to create a resistant crop. The task is proving onerous, as the plants are only distantly related and the progeny are largely sterile. The tiny seeds of Australian *Glycine* are not considered

Coastal bean (*Vigna marina*) supplied Aborigines with a slender starchy taproot. The small beans appear to be inedible, although in South-East Asia, where this creeper also grows, the young leaves have been cooked and eaten. Photographed on Bribie Island near Brisbane.

One of many tropical beans with an edible taproot, *Austrodolichus errabundus* is a slender creeper from open woodlands in northern Australia. Photographed on Horn Island, north Queensland.

edible, although Aborigines ate the root of one species.

Australian agronomists have also suggested breeding our native *Desmodium* and *Atylosia* species with crop relatives overseas, though nothing has come of this. In north Queensland the root of *A. reticulata* was an Aboriginal food, eaten after roasting and hammering. Other beans eaten by Aborigines, but about which little is known, were hovea (*Hovea longipes*), flax-leaved indigo (*Indigofera linifolia*) and sesbania pea (*Sesbania benthamiana*). Aborigines also ate the taproots of some native beans.

Before finishing with the beans,

mention might be made of our legume weeds. Among these are the vetches (*Vicia* species), certain lupins (*Lupinus* species) and related weeds from overseas with nutritious edible seeds. Especially noteworthy is lucerne (*Medicago sativa*), a source of nutritious hay for cattle and a weed of roadsides and orchards. Lucerne is a pretty weed with violet flowerheads and curly pea pods. The tiny seeds gathered from roadside plants can be kept in a bottle and watered daily. When sprouted, they become that familiar salad food, alfalfa sprouts. For though it is not well known, alfalfa and lucerne are the same plant.

Lucerne, alias alfalfa (*Medicago sativa*), is a common roadside weed, growing wherever its seeds fall from trucks carrying hay. The pretty mauve flowers are followed by tiny curly pods, which contain seeds that can be sprouted as alfalfa sprouts.

TUBERS

WILD
TUBERS

There is a rare satisfaction that comes
from being able to find tubers in the
bush. To know which stalk or sedge
points to an underground store of food is
to own the key to living off the land.
Tubers are easily the most important of
plant foods, but also the hardest to find;
unlike fruits, seeds and leaves, they are
well concealed from view.

Tubers provided the staple diet of
Aborigines over most of Australia.
Various yams, corms, rhizomes and roots
were the major forms of sustenance,
except when cycads and other large seeds
came into season. Only in the deserts,
where bread was baked from grain, were
they secondary in importance.

Early settlers appear to have made
little use of tubers. The few records

indicate that South Australian colonists
ate murnong roots, that arrowroot flour
was made from Darling lily (*Crinum
flaccidum*), and that country boys often
ate orchid tubers, calling them "yams".

The tubers used by Aborigines were
often very small. Nalgoo (*Cyperus*
species), a staple of outback tribes, has
tubers as tiny as peas. Murnong
(*Microseris scapigera*), ground orchids and
lilies, the main staples in Victorian
woodlands, are substantially smaller than
baby carrots. These tiny morsels were
valued because they could be readily
gathered in large numbers from shallow
soil. Big tubers, of potato size or larger,
were found in rainforests and tropical
woodlands, but were usually deeply
buried and difficult to dig, and required

Australian pioneers
sometimes harvested
forest tubers. Murnong
and ground orchid tubers
were dug up and eaten,
and the starchy stem
bases of epiphytic
orchids were taken as
medicines.

leaching to extract bitter or acrid toxins. Aboriginal women were very adept at removing poisons, and only a few kinds of tubers were not able to be used (for example, those of tar vine [*Stephania japonica*], which contain alkaloids).

Tubers are storage organs produced by plants for storing spare sugar, starch or water. Fewer than one in twenty plants produce them. They are rare among trees and shrubs, which have woody trunks for storage, but common among four groups of non-woody plants—water plants, vines, ground orchids and lilies. These plants hold special interest for foragers.

Plants at the water's edge live in a fluctuating environment and often bear starchy underground stems or tubers to tide them over through dry spells. The list of tuberous water plants includes many of Australia's key foods—bungwall fern, the mainstay of Brisbane tribes; bulrushes, a staple along the Murray River; spike rush, a major food in the tropics; and various sedges, waterlilies, lotus and taro. In no other environment do so large a proportion of plants store starch, and in all of the plants, apart from taro, it is edible raw. Taro, incidentally, may have been introduced into Australia by early travellers from New Guinea or Indonesia.

Ground orchids and lilies are plants with a niche in time. In temperate Australia they live for the spring, when the soil is moist but the sun not too hot. After they seed in early summer their flimsy leaves die away, and they survive the hot seasons as tiny underground tubers. In the tropics, lilies and their kin are dormant in the dry season. Some, such as Polynesian arrowroot (*Tacca leontopetaloides*), are hefty plants with two-metre flowering stalks and potato-like tubers. Lilies in temperate Australia are much smaller. Ground orchids, and the smaller lilies (in family Liliaceae and related groups), are considered in detail in the following chapters.

Vines, like other non-woody plants,

often use underground tubers to store spare starch, which would be vulnerable to rats and insects if kept anywhere else. Tuberous vines used by Aborigines included wild bean vines (see Native Beans and Peas chapter), the tar vines (*Boerhavia* species), various close relatives of the sweet potato (*Ipomoea* species) and, of course, the yams.

Early colonists often referred to any of

Tar vine (*Boerhavia* species) sprouts from a stout starchy taproot, once an Aboriginal food but now rarely eaten. One nutritional test of the roots revealed an extraordinarily high yield of potassium.

Of the long yam (*Dioscorea transversa*), colonist C. Petrie noted: "The gins would have to dig three feet sometimes for this root ('tarm') which was very nice roasted." The winged seedpods of this vine, growing on Horn Island, Torres Strait, hang in clusters behind the leaves.

So common are round yams (*Dioscorea bulbifera*) at Cape York, it is easy to see why local Aborigines did not follow the agricultural practices of their islander neighbours in Torres Strait. This plant is flowering.

"Cheeky" tucker: the tuber of the round yam vine was a staple across northern Australia. The Aboriginal slang "cheeky" aludes to the poisons in the tuber, which must be leached away before the tuber can be eaten. It has an excellent floury flavour.

the roots used by Aborigines as "yams", but true yams are vines of genus *Dioscorea* with wiry stems and (usually) heart-shaped leaves. Australia has at least three native species, although, surprisingly, the identification of Australian yams is very confused. I strongly suspect that the so-called long yam (*Dioscorea transversa*) is two species masquerading under one name, one inhabiting eastern rainforests, and the other, northern beaches. The tuber is long, white and slender, can be eaten raw, and has a delightful potato taste. The eastern form is found on rainforest edges south to Sydney.

The round yam (*D. bulbifera*), also known as hairy yam and cheeky yam, was a staple in northern Australia, where it

grows in woodlands, vine-thickets and monsoon forests. The yellow-fleshed tuber is poisonous unless grated, soaked and baked. Round yam is found also in Asia and Africa, and is one of the plants that may have been introduced into Australia in the canoes of early Aboriginal immigrants.

The other native yam is warrine (*D. hastifolia*) of south-western Australia. The explorer George Grey referred to this yam when he wrote of seeing "tracts of land several square miles in extent, so thickly studded with holes, where the natives had been digging up yams (*Dioscorea*), that it was difficult to walk across it".

Apart from these native yams, three introduced species grow wild in Australia, from early introductions by islanders. The oddest of these is the five-leaf yam (*Dioscorea pentaphylla*), with leaves shaped like a hand. Until recently this yam, widespread in Asia, was known in Australia only from a single specimen collected on Thursday Island in 1898. Almost a century later, in April 1988, I visited Thursday Island hoping to rediscover this long-lost species. I was

Never before photographed in Australia, a five-leaf yam (*Dioscorea pentaphylla*) thrives in the gloom of a jungle clearing on Thursday Island, Torres Strait. The vine produces small tubers along its stems, which fall off and sprout like seeds.

overjoyed to find it growing in a clearing in scrub near the Thursday Island dam, and collected it also in rainforest on nearby Hammond Island. In the *Flora of Australia* this species is considered native to Australia, with the footnote "perhaps of pre-European introduction". After seeing the disturbed scrubs where it grows on Thursday Island I feel sure it is an old islander crop gone wild—although the locals did not recognise it. The small tubers taste delicious.

Yams are often thought to be the typical food of Aborigines, but because of their coastal, mainly tropical, distribution they were unavailable to most tribes. Elsewhere in Australia, a variety of tubers took their place.

Bracken fern (*Pteridium esculentum*) was important in south-eastern Australia, where the rhizomes were roasted and chewed to extract the bland white starch. This may be the "fern" which the

This small tuber of a five-leaf yam, which was dug on Hammond Island, had a delicious floury taste. Early travellers probably brought the plant to the Torres Strait islands from New Guinea or Indonesia, where it has been cultivated for hundreds of years.

An Aboriginal woman and five sprouting round yams, as depicted by a Kakadu cave artist. In parts of the Northern Territory the round yam was so important that ceremonies were performed to increase the supply.

Once an Aboriginal staple, now a weed to graziers, the hardy bracken fern (*Pteridium esculentum*) grows well in the foothills of mountain ranges where bushfires are common.

Top right: A dandelion look-alike, the flower heads of murnong (*Microseris scapigera*) signal the presence of sweet starchy tubers.

Below right: Small but numerous, the tasty tubers of murnong sustained dozens of Aboriginal tribes in Victoria, New South Wales and South Australia. These tubers were dug in the Adelaide Hills, where this plant is still common.

officers of the First Fleet saw Aborigines harvesting around Sydney, and flavouring with crushed ants. (Bungwall fern is another possibility.)

It is worth noting that the part of the fern eaten by Aborigines was not the root but the underground stem. Botanists are very fussy about the distinction. Strictly speaking, tubers are swollen roots or stems, bulbs are swollen shoots, rhizomes are underground stems, and corms are underground stems replaced by the plant each year.

In Victoria the most important staple was the yam daisy, or murnong, (*Microseris scapigera*), a relative of the dandelion found abundantly in woodlands amongst grass. The raw tubers

taste bland, even bitter, but when roasted in a stone oven become sweet and syrupy, like the skins of baked sweet potato. It is an appalling tragedy that sheep introduced into Victoria decimated the murnong and destroyed forever the Aboriginal way of life.

Murnong thrived in large numbers alongside edible lilies and orchids, and after flowering in spring and summer survived the autumn heat as dormant tubers. Two other edible herbs grew in the same woodlands, Australian bindweed (*Convolvulus erubescens*) and native cranesbills (*Geranium* species). These have fibrous and not especially tasty roots.

Along rivers and creeks, and especially

the Murray River, the floury rhizomes of bulrushes (*Typha domingensis, T. orientalis*) were staple fare. Explorer Major Thomas Mitchell in 1839 described how this food was prepared: "They take up the root of the bulrush in lengths of about eight or ten inches [20 or 25 centimetres], peel off the outer rind, and lay it a little before the fire; then they twist and loosen the fibres, when a quantity of gluten, exactly resembling wheaten flour, may be shaken out, affording at all times a ready and wholesome food. It struck me that this gluten which they call Bàlyan, must be the 'staff of life' to the tribes inhabiting these morasses." The Aborigines used the leftover fibre to make string, and Mitchell noted "about the fires of the natives, a number of small balls of dry fibre, resembling hemp".

Growing alongside bulrushes were many other sedges used by Aborigines. The clubrushes (*Bolboschoenus* species) are coarse grass-like plants bearing sweet grape-sized tubers in the mud beneath new shoots. Sea clubrush (*B. caldwellii*), a rush found worldwide, has become a weed of drains in Brisbane, Adelaide and Wollongong. Water ribbons (*Triglochin procera*) produces up to two hundred (but usually far fewer) bullet-shaped tubers which are crisp and refreshing but very fibrous. Grey sedge (*Lepironia articulata*) has woody rhizomes yielding a meagre layer of starch.

In northern Australia the spike rush (*Eleocharis dulcis*) provided small onion-shaped tubers that were staple foods, eaten raw or cooked. Feral pigs cause enormous damage to wetlands when grubbing for these. The water chestnuts used in Chinese cooking are the same plant, grown on farms in China.

In Moreton Bay the semiaquatic fern called bungwall (*Blechnum indicum*) was the mainstay of local tribes. Early settler Constance Petrie described how the starchy rhizomes were "first roasted, then scraped and cut up finely with

A staple for riverine Aborigines, bulrushes (*Typha* species) are a botanist's nightmare. The two native species are exceedingly difficult to distinguish from one another and, when illustrated in books such as this, are usually presented without precise identification.

A gleaming white tuber of sweet starch swells in the mud at the base of each young stalk of the sea clubrush (*Bolboschoenus caldwellii*), providing easy pickings for the forager.

An unassuming source of food, the sedge called water ribbons (*Triglochin procera*) was probably an Aboriginal staple over much of Australia. Photographed on Moreton Island near Brisbane.

Right: This bounty of tubers produced by an undescribed species of sedge (*Triglochin*), which is closely related to water ribbons, was found growing in a seasonal drainage channel in tea-tree woodlands near Bamaga in north Queensland.

sharp stones on a log, when it was ready to eat. 'Bangwall' was generally eaten with fish or flesh, as we use bread, though also eaten separately. In a camp, my father says, one would hear the chop-chop continually all over the place, as this food was prepared."

Bungwall is found in coastal swamps throughout eastern and northern Australia, but is nowhere as numerous as in Moreton Bay, and only there served as a staple food. Although resort development has destroyed most of its habitat, it can still be seen lining creeks in the Sunshine Coast hinterland. The

similar mangrove fern (*Acrostichum speciosum*) provides a much smaller yield of starch.

The most colourful of all water plants are the waterlilies (*Nymphaea* species) and the lotus lily (*Nelumbo nucifera*), and these also supplied Aborigines with tubers. Waterlilies are surprisingly useful plants, yielding edible pods, seeds and celery-like stalks as well as coarse tubers. Lotus lilies are more common in Asia, where they feature prominently in art and religion. Their nutty seeds are edible.

Many other rootstocks were eaten— the slender roots of Australian hollyhock (*Lavatera plebeia*), the sweet root bark of certain eucalypts (*Eucalyptus* species), the rhizomes of kangaroo paws (*Anigozanthos* species) and the hefty roots of gymea lilies (*Doryanthes excelsa*). In Western Australia the roots of the Christmas tree (*Nuytsia floribunda*) were harvested, as recorded by settler Ethell Hassell: "The natives dug up the suckers, which are numerous, peeled off the pale yellow outer bark, and ate the moist brittle

centre which tastes like sugar candy." In Queensland rainforests starch was extracted from the cunjevoi (*Alocasia macrorrhizos*), probably the most toxic of all tuber crops, by repeatedly baking and pounding the rhizomes. Potato-like tubers of Polynesian arrowroot (*Tacca leontopetaloides*) were grated or pounded, soaked, and then baked. Black arum lilies (*Typhonium* species) and *Amorphophallus galbra* were treated similarly.

Related to these are the bloodroots (*Haemodorum* species) of Western Australia, grass-like plants which appear to have been among the most unappetising of Australian bush foods. Explorer George Grey said the roots caused dysentery unless first pounded and mixed with earth. James Backhouse said the Aborigines called them "Mean; and poor fare, it truly is, occasioning their tongues to crack grievously".

An abundance of bungwall (*Blechnum indicum*) in this paperbark tea-tree swamp on Bribie Island must have signalled easy living for the Aborigines, who feasted on the starch. Special rocks were used for pounding the rhizomes.

Throughout Sydney's sandstone belt grows the gymea or flame lily (*Doryanthes excelsa*), with its thick root which was once eaten by Aborigines. Missionary James Backhouse noted that "The Blacks . . . roast the roots, and make them into a sort of cake, which they eat cold". Photographed at Waterfall.

FOREST
LILIES

The delectably fragrant chocolate lily (*Dichopogon strictus*) "during spring gives to many of our meadows by its frequency quite a purple hue," said colonial botanist Baron Ferdinand von Mueller. Photographed in Morialta Conservation Park near Adelaide.

In the Adelaide Hills the nodding chocolate lily (*Dichopogon fimbriatus*) grows alongside the common chocolate lily but has a later flowering season. Photographed at Belair.

Australia's Aborigines knew the smell of chocolate for thousands of years before they encountered the taste. The aroma is carried by the mauve flowers of two little lilies found among grass in the woodlands of southern Australia. Chocolate lilies (*Dichopogon strictus* and *D. fimbriatus*) were important to Aborigines, not for their smell, but for their small translucent tubers which Aborigines dug as food. These are watery and bittersweet and don't taste at all like chocolate.

Chocolate lilies were but one of many kinds of small native lily the Aborigines gathered for their roots. Fringed lilies, bulbine lilies, milkmaids, early nancy and grass lilies were also part of the harvest. Most of these lilies are well-known wildflowers, much beloved by naturalists and bushwalkers. Their importance as Aboriginal foods is largely forgotten.

The common fringed lily, or violet lily, (*Thysanotus tuberosus*) is famous for its

feathery fringed flowers, so frail and ephemeral, which open only for a single morning, to be pollinated by small native bees, and close about midday or shortly after. The plants are then nearly impossible to find in the grass where they grow. Under the ground the roots swell into small sugary tubers which Aboriginal women dug up with digging sticks as sweet treats.

The related twining fringed lily (*T. patersonii*) is a delicate creeper found twining about grass stalks and the low branches of shrubs. Its leaves fall away each spring and the plant photosynthesises through its wiry stems.

At Mingenew in Western Australia Aborigines called this creeper "tjungoori". The vine and leaves were rolled into a ball, placed on the edge of a fire and covered with hot ashes. They were then ground to a green powder and eaten with the sweet root of york gum (*Eucalyptus loxophleba*). In eastern

Australia the watery bittersweet tubers were dug and eaten. Twining fringed lily is common in sunny glades in the forests and heaths of southern Australia; it flowers during the morning in winter, spring and summer.

In the deserts of the Northern Territory the desert fringed lily (*T. exiliflorus*) was an important source of water for travelling Pintupi. During long treks across barren plains they pulled up the tiny tubers and squeezed the juice into their mouths. The bitter skins were discarded. Western Aranda applied the root juice as a hair lotion.

Australia has another forty-four different fringed lilies, at least half of which bear tubers, and were probably Aboriginal foods. In South Australia Aborigines ate the mallee fringed lily (*T. baueri*), but nothing is known of their use of the other species—the anthropological record is too patchy. Some fringed lilies are now extremely rare plants, especially in Western Australia, where six species face extinction.

The season for flowering lilies is spring, especially the month of October. A few species open as late as summer, but none flowers earlier than early nancy (*Wurmbea dioica*), which blooms in late winter. Colonial botanist Baron Ferdinand von Mueller declared this the "first harbinger of the spring, as it bursts forth into flower, much like the

One of Australia's most famous wildflowers, the common fringed lily (*Thysanotus tuberosus*) decorates the forest floor with its elegant fringed blossoms. As its Latin name indicates, the roots are tuberous. Photographed at Westlake near Melbourne.

Ephemeral flowers of the forest floor, the little blooms of the twining fringed lily (*Thysanotus patersonii*) open but once during sunny mornings. Baron von Mueller called the plant "a delicate humble climber".

A pretty wildflower with an ugly name, *Wurmbea biglandulosa* sprouts among grass at Girraween National Park in southern Queensland. *Wurmbea* is an ancient genus harking back sixty-million years; members of the genus are found in southern Australia and South Africa.

snowdrop indicates the first effects of the warming rays of the spring-sun in the European North".

The flowers of early nancy have six white petals, often with an inner band of pink, green or yellow, or small insect-guiding spots. In olden times this wildflower had quaint colloquial names such as "pepper and salt", "harbinger of spring" and "blackman's potatoes". The bitter tubers are not especially palatable, even after baking.

One of a group of lilies, the nancies (formerly in genus *Anguillaria*) have soft green leaves with broad sheaths encircling the stems, and tiny round tubers, usually smaller than peas. *W. biglandulosa* and *W. dioica* are common wildflowers in south-eastern Australia, growing amongst grass.

Desert nancy (*W. centralis*) is an odd member of the group with pink flowers and an eccentric distribution. It is known only from the Flinders Ranges and southern districts of South Australia, and from the Olgas six hundred kilometres to the north-west, where it grows in deep sand in gullies. Unlike the other nancies, which flower each year, this hardy desert-adapted plant grows and flowers only after rain. To help it through drought, its starchy tuber is much larger and carried much deeper than those of other nancies. The grape-sized tuber has a rich nutty taste. Once a food of the Pitjantjatjara, its use has been forgotten, and present-day Aborigines deny that it is edible.

Milkmaids (*Burchardia umbellata*) is another of the prettily named wildflowers, known also as "star of Bethlehem". One of the commonest wildflowers in south-eastern and south-western Australia, it decorates the forest floor each spring with clusters of dainty white flowers, the petals of which are concave. Of all the forest lilies, I think milkmaids presents the tastiest tubers. These are crisp and starchy, looking like tiny carrots, with a pleasant potato taste.

Milkmaids (*Burchardia umbellata*) is one of the characteristic wildflowers of southern Australia. Although it was probably a staple food of Aborigines, their harvesting of the tubers is mentioned only twice in the historical records.

Lilies of the field: a dense colony of milkmaids in the Mount Lofty Ranges near Adelaide speaks of an abundance of bush tucker. Chocolate lilies, orchids and murnong grow in the same forest glades but are rarely so conspicuous.

They are carried in clusters of three to ten at the base of each plant, several centimetres into the soil. Milkmaids is common in the ranges behind Adelaide and Melbourne.

Bulbine lily (*Bulbine bulbosa*) has golden flowers in small heads carried on waving stalks a half-metre or so tall. Like the other lilies, it is a colonial plant, and one may stroll through sun-dappled forests in late spring and see dozens of the yellow flower heads nodding in the breeze. Von Mueller praised the flowers for contributing "much to the gayness of our flower-fields during spring". To the Aborigines these blossoms signalled plentiful food, for the rounded tuber is large and starchy.

Bulbine lily is probably not a single species but rather a group of two or more similar plants that botanists have not as yet delineated. This seems likely because the distribution of these lilies is so peculiar: there are bulbine colonies in arid central Queensland, and others in cool wet forests in subalpine New South Wales. Bulbine lilies are probably affected by grazing: explorer Major Mitchell collected specimens in the north-west corner of New South Wales, where they have not been seen since.

The tiny tubers of milkmaids are one of the tastier root crops of woodlands in temperate Australia. These were dug near Mount Gambier.

Bulbine lily (*Bulbine bulbosa*) is known to some country people by the telling names of "wild yam" and "gin's onion", suggesting it was once a significant Aboriginal food. Photographed at Belair in Adelaide.

The tubers of bulbine lily are 7.5 per cent carbohydrate and about 80 per cent water, and contain very large amounts of calcium and iron.

Below left: These tubers of golden stars (*Hypoxis pratensis* var. *tuberculata*) were dug by Lennie Duncan at Cherbourg in southern Queensland. Lennie remembers his mother's people at St George gathering the tubers of yellow-flowered lilies, possibly those of golden stars.

Right: The golden star (*Hypoxis marginata*) is one of ten *Hypoxis* in Australia, four of which were named only in 1987. The genus is found also in America, Africa and Asia and embraces 150 species worldwide. The tubers were harvested as food by Aborigines and by the Kanaks of New Caledonia. Photographed at Cape York.

Among the tiniest of lilies are the golden stars (*Hypoxis* species), small grass-like plants with dainty yellow blooms, found widely throughout Australia on coasts and inland plains. There are several accounts of Aborigines eating the minute tubers, from regions as disparate as the Kimberleys, Keppel Island in Queensland, western New South Wales and central Queensland. I find these records surprising, for every time I have cooked up the tubers I have been repelled by the earthy, bitter, often irritant, taste.

A friend of mine, Geoff Monteith, 47, remembers eating the tubers as a small boy in the Burnett Valley of southern Queensland. During lunch hours at school his chums squatted on the ground digging up the tubers, cupfuls of which were washed under the tap and eaten raw. "That was what we did in those days when their wasn't any television," Geoff recalls.

Another group of small lilies with grass-like leaves are the aptly named grass lilies (*Caesia* species). The tiny flowers have blue, purple or white petals, with a darker mid-stripe. After unfurling for a day, the flowers close again and the petals become twisted, providing an aid to identification.

No-one is really sure how many kinds of grass lily there are in the south, and wildflower books often list the blue grass lily (*C. vittata*), which is probably only a colour form of the widespread pale grass lily (*C. parviflora*). The tubers were a food of Aborigines in Victoria and New South Wales.

All of the lilies harvested by Aborigines have similar habits. They are woodland plants dependent on their starch- or water-filled tubers to tide them over through hot summers or seasonal droughts. Most of these species wither during summer, surviving only as underground tubers. During late winter the leaves re-emerge and the flowers follow. The tubers swell up after the foliage has died away, and Aborigines were no doubt very adept at spotting the dried stalks in the grass.

Most of these lilies are colonial plants, and large numbers can be found close together. Aboriginal women could easily have turned the soil with digging sticks, and though the tubers are tiny, enormous numbers could be gathered with little effort. So prolific are these plants in shallow woodland soils in southern Australia, that tubers of different species can be found entwined, forming in some areas an underground layer of starch. Tuberous ground orchids and murnong grow in the same soils and contributed to what must have been an extraordinary harvest of food.

These rich tuber beds were probably major resources for Aborigines in southern Australia prior to European settlement. Unfortunately the soft leaves (they are tender because they are produced each year anew) are avidly eaten by cattle, rabbits and sheep, and lily fields nowadays survive only in hilly regions free from grazing pressure, such as the Dandenongs, Grampians and Mount Lofty Ranges.

Although lily beds are mainly a feature of southern forests, there is a suite of liliaceous plants found growing in the far north. For the most part these lilies do not grow in dense fields, and they are not well-known wildflowers. They featured less prominently in the Aboriginal diet, presumably because yams and other large tubers provided a better yield.

Perhaps the most important of the small northern lilies was the grass potato (*Curculigo ensifolia*). More like a runt carrot than a potato, the tuber of this lily is brown and slender and up to ten centimetres or more long. On Groote Eylandt in the Northern Territory it goes under the jaw-breaking name of amurndangirringirra. The roots are roasted in hot sand and ashes and, before

The pale grass lily (*Caesia parviflora*) is common along walking tracks in the heathlands of the Royal National Park, just south of Sydney, where it flowers alongside fringed lilies and edible ground orchids.

But for its tiny yellow flower, the grass potato (*Curculigo ensifolia*) could be mistaken for a tuft of grass. The flower probably attracts a specialised pollinating insect, which knows to search for it beneath the concealing foliage. Photographed at Cape York.

Tubers of the grass potato neither look nor taste like potatoes, although the leaves closely resemble grass. This plant is not well known today but was probably a very important Aboriginal food.

being eaten, are often hammered between stones to break the fibres.

Grass potato is a common enough woodland plant, but its harvest demands skilful observation. The leaves are very grass-like, and the plants grow mainly within stands of blady grass. Although the small yellow flowers betray it to be a lily, not a grass, they are carried so close to the ground, and amongst such thick grass, that they are easily overlooked. I am curious to know what pollinates such well-concealed flowers.

Pink swamp lily (*Murdannia graminea*), like the bulbine lily, is almost certainly two plants under the one name. Northern plants have bilaterally symmetrical flowers on beaded stems;

The use of food plants by Aborigines varied from place to place, and the pink swamp lily (*Murdannia graminea*) is a case in point. The small tubers were widely eaten along the Northern Territory coast, but the Warnindilyakwa of Groote Eylandt say they are not edible.

Above: This bunch of tubers of arda (*Cartonema parviflorum*) was gathered on Horn Island in Torres Strait towards the end of the wet season. Although the tubers are tiny, they are borne so abundantly they could serve as important foods in season.

Far left: On the sandy low-lying plains of northern Australia, prickly arda (*Cartonema spicatum*) sprouts in large numbers each wet season. The starchy tubers do not develop until the end of the Wet, by which time the leaves and flowers have withered.

Left: The small fragile blossom of arda (*Cartonema parviflorum*) opens only for a single morning, withering shortly after midday. Vast fields of these lilies brighten the forest floor in tropical woodlands.

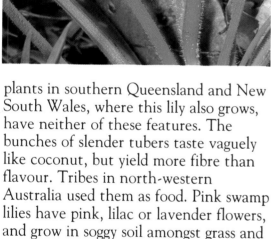

plants in southern Queensland and New South Wales, where this lily also grows, have neither of these features. The bunches of slender tubers taste vaguely like coconut, but yield more fibre than flavour. Tribes in north-western Australia used them as food. Pink swamp lilies have pink, lilac or lavender flowers, and grow in soggy soil amongst grass and rocks.

"Wandering jew", the name given to garden plants of genus *Tradescantia*, is often applied to related native plants (*Commelina*) with delicate blue flowers. These plants, relatives of the lilies, are also called "scurvy grass" after their use by early outback settlers as emergency vegetables. In northern Australia one species, *C. ensifolia*, has slender tubers. It grows in sandy and loamy soils, often on the edges of swamps. Aborigines nibbled the tubers, but probably only as minor snack foods, as my field notes record them as being "chewy, tasteless, low grade, but not bitter".

Other edible lilies of the north include various golden stars (*Hypoxis* species), a

fringed lily (*Thysanotus banksii*) and the hairy grass lily (*Caesia setifera*), the latter forming colonies of pretty blue flower heads on deep siliceous sand beside streams. Arda (*Cartonema parviflorum* and *C. spicatum*) furnishes bunches of starchy tubers which my notes say are "very tasty, floury, potato-like, nourishing, and very slightly bitter". *C. spicatum* is a small thistle-like plant found in open woodland; *C. parviflorum* is a softer plant forming very dense colonies which were probably a major source of food for Aborigines (and possibly Torres Strait islanders). The flowers of arda are yellow with three petals; they open during autumn mornings. The plants wither at the end of the wet season and then are dug by Aborigines.

Next time you are strolling in the bush, spare a thought for the dainty forest lilies at your feet. The tubers hidden beneath those insignificant-looking wildflowers were once the vegetable staples of whole Aboriginal nations.

WILD
ORCHIDS

Left: Common waxlip (*Glossodia major*) sprouts from a small tuber which was almost certainly an Aboriginal food. Colonial botanist Baron von Mueller provided the main record of Aboriginal use of orchids, and he listed *Glossodia* species. Photographed in the Grampians.

Right: One of the donkey orchids, so named because of their ear-like petals, the leopard orchid (*Diuris maculata*) has flowers with both appealing colours and an unusual shape. Some country people know it as "nanny goats". Photographed in the Grampians.

Ground orchids are enchanting plants. Each spring they brighten the forest floor with dainty blooms of the oddest colours and shapes. Enjoy them while you can, for they flower but briefly; each summer the leaves, stems and flowers die away.

Ground orchids sprout from small starchy tubers, which colonial writers often listed as foods of Aborigines. During my first years studying Aboriginal diet I paid them little heed, for I rarely encountered orchids and the tubers I dug up were tiny. But then I came upon an intriguing article by Melbourne botanist Beth Gott. She wrote: "Accustomed as we are to the total protection of orchids in most states of Australia, we tend to dismiss the Orchidaceae [orchid family] as an important food source, considering them to be rare; yet orchids are widespread, even in quite dry areas, and are often locally abundant. They were widely exploited as a food source."

Beth wrote of finding nodding greenhoods (*Pterostylis nutans*) at the extraordinary density of 440 plants per square metre, yielding 800 tiny tubers, with a combined weight of only 126 grams. Orchid tubers are easy to dig and, at densities like this, could serve as important foods.

I began looking out for orchids, and one spring reaped a bountiful reward. It began in southern Australia on a small rocky knoll where I chanced upon four species growing side by side. The first, a common waxlip (*Glossodia major*), sported a single egg-shaped tuber with a pointed tip. This tuber tasted watery and slightly sweet, with a bitter aftertaste. It was not nice. The second, a leopard orchid (*Diuris maculata*), had two bullet-

A common but rarely noticed ground orchid, pink fingers (*Caladenia carnea*) has delicate pink petals suggesting an outstretched hand. It grows in heaths and forests in south-eastern Australia, New Zealand, Indonesia and Malaysia. Photographed at Berowra near Sydney.

shaped tubers three centimetres long and six to seven millimetres wide, with a glutinous sticky taste. The arrowroot-like starch, although filling, stuck cloyingly to my gums. The third orchid, a tall greenhood (*Pterostylis longifolia*), had a pair of globular tubers, the size of grapes, with a watery bitter taste. The fourth orchid, pink fingers (*Caladenia carnea*), had two pea-sized white tubers, tasting sweet and juicy.

I was intrigued by this hilltop orchid entree. The tubers of these four plants were as varied in flavour and form as were the flowers in colour and shape. Although some of the tubers were not appetising, altogether they afforded a most interesting wild food snack.

Since then I have sampled the tubers of fourteen genera and more than twenty-five species of ground orchid. Some were to me quite unpalatable, although all were obviously edible, and a few were exceptionally tasty—especially the walnut-sized "potatoes" of brown

Some of the starchiest of orchid tubers are found among the sun orchids, such as this scented sun orchid (*Thelymitra nuda*) growing in woodland in the Mount Lofty Ranges. Sun orchid flowers have symmetrical petals and closely resemble lilies.

A hardy survivor, this hyacinth orchid (*Dipodium punctatum*) was growing in weed-infested bushland beside a highway in western Brisbane. The hyacinth orchid is among the most durable of native orchids, often persisting in disturbed habitats.

This pale form of hyacinth orchid was growing at the western limit of its range in the Mount Lofty Ranges behind Adelaide. Colonists sometimes called this the "plum pudding flower", presumably because of the spots.

beaks (*Lyperanthus suaveolens*) and the fragrantly flavoured starch of the horned orchid (*Orthoceras strictum*). Most filling were the glutinous tubers of donkey orchids (*Diuris* species) and sun orchids (*Thelymitra* species), and I have no doubt these were important Aboriginal foods.

Although most of the tubers were tiny, those of the common hyacinth orchid (*Dipodium punctatum*) were hefty. One plant had six long tubers, each as thick as a pencil and longer than my fingers. The tubers were watery and, for an orchid, unusually fibrous—although less so after baking. These were the only orchids that improved much with cooking; the others I was able to eat raw.

Incidentally, hyacinth orchids are mysterious plants. Lacking leaves, they grow only beneath certain kinds of eucalypts and are said to be parasitic on a fungus. They have exceptionally large tubers, as does the potato orchid (*Gastrodia sesamoides*), another leafless saprophyte, once an important food of Tasmanian Aborigines.

Hyacinth orchids flower through summer, but most orchids bloom in spring, which is when the leaves appear. Ground orchids are not leafy plants, and many produce only a single leaf, others two or three. These soft, succulent leaves cannot withstand the scorching summer sun, and the plants "gestate" through summer in the form of those starch-filled tubers, so important as foods.

Tuber producing is a common tactic of small plants with soft leaves growing in a harsh climate with seasonally dry soil. Besides the orchids, many of the smaller lilies and murnong depend on tubers. These plants grow together in shallow soils and Aborigines harvested them in huge numbers.

The tiny tubers could have served as staple foods in spring, when these plants are in flower, but I was curious to know if Aborigines would have harvested them in other seasons, when the plants are less obvious.

At first it seemed unlikely. I was in the granite mountains near Stanthorpe, where I found colonies of brown beaks in which only half the plants were flowering. This orchid has a single leaf remarkably similar to blady grass (*Imperata cylindrica*), and these plants often grow together, rendering the orchid extremely difficult to find without its flowers. On open ground the leaf is discernible but still easily overlooked. Could Aborigines have gathered orchids like this outside the flowering season?

The following summer I stumbled upon the answer. I was photographing hyacinth orchids in disturbed bush in suburban Brisbane where this orchid is surprisingly common. Many of the orchids were past flowering and I noted their distinctive oval capsules full of tiny seeds. Two weeks later I was in South Australia in the hills behind Adelaide, when I noticed a similar capsule in the dried grass. Could this be an orchid? I clawed into the dirt and, to my astonishment, unearthed a shiny white tuber shaped like a grape. This was no hyacinth orchid, but was obviously an orchid's tuber. Its crisp white starch tasted sublime. Excitedly I scanned the nearby forest floor, and realised there were dozens of these dried pods, all

This green-flowered form of brown beaks (*Lyperanthus suaveolens*), an unusual orchid with spider-shaped flowers, was growing on the dark forest floor among granite outcrops at Girraween National Park in southern Queensland.

A tuberous treat, the small "potatoes" of brown beaks are tasty tucker, having a fragrant starchy flavour. Most orchid tubers are much smaller than these.

This spider orchid, allegedly a hybrid between *Caladenia dilatata* and *C. patersonii*, was growing in woodland just east of Mount Gambier. Orchid specialists have split Australia's orchids into scores of difficult-to-distinguish species which readily hybridise, creating the suspicion that many of these species exist only in the minds of orchid specialists.

signalling tiny stores of food hidden in the hot earth. The tubers were so common that a forager could have lived happily off the land. The different shapes and tastes of the tubers confirmed that several orchid species were present.

Elsewhere in south-eastern Australia it was the same. In southern Victoria, in coastal New South Wales, wherever I looked I found tubers, sometimes by spotting a dainty flower but more often by finding dried pods in the wiry grass. Occasionally I made a mistake, confusing the capsules of trigger plants (*Stylidium* species) with orchids. But there could be no mistaking the significance of my

find—that, for Aborigines, orchids were a source of sustenance all the year round.

Ground orchids are no longer on my menu. I cannot justify the continued harvest of these beautiful plants. Nor would I want others to follow my example. Orchids are protected in some States, and rightly so. It is worth noting, however, that in colonial times orchids were eaten by Europeans. The tubers were a favoured vegetable of Sydney's first convict colony, according to Captain Watkin Tench, writing in 1789. And colonial botanist Joseph Maiden recorded in 1898 that "There is hardly a country boy who has not eaten so-called

Yams, which are the tubers of numerous kinds of terrestrial or ground-growing orchids".

Surprisingly, the starch in orchid tubers, known as "saloop" or "salep", was once an esteemed food in Europe. The English plant writer Anne Pratt in 1891 spoke of its significance: "Salep is little used now in this country; but less than a century since, the Saloop-house was much frequented, and the substance was a favourite repast of porters, coal-heavers, and other hard-working men. It is said to contain more nutritious matter, in proportion to its bulk, than any other known root, and an ounce of salep was considered to afford support to a man for a day; hence, those who travel in uninhabited countries have greatly prized so portable a vegetable food."

I have not tasted European salep, but Pratt's description rings true for the remarkably starchy tubers of sun orchids and donkey orchids. Indeed, Australian colonial botanists suggested that salep might be extracted from local species.

Ground orchids thrive mainly in south-eastern and south-western Australia, and only a few species grow in the tropical north (for example, *Habenaria*). There are, however, a variety of epiphytic orchids found in the tropics and subtropics, and some of these supply starch. The black orchid (*Cymbidium canaliculatum*) and the king orchid (*Dendrobium speciosum*) have no tubers, but their thick leaf bases are swollen with starch grains which Aborigines used as food. In colonial times black orchid was known to settlers as "native arrowroot" and, according to one early writer, "delicate children have been reared on this when accidents have cut off from them other supplies".

A favourite of gardeners, the king orchid (*Dendrobium speciosum*) is often planted in the crotches of backyard trees, where it flowers freely. Gardeners are generally unaware that the stems contain edible starch.

GREENS

WILD
GREENS

Leaves are the plebeians among plant foods. They lack the glamorous flavours of fruits and nectars and the sustenance of seeds and roots. They were only minor foods of Aborigines.

But to colonial Australians leaves were important. Highly valued as vegetables and scurvy cures, they were the most widely harvested of plant foods after the fruits. The first Australian plant ever to be cultivated as food was a native "spinach".

The inner shoots of wild plants are greens of a different sort. Growing hearts of palms and tree ferns were Aboriginal staples, but were little used by colonists. The starchy nutritious buds were hacked from the upper trunks of the trees.

There are surprisingly few accounts of Aborigines eating leaves. In northern Australia especially, food lists compiled by anthropologists rarely mention leaves. For all of coastal Queensland I can find only two listings, both from north

Queensland. One refers to a fig, the leaves of which were eaten raw, the other to native rosella (*Hibiscus heterophyllus*—"young shoots, and leaves eatable").

In southern Australia there are records aplenty of Aborigines gathering cresses and sowthistle, but not much else. These plants feature in later chapters (Cresses and Mustards, and Weeds, respectively). By far the greatest range of leaves was eaten in the deserts, presumably because food choices were fewer. Outback tribes ate leaves of various pigweeds (*Portulaca* species), parakeelyas (*Calandrinia* species), wood sorrels (*Oxalis* species), twin leaves (*Zygophyllum* species), peppercresses (*Lepidium* species), Cooper clover (*Trigonella suavissima*), doubah (*Leichhardtia australis*) and desert mustards.

From the pen of colonial cookery writer Mrs Lance Rawson we have a rare record of Kanakas in Queensland eating

A versatile vegetable, native rosella (*Hibiscus heterophyllus*) has buds that can be stewed as rosellas, leaves tasting like sorrel, roots like woody parsnips, and bark that Aborigines spun as string. I have made excellent "spinach" pie from the exquisitely sour leaves.

The bruised leaves of fishweed (*Einadia trigonos*) smell like the sea, hence its odd name. Boiled, the leaves taste like premium spinach. Although a native plant, fishweed sometimes grows as a weed; this plant was growing in an unkempt park in Brisbane.

Top left: Dainty twiner of the outback, the climbing saltbush (*Einadia nutans*) has both leaves and fruits that are edible. Aborigines in Bedourie call it "tomato berry", although the fruits are smaller than apple seeds. Photographed on the Birdsville–Bedourie "highway".

Below left: On the harsh saline plains of the Coorong in South Australia, the marsh saltbush (*Atriplex paludosa*) is one of the few edible plants. The younger leaves can be boiled like spinach.

Below right: A tender succulent vegetable can be prepared by steaming the leaves of Mueller's saltbush (*Atriplex muelleri*), a shrub of outback plains, photographed here at Glengyle, western Queensland. It seems likely that most species of *Atriplex* are edible.

wild leaves. In amongst praise for pigweed and thistle tops, she speaks of the "tender young top shoots of the wild rough leaved fig; the Kanakas used to gather these, tie them in bundles and boil them with their meat and eat them like cabbage". She rated them an "excellent spinach". Mrs Rawson followed an adage that kept her in good stead: "Whatever the blacks eat the whites may safely try."

The leafy foods of the colonists are recorded in the Colonial Greens chapter.

A large proportion of the plants used were members of just two families, the mustard-cress family (Brassicaceae), and the saltbush family (Chenopodiaceae). These families are rich in food plants, and the number could probably be greatly extended by experimentation. Among the chenopods I have tried boiled fishweed (*Einadia trigonos*), berry saltbush (*E. hastata*), Mueller's saltbush (*Atriplex muelleri*) and marsh saltbush (*Atriplex paludosa*), and all proved delectable vegetables. These plants are halophytes

Aborigines made better use of the starchy inner shoots of palms, tree ferns and grass trees. In Tasmania tree fern cores were a staple food, and in the tropics palm hearts were heavily exploited. Removing the core kills the plant, and it is evident that Aborigines diminished the numbers of these trees. In sheltered gorges in central Australia desert cabbage palms (*Livistona mariae*) are proliferating since Aborigines stopped harvesting them sixty years ago.

Inner palm shoots, called "cabbages", were sometimes eaten by Europeans. Captain Cook's men ate palm cabbages at Endeavour River, although Cook complained that the palms "were in General small, and yielded so little Cabage that they were not worth the Looking after, and this was the Case with most of the fruit, etc., we found in the woods". The cabbage palm (*L. australis*) of eastern Australia is so named because its top was eaten by colonists around Sydney. According to Surgeon Worgan of the First Fleet, "The Cabbage eats something like a Nut."

No mountain-top panorama would be complete without grass trees (*Xanthorrhoea* species). Aborigines used the gum to haft spears and gouged nutty-tasting starch from the top of the trunk. Photographed atop Mount Mitchell, Cunninghams Gap near Warwick.

Right: In the highlands of Victoria and Tasmania, the soft tree fern (*Dicksonia antarctica*) was probably a staple Aboriginal food. The starchy inner trunk is about twelve per cent carbohydrate. Photographed in the Grampians.

(see Foods of the First Fleet chapter) and seem to depend mainly on their saltiness to repel plant-eaters. Boiling removes the salt and renders them tender and tasty.

In northern Australia there grow a handful of plants, mainly seashore trees, the leaves of which have been used as vegetables overseas. Shoots and leaves of octopus bush (*Argusia argentea*), great morinda (*Morinda citrifolia*), pisonia tree (*Pisonia grandis*) and pemphis (*Pemphis acidula*) are cooked by islanders in the Pacific, where these plants also grow, but were apparently never used by Aborigines or colonists. The ones I have tried were not tasty.

A few kinds of leaf stalks were Aboriginal foods. In the north, waterlily (*Nymphaea* species) stems were nibbled like celery, and in Queensland the stalks of tree orchids were baked and chewed for their starch. The ends of bulrush stems were eaten in New South Wales. In South Australia colonists ate the inner white leaf bases of the coast sword sedge (*Lepidosperma gladiatum*), a coarse sedge of coastal dunes which was lauded as a source of fibre for paper making. The basal core of the long-leaf mat-rush (*Lomandra longifolia*) can be chewed and tastes like green peas. Another green eaten by Aborigines was the young underground shoot of the common reed (*Phragmites karka*). Aborigines no doubt nibbled many other kinds of shoots and sedge bases for which no record now survives.

In Australia today, edible greens are easiest to find around human habitation. A surprising proportion of farm and garden weeds have edible leaves. Such

One of Australia's more beautiful bush foods, the waterlily (*Nymphaea gigantea*) has leaf stalks tasting like celery. Aborigines in northern Australia chew them as snacks. The seeds and tubers are also edible. Photographed near Injune in central Queensland.

Beloved by basket weavers for its long pliable leaves, the long-leaf mat-rush (*Lomandra longifolia*) also has edible leaf bases, tasting exactly like raw green peas. This sedge is often cultivated outside city banks and offices.

Villagers throughout the world know that the young leaves of pumpkin vines (*Cucurbita maxima*) can be boiled as a vegetable. In our own affluent society this knowledge has been largely lost.

weeds are quick-growing plants producing flimsy, and therefore very tender, leaves. They grow in soils enriched by dog manure and refuse and this makes them nutritious to eat. Some garden weeds, such as fat-hen and chickweed, were ancient European foods—the bush tucker of our Caucasian forebears. These and other weeds are featured in the chapter on Weeds.

Among garden shrubs there are some with edible leaves. The new foliage of mulberry trees (*Morus alba*) and garden hibiscuses (*Hibiscus* species) can be used in place of spinach. Hollyhock and celosia leaves are edible. Also, most garden vegetables bear edible leaves— pumpkin, carrot, onion, beetroot,

zucchini, marrows, radish, choko and celery (but not potatoes and tomatoes, which have poisonous leaves).

A light-hearted warning about wild greens—eat too many and your skin may turn yellow. During the food shortages that followed the bombing of Dresden in World War II, some Germans took to eating two or three meals a day of fat-hen, nettles and other wild greens sprouting in the rubble. After several months on this diet these people became fatigued and found their skin turning yellow, especially on the palms and soles. Fortunately, the colouring is harmless and reversible. Overconsumption of vegetables and citrus fruits can have the same effect.

COLONIAL
GREENS

The little plants called plantains are among the more obscure of our forest herbs, and few people would consider them seriously as a food. Yet French botanist Labillardière, exploring Tasmania in 1793, wrote glowingly of a wild plantain he sampled: "This must be reckoned among the most useful plants, which this country affords for the food of man. The hope of finding some vegetables fit to eat as sallad had induced the most provident among us, to bring the necessary sauce, and the sallad furnished by the leaves of this plant, which were very tender, was highly relished by all the company."

Nowadays we would not become excited over wild greens, but nineteenth-century Europeans much appreciated the flavours of different leaves, and in English markets could be found for sale sorrel, beets, spinach, watercress, mustards, good king henry and other table greens. It is much to our loss that these nutritious vegetables have fallen from favour; sad to say, modern Australians have little appreciation for the culinary virtues of greens.

Colonial Australians were more adventurous, and the history of leaf eating in Australia is an interesting tale, starring many of Australia's most eminent explorers, and featuring many of our forgotten pioneers.

Captain Cook was the first Englishman to nibble our native greens. A great humanitarian, he was the first mariner to diligently supply his crew with fresh vegetables as protection against scurvy. At Botany Bay he served up New Zealand spinach (*Tetragonia tetragonoides*) and sea celery (*Apium prostratum*), and at Endeavour River, sea purslane (*Sesuvium portulacastrum*) and taro (*Colocasia esculenta*). All of these are interesting plants.

The tender young leaves of shade plantain (*Plantago debilis*) can be cooked and eaten and the seeds soaked in boiling water to make a jelly drink. European and Asian plantains are used in the same way. Photographed at Cunninghams Gap near Warwick.

At Endeavour River Captain Cook ate taro (*Colocasia esculenta*): " . . . we found some Wild Yamms or Cocos growing in the Swampy grounds, and this Afternoon I sent a Party of Men to gather some. The Tops we found made good greens . . ."

Right: The salty succulent leaves of pink purslane (*Sesuvium portulacastrum*) were considered by Captain Cook to be "very good when boiled".

Sea purslane is a small fleshy herb of beaches and estuaries in the northern half of Australia. Like many seashore plants it occurs worldwide, and was harvested as a vegetable in Java and tropical Africa. It makes an excellent spinach substitute in spanakopita. Joseph Banks's journal refers to it as "Red flowerd purslane", which at first puzzled me, as the flowers are pale pink. But consulting the Oxford Dictionary I found that the word "pink" originally referred, not to a colour, but to the garden flowers

of genus *Dianthus*. The newer meaning was probably unknown to Banks, who would have described the starry flowers as pale red.

New Zealand spinach (*Tetragonia tetragonoides*) is so named because Cook first found the plant growing along the rugged shores of New Zealand. The seed pods of this delicious vegetable float freely on ocean currents, and the plant has spread naturally from Australia to New Zealand.

Of all the plants tasted by Banks and Cook during their voyage, this "spinach" (no relation to the real thing) made the strongest impression, and Banks took seed back to England, where it was grown in Kew Gardens. By the nineteenth century New Zealand spinach, known also as "Botany Bay greens", had become · a popular summer spinach in England and America, appearing for sale in seed catalogues in the 1820s. According to the Reverend William Woolls, "during the whole summer of 1821, no other spinach was used in the Earl of Essex's family at Cashiobury". New Zealand spinach is no longer popular, but still rates a listing in seed catalogues and vegetable dictionaries.

Banks's fondness for this food may have helped seal the fate of Australia as a convict settlement. When called to testify to a 1779 House of Commons

Committee on the suitability of Australia as a colony, Banks testified that at Botany Bay "The grass was long and luxurient, and there were some eatable Vegetables, particularly a Sort of Wild Spinage; the country was well supplied with Water". Botany Bay won the vote despite stiff competition from West Africa.

Two close relatives of New Zealand spinach deserve mention. Bower spinach (*T. implexicoma*) is a creeper of southern beaches, forming dense mats on sand or trailing through low branches, creating thick curtains of bright green edible foliage. Colonial botanist Baron von

Mueller suggested this "spinach" was worthy of cultivation. The leaves are almost as tasty as those of New Zealand spinach.

The South African sea spinach (*T. decumbens*) has escaped from cultivation in southern Australia and forms large mats on beaches around Perth and Adelaide. It, too, has tasty edible leaves. South Africa has several different *Tetragonia* species, some of them eaten as vegetables, and it is likely that all the Australian species evolved from seeds that long ago floated across from Africa.

The sea celery eaten by Cook and Banks is another vegetable of great interest. It became one of the scurvy cures of the First Fleet. Curiously, the botanist Joseph Banks took no specimens back to England, and it was left to Labillardière in 1792 to collect and later name the species. Perhaps Banks was too besotted by Australia's spectacular banksias and hakeas to bother with a mere celery; or perhaps the collections of celery were all consumed by the crew. Labillardière was very appreciative of the plant, although like Banks he referred to it as a "parsley": "I discovered at a little distance . . . a new species of parsley, which I named *apium prostratum* on account of the position of its stem, which always creeps along the ground. Its

On Adelaide beaches South African trailing spinach (*Tetragonia decumbens*) forms sprawling mats of edible foliage up to three metres wide. This creeper is distinguished by its thick blunt leaves, pale yellow flowers and papery seed pods.

Centre: Despite its name, New Zealand spinach (*Tetragonia tetragonoides*) is an Australian native. Identifying features are the yellow flowers with four petals, and rhomboidal leaves with glistening undersides. Photographed at Burleigh Heads on the Gold Coast.

The shiny red fruits of bower spinach (*Tetragonia implexicoma*) are beloved by seagulls, and dozens of the seeds may be found in their pellets. The leaves were a spinach of early pioneers and were thought to prevent scurvy.

On the muddy banks of the Brisbane River, even in inner suburbs, sea celery (*Apium prostratum*) is a common wild vegetable, often growing alongside seablite beneath a canopy of grey mangroves. Photographed in Sherwood.

analogy with the other species of the same genus, led me to think it might be good to eat, and it answered my expectations. We carried a large quantity of it on board with us, which was acceptable to mariners who felt the necessity of obviating, by vegetable diet, the bad effects of the salt provisions on which we had lived during the whole of our passage from the Cape of Good Hope to that of Van Diemen."

Sea celery was also highly praised by an early visitor to Tasmania, Daniel Bunce, who botanised along the Tamar River in the 1830s, "where the inhabitants of Launceston were in the habit of washing their clothes and linen". He found that "native parsley, was . . . abundant on the bank of the stream, and forms an excellent ingredient in soup, and otherwise may be used as a potherb".

Sea celery is common on beaches and estuaries in southern and eastern Australia. Although it doesn't look much like commercial celery, it does bear close resemblance to the wild European herb from which celery was originally bred. Indeed, kitchen celery now runs wild in southern Australia, where even botanists confuse the two. This suggests that, with a careful program of selective breeding, our native celery could be bred into a vegetable of commercial standards.

Australia has two other native celeries. Dwarf celery (*A. annuum*), a tiny herb of southern beaches, can be used like parsley as a garnish. The other wild celery (*A. insulare*) grows only on Bass Strait islands and Lord Howe Island, an unusual distribution for what is an obscure plant. I don't know if it has been used as food but, being the largest of our celeries, it could prove promising.

The founding of Sydney as a convict settlement in 1788 brought hundreds of hungry mouths to feed, and all manner of wild greens were gathered as foods. In

On Melbourne beaches grey saltbush (*Atriplex cinerea*) forms large clumps of tasty foliage which are nowadays almost forgotten as a source of sustenance. The burnt leaves were an important source of lye for colonial soap makers.

an earlier chapter I note that samphire, grey saltbush, wood sorrel, New Zealand spinach and sea celery became valued potherbs. Their use apparently persisted well into the nineteenth century, for the roving Quaker missionary James Backhouse could assert in 1843 that two kinds of samphire and four different genera of saltbushes were used.

Another man of the cloth, the Reverend William Woolls, was also interested in wild greens, and in 1867 recorded colonists eating New Zealand spinach, "fat-hen" (*Chenopodium erosum*), pigweed (*Portulaca oleracea*), the samphire *Halosarcia indica* and various cresses (see Cresses and Mustards chapter). Of the fleshy-leaved seablite (*Suaeda australis*) he declared, "I have frequently used *C. Australe* for pickle, and have found it far from contemptible."

Not all the greens of the colonists were native plants. Colonial botanist Joseph Maiden in 1889 wrote enthusiastically of the green amaranth (*Amaranthus viridis*), a garden weed from overseas: "It is an excellent substitute for spinach, being far superior to much of the leaves of the white beet sold for spinach in Sydney. Next to spinach it seems to be most like boiled nettle leaves, which when young are used in England, and are excellent. This amarantus should be cooked like spinach, and as it becomes more widely known, it is sure to be popular, except amongst persons who may consider it beneath their dignity to have anything to do with so common a weed."

In the Kakadu region, Aborigines today boil up or fry the leaves of this exotic weed, a practice learned from the Chinese community of Pine Creek. The Aboriginal name means "plant with no name"; they also call it "Chinese cabbage".

In outback areas pioneers used a great variety of wild greens, including New Zealand spinach, scurvy grass (*Commelina*

Wallaby bush (*Threlkeldia diffusa*), a vegetable of early colonists, grows here surrounded by edible bower spinach at Beachport, South Australia. Wallaby bush bears tiny, red, barrel-shaped fruits which are edible.

Centre: A pickle plant of pioneers, seablite (*Suaeda australis*) can also be eaten as greens. It is one of the most common saltmarsh plants in eastern and southern Australia. Photographed on St Helena Island, an old convict colony near Brisbane.

William Woolls in 1867 commended green amaranth (*Amaranthus viridis*) and a related species, saying that "in seasons of scarcity they might be eaten as pot-herbs, and in some countries they are employed as emollient poultices". Photographed in Brisbane.

Parakeelya (*Calandrinia balonensis*) supplied Aborigines with edible leaves and seeds, and colonists cooked the leaves like spinach. The plant provides valuable forage for outback cattle and sheep, especially in spinifex country. Photographed at Uluru.

Above right: The tiny button fruits of ruby saltbush (*Enchylaena tomentosa*) were eaten by inland Aborigines. Although usually red when ripe, the fruits of this plant growing at Broken Hill are yellow.

Below right: On the edge of a swamp north of Birdsville, a clump of ruby saltbush spreads its arching stems, partly concealing an old truck. While camped beside this wreck, I gathered the saltbush leaves to enliven the evening stew.

and a desperate Colonel Warburton dined on samphire: "I endeavour to eke out my meagre fare with a mess of boiled salt-plant." Major Mitchell harvested fragrant saltbush (*Rhagodia parabolica*)—"a tender and palatable vegetable"—and Cooper clover (*Trigonella suavissima*), which greatly impressed him: "The perfume of this herb, its freshness and flavour, induced me to try it as a vegetable, and we found it to be delicious, tender as spinach, and to preserve a very green colour when boiled. This was certainly the most interesting plant hitherto discovered by us."

For later waves of settlers, the most important outback vegetable was the succulent yellow-flowered plant called pigweed, purslane or munyeroo (*Portulaca oleracea*). Throughout the vast outback pigweed was valued in homestead kitchens as a vegetable and

ensifolia), showy groundsel (*Senecio magnificus*), old man saltbush (*Atriplex nummularia*), and various cresses and mustards.

Alice Duncan-Kemp, writing from Windorah at the turn of the century, described how white children learned of these foods: "Little black children and their white playmates gathered armfuls of Bogil-a-ri or Wild Spinach from the sandy stretches, and red rosy Pigweed for salads, and Mungaroo, a fleshy-leaved plant, or the water-bearing Par-a-keel-ya [*Calandrinia balonensis*]—all were palatable vegetables when cooked and dressed with seasoning or white sauce."

The first Europeans to sample outback greens were the doughty explorers. Burke and Wills ate pigweed—which may have prolonged their lives; Charles Sturt ate ruby saltbush (*Enchylaena tomentosa*);

salad plant. The succulent, somewhat slimy leaves and stems were believed to cure scurvy—although recent tests by the Department of Defence Support showed only traces of vitamin C.

Pigweed also grows near our coasts, and was one of many wild plants tried by northern explorer Ludwig Leichhardt. Along the Mackenzie River in February 1845 he recorded that "A crow was shot and roasted, and found to be exceedingly tender, which we considered to be a great discovery; and lost no opportunity of shooting as many as we could, in order to lessen the consumption of our dried meat. We again enjoyed some fine messes of Portulaca [pigweed]."

The last word on the matter comes from the pen of Rachel Henning, writing from the beleaguered Exmoor Station in Queensland. "We get along with wild vegetables till the tame ones see fit to flourish," she wrote in 1865. "We have a wild plant which makes a capital salad and which we seldom dine without. It rejoices in the name of pigweed."

The Aboriginal name "munyeroo" is widely used in the outback for a plant better known in the cities as pigweed (*Portulaca oleracea*). Americans call this cosmopolitan weed "purslane". Photographed at Bondi Beach.

Goldminers in colonial Australia were often troubled by scurvy. Wild plants, mainly leafy vegetables, were widely used as cures.

CRESSES AND MUSTARDS

Containing up to twice the vitamin C of oranges (weight for weight), the foliage of watercress (*Rorippa nasturtiumaquaticum*) makes a nutritious salad, especially since it is also rich in minerals and vitamin A. Photographed at Bondi Beach.

Look up Australian nutritional tables and you may be surprised to find that, weight for weight, raw watercress contains much more vitamin C than oranges. This is actually one of those misleading statistics, for it is next to impossible to eat, in one sitting, an orange's weight in raw cress— the leaves are just too piquant.

The spice in watercress comes from mustard oils released in the leaves when the foliage is chewed. The plant produces these oils to deter grazing animals. These same oils give cabbage and brussels sprouts their flavour, and radishes and mustard seeds their bite. Indeed, all of these vegetables are related members of the mustard family (Brassicaceae or Cruciferae).

Australia has more than a hundred native members of this family, all of them soft-leaved herbs with pungent-tasting leaves. They are common on outback flood plains and in southern coastal forests. Aborigines and pioneers often gathered and cooked them as nutritious vegetables.

As well, colonial immigrants accidentally carried in seeds of foreign mustards in potting soil or seed packets. Some of these became established here as weeds and make interesting potherbs. Watercress was even subjected to a concerted program of acclimatisation.

Watercress (*Rorippa nasturtiumaquaticum*), the little herb with the big name, is noteworthy as the only well-known vegetable that has not been transformed by centuries of horticulture. Look closely at the wild plants growing in ditches and drains and you will find they are identical to the cress sold in greengrocer's stores. (By comparison, wild forms of carrot, beetroot and celery are unrecognisable.)

From the earliest days of white settlement in Australia, attempts were made to establish watercress in the wild. Labillardière, the French botanist accompanying D'Entrecasteaux during his forays in the South Pacific, was surprised to find a plot of cresses growing untended on the rugged coast of Van Diemen's Land (Tasmania) in 1793. The Frenchman had stumbled upon a garden planted by Captain Bligh of *Bounty* fame as a supply for passing seafarers. Here were scrawny fig, quince and pomegranate trees growing beside clumps of celery and cress.

The dark forests of Tasmania probably reclaimed this valiant attempt at cultivation, but later introductions of watercress proved highly successful. The colonial botanist F. M. Bailey lauded a Mrs Davenport for liberating watercress into South Australian streams in about 1842. Bailey considered watercress a wonderful addition to the flora, and in 1898 in Brisbane lamented, "I am sorry I cannot give the name of the public benefactor who introduced this wholesome and useful plant into our Queensland streams." The *Queensland Agricultural Journal* at the turn of the century advised that watercress would "thrive well and yield good crops if sown amongst weeds on a creek bank or on the edge of a waterhole or swamp". There was said to be "excellent cress" growing in pools beneath the Dividing Range below Toowoomba. The only sour note came in the anonymous article of 1907, "Nations which have been ruined by weeds", which asserted that "Tasmania has lost the use of its finest river by the spread of watercress, planted years ago by an enterprising farmer and allowed to go unchecked".

This statement is almost certainly hearsay, for wild watercress is nowadays a benign and insignificant weed. It thrives in polluted streams and drains in coastal cities and towns, and sprouts in wet pockets along the cliff lines of Sydney's Bondi Beach. I have seen plants growing beneath picnic tables at Yuraygir

National Park near Grafton, showing how easily the plants spread from lunch litter. No longer is there "excellent cress" in the ponds below Toowoomba, but succulent thickets thrive in the drains of Toowoomba's city parks, as they do in suburban Brisbane further east.

You can recognise watercress by its tiny white flowers with four white petals, by its bright green pinnate leaves, and by its sausage-like pods a centimetre or two long. The stems are hollow and brittle, and trail over gravel or into water, shooting out numerous soft white roots.

Cress often grows in polluted sludge, or on farms where there is the risk of liver flukes, so take care when harvesting from the wild. Store the whole plants in bowls of water but do not refrigerate—cresses wilt easily.

The native cresses, unlike watercress, are uncommon and poorly known plants. Trampling cattle have probably eliminated them from many districts. The one common species is marsh or yellow cress (*R. palustris*), an untidy plant of disputed origins. Colonial botanist Joseph Hooker stated that "This and other species afford excellent pot-herbs when luxuriant and flaccid", and an early visitor to Tasmania noted that the plant

Brisbane drains provide the habitat for luxuriant watercress, but plants such as this one, growing in Toowong, are too contaminated to be safe to eat.

Aborigines would have eaten an exotic herb, particularly one so unlike their native cresses. Also, there is a record of Joseph Banks collecting marsh cress in New Zealand in 1769, proving the plant existed in this corner of the globe in pre-European times. The seeds probably came in thousands of years ago on the feet of migrating waterbirds, for this cress is common along the edges of rivers and lagoons where ducks and egrets roost. It often grows beside dams and drains, and has probably increased in range and abundance since European settlement. Marsh cress has tiny yellow flowers (other cresses have white flowers), and crinkled lobed leaves with serrated edges. The steamed leaves have a mustardy taint and I don't much enjoy their taste.

The other native cresses are small herbs of damp forests and creek banks in south-eastern Australia. Although poorly known, most of them seem to have edible leaves used as potherbs by early settlers. Quaker missionary James Backhouse recorded that in Tasmania three kinds (*R. dictyosperma, Cardamine*

Colonial botanist Daniel Bunce, in the ponderous botanical prose of the nineteenth century, wrote of marsh cress (*Rorippa palustris*) as "half pinnated mustard, forming a good salad".

Right: Native cresses (*Rorippa* species) kept scurvy at bay among bushmen and drovers. In Australia cress identification is sorely confused, and young plants such as these, lacking flowers and pods, are impossible to identify. Photographed at Cunninghams Gap, Queensland.

forms "a good salad". Along the Nepean River the herb was called "native cabbage", and in nineteenth-century Victoria, Aborigines were recorded eating the leaves.

Yet according to the authoritative *Flora of Australia* published in 1982, marsh cress is not native to Australia but an introduced weed. The species is widespread in Europe where it is sometimes eaten as cress, and most botanists assume it was brought into Australia accidentally by early immigrants.

I believe these botanists are wrong. It is unlikely that nineteenth-century *gunnii* and *C. tenuifolia*) "might be eaten like the Common Cress; although generally, when in a wild state, or not growing luxuriantly, they are slightly acrid". The Reverend William Woolls said of *C. tenuifolia*, in 1867, that it "resembles the garden cress in flavour, but it is far too rare to be of any utility". In the Otway Ranges of Victoria, journalist Donald Macdonald wrote in 1887 of one of the native cresses, probably woodcress (*C. gunnii*): "A variety of mustard growing along some of the mountain creeks is the one salad amongst the marsh plants."

Tribal Aborigines probably ate all of these cresses, although there is scant written record of this. In Victoria, they were recorded eating marsh cress, woodcresses (*Cardamine* species) and peppercresses (*Lepidium* species). In the Coorong of South Australia the Taganekald tribe wrapped their game in cresses (and seaweeds) before baking it.

A recent account of Aborigines using cress comes from an elderly Aborigine, Mrs Ivy Sampson, who once lived at Coranderrk Mission near Healesville in Victoria. She remembered eating "watercress", perhaps one of the native cresses, growing along the banks of streams. Such memories are now very rare.

Among the introduced cresses that have found their way to Australia are some very interesting plants. Lesser swinecress or wart cress (*Coronopus didymus*) is a tiny lawn weed with fiery hot leaves that were eaten in New South Wales last century. The crushed leaves smell horrible, but cooking removes both the smell and the heat and the steamed leaves furnish a pleasantly bland vegetable. The raw leaves give real bite to salads and sandwiches.

Common bittercress (*Cardamine hirsuta*) is another lawn weed worth eating. Colonial botanist Joseph Maiden rated it an "excellent" potherb. In Japan the young roots and leaves were eaten

raw with vinegar and soy sauce. This dainty weed has a curious affinity for nurseries, and may be found sprouting prolifically in pots and pavement cracks in almost any nursery, from which it eagerly spreads to gardens. It also thrives along the sandbanks of forest streams.

Related to the true cresses are the peppercresses (*Lepidium* species), tall scrappy herbs of unkempt road verges and vacant allotments. Peppercress leaves are very peppery, and the seeds are hot enough to grind up and serve as mustard. There are several weedy peppercresses, all from overseas, with telling names such as Argentine

Top: A herb of old England, common bittercress (*Cardamine hirsuta*) was known as splitting jenny because the slender pods burst when ripe, scattering the seeds afar. The soft pinnate leaves have a delicate cress-like flavour, much milder than true watercress.

Below: Lesser swinecress (*Coronopus didymus*) was known in Queensland last century as watercress, suggesting that it was used like watercress as a flavouring herb, for which it is well suited. It certainly looks nothing like watercress.

peppercress, Virginian peppercress and common peppercress (*Lepidium africanum*).

Australia also has native peppercresses, found mainly on flood plains in the outback. J. Harris Browne in 1897 told of the elaborate techniques by which Aborigines in South Australia steamed the leaves:

"A circular hole was dug in the ground, two feet [0.6 metre] deep by three feet [0.9 metre] diameter, and into the bottom of the hole large pebbles were placed; a fire was kindled and kept burning until the stones were red hot. The embers were then taken out and sticks laid across the hole; on these a layer of reeds or damp grass was placed, and on them the cress in concentric layers, the root-ends to the outside; over the cress another layer of grass was laid and more grass round the outside of the heap. A 'yam stick' was then thrust through the heap from the top, and when withdrawn water was poured down the hole thus made; this reaching the hot stones, came up in steam that permeated the whole heap, more water being added from time to time when necessary. In about an hour the cress was well cooked, and the oven ready for another fire as before."

Peppercresses are still eaten occasionally by desert tribes. Anthropologist Peter Latz says they have "a strong flavour, similar to watercress. Steaming, however, nullifies the sharp taste and enables large amounts to be eaten. The small seeds, contained in the pods, would add to the nutritional value of this food. This is not a particularly tasty food; it was, however, available at a time of the year when other more favoured foods were scarce."

Not all desert tribes ate these cresses. Anthropologists Cleland and Tindale said of 'enmarta (*L. phlebopetalum*): "Aranda eat it after steaming; Pintubi do not use the steaming method of cooking greens and make no use of 'enmarta."

The native peppercresses, of which there are thirty-five species, are greedily grazed by cattle and rabbits, and it is sad but true that since European settlement four species have vanished, presumably into extinction, and another two are endangered. Botanists Leigh, Boden and Briggs discussed the demise of the winged peppercress in terms that could be applied to all the rare peppercresses: "Once widespread through drier areas of Victoria and New South Wales but it now appears to be very rare and possibly on the verge of extinction. The reasons for its decline are most probably grazing by domestic stock, rabbits, increased numbers of kangaroos and land clearing for agriculture (largely cereal cropping). These factors, particularly grazing, are likely to be continuing threats." Those conservationists who oppose kangaroo culling must recognise that the exploding populations of these marsupials, triggered by the provision of watering troughs in the outback, are promoting the demise of endangered plants like peppercresses.

The coast peppercress (*L. foliosum*) of southern Australia is a cress of special interest, being entirely restricted to small offshore islands, where it is sometimes the dominant plant. The tiny seeds are probably carried about on the feathers of birds, but why the plants sprout only on islands is difficult to say. At Beachport in South Australia I was able to collect this

rarely seen cress by swimming out to an offshore rocky shelf. The cress was thriving amongst the burrows of fairy penguins and the nests of angry seagulls. I took sprigs back to show naturalists in Beachport who had never seen the plant before. I thought perhaps this cress could grow only in guano, but a search through dozens of specimen labels in the herbaria of Adelaide and Melbourne lent no support to this view. I also wondered if the plants were grazed out on the mainland by wallabies or rabbits, but carefully searched many jagged headlands at Beachport, completely inaccessible to grazing animals, and found no peppercress. This greatly puzzles me. I can report, however, that the steamed leaves make a good vegetable, and I think it likely that all the peppercresses are edible, although of course in the case of the extinct species we will never know.

As well as peppercresses, Aborigines in desert areas ate the leaves of related native plants, such as unmuta (*Stenopetalum lineare*), downy thread-petal (*S. velutinum*), and priddiwalkatji (*Arabidella eremigena*). The last of these is probably the "scurvy-grass" described by Alice Duncan-Kemp in her evocative memoirs of life on a station west of

Never before photographed, the coast peppercress (*Lepidium foliosum*) is a mysterious herb known to grow only on tiny islands off the coast of southern Australia. This plant, which I collected in 1987, is only the second specimen recorded from the south-east of South Australia.

Flowers with four petals shaped like crosses, or crucifixes, led early botanists to nominate the family name Cruciferae for all mustard and cress plants, such as this wild radish (*Raphanus raphanistrum*). The buds and flowers can be cooked as a broccoli substitute.

Right: A tangle of wild radishes decorates a verge near Casino, providing nectar for dozens of humming bees. The wild radish, like most wild mustards, grows mainly in the cooler months.

Windorah at the turn of the century (*Our Sandhill Country*).

Thus far I have described members of the cress family that can loosely be termed "cresses". Mention should also be made of the other edible members of this remarkable family.

None is more noteworthy than the wild cabbage (*Brassica oleracea*), a plant of unparalleled versatility, from which have been bred cabbage, cauliflower, broccoli, brussels sprouts and kohlrabi. Wild cabbage and several allied plants have become weeds of farms and pastures in eastern Australia, and all of these plants make very interesting vegetables.

The leaves can be cooked as cabbage, the buds and flowers steamed as broccoli, and the seeds ground as mustard.

The wild radish (*Raphanus raphanistrum*), probably the ancestor of the cultivated radish, can be used in the same way. In nineteenth-century England its seed was separated from grain and sold as "Durham mustard"—a highly regarded condiment.

Many other common mustard weeds of Australian farms can be substituted for cabbage or mustard. These plants, all native to Europe and western Asia, are unknown to most Australians, but farmers will recognise such pests as hedge mustard (*Sisymbrium officinale*), buchan weed (*Hirschfeldia incana*), hoary cress (*Cardaria draba*—a declared noxious weed in Victoria), charlock (*Sinapis arvensis*), Indian mustard (*Brassica juncea*), and shepherd's purse (*Capsella bursa-pastoris*). Of the eighty or so introduced members of the mustard family growing in Australia as weeds, more than half are edible. No other plant family is so acceptable to human tastes.

Most gardeners would not know that sweet alyssum (*Lobularia maritima*), a small ornamental plant with white or mauve flower heads, is a member of the mustard family and has spicy edible leaves. It is naturalised along seashores in south-eastern Australia and may be seen

growing wild in small colonies on cliffs at Bondi, Kiama and elsewhere.

Probably the most unusual of the mustards are the sea rockets (*Cakile* species). These shrubby herbs have adapted to life on seashores by evolving thick fleshy leaves and succulent seed pods that float on ocean currents, carrying the seeds to isolated shores. Sea rockets hail from Europe and North America, but so successful has been their colonisation of Australia's shores that on many beaches, even in remote national parks, they are the dominant strandline plant. Indeed, there is scarcely a beach in temperate Australia where they do not grow. American sea rocket (*C. edentula*) was first recorded in 1863 on Phillip Island and was probably introduced accidentally in ballast from New England sealing ships. European sea rocket (*C. maritima*) appeared in Australia in 1897. These rockets spread so widely and prolifically that colonial botanists believed them to be native plants.

Young shoots of seedling sea rockets can be eaten as condiments, tasting hot and spicy like typical mustard greens. The seeds can be ground as mustard. During famine in Canada in the eighteenth century the roots were pounded, mixed with flour and eaten. In Australia their potential as food is virtually unknown. It is noteworthy that emus eat the young shoots and the seeds are a major food of orange-bellied parrots—one of Australia's rarest birds.

Before finishing with the mustards it is worth mentioning that among plants belonging to other families, a few have evolved mustard oils identical to those found in the mustards and cresses.

The garden nasturtium (*Tropaeolum majus*) is one such plant. Not only does this garden plant have mustardy leaves

The vast shifting sand dunes of Little Dip in South Australia are home to large numbers of European sea rockets (*Cakile maritima*), which stabilise the dune crests. The seed pods of this plant are scattered by the strong onshore winds.

Top left: On the headlands at Bondi Beach the garden plant called sweet alyssum (*Lobularia maritima*) has become a feral plant. The young leaves have a peppery taste and may be used in salads or as cooked vegetables.

Centre: Viewed closely, the purplish, fleshy, lobed leaves of the sea rocket are an eerie sight. They make a reasonable vegetable when boiled.

Below: Very few beaches in temperate Australia do not carry large colonies of introduced sea rockets on their fore dunes. These plants have filled a niche left vacant by Australian plants.

Nasturtium flowers (*Tropaeolum majus*) are followed by fleshy seeds, which during World War II were used in England as a pepper substitute, though they are scarcely spicy enough. The leaves can be used instead of vine leaves in Greek cookery.

and stems, it even takes its name from watercress (*Nasturtium* is the Latin name for watercress, and means "nose-twisting", alluding to the pungent leaves). Leaves of garden nasturtium can be cooked as vegetables, and the young seeds pickled like capers. True capers are members of the caper family (Capparaceae), a group closely allied with the mustards (plants of both families have flowers with only four petals, an uncommon feature). Mustard oils are found widely within the caper family, and in Queensland last century a mustard substitute was even fashioned from caper rinds.

The leaves of the mustard tree (*Codonocarpus cotinifolius*) of outback Australia also taste strongly of mustard. One colonial writer exclaimed that it had "a very suitable name, for the leaves of it have a remarkable pungent taste very like mustard". The leaves have no culinary use, although Aborigines ate the sappy roots. Crushed pawpaw seeds also taste of mustard, and contain mustard oils.

Not surprisingly, Aborigines had no taste for mustard. Explorer George Grey noted that they "dislike mustard, sauces, &c. when they first eat them, and nothing can be more ludicrous than their grimaces are the first time mustard is given them upon a piece of meat".

WEEDS

Along road verges in eastern Australia there grows an untidy weed with coarse leaves and bristly stems. Farmers, who spray 2,4-D to control this pest, know it as compass plant, or prickly lettuce, (*Lactuca serriola*). The blue-green leaves usually grow flat, as if pressed between pages of a book, hence compass plant. "Prickly lettuce" is the less obvious name but the more apt, for, despite its harsh appearance, this is the ancestor of the cultivated lettuce.

Prickly lettuce bears scant resemblance to its modern-day descendant, but we know from Egyptian wall paintings that lettuces grown thousands of years ago looked like this weed, as do some lettuce breeds farmed in China today. Breeding experiments confirm the ancestry. If you let a garden lettuce run to seed, it soon sprouts the tall stalk, yellow flowers and milky sap of its spiky forebear.

Prickly lettuce cannot be substituted for the modern vegetable. The coarse leaves taste far too bitter. They can, however, be used in soups and as a substitute for spinach. In Sudan, an oil in the tiny seeds is extracted for cookery.

Prickly lettuce is but one of about three hundred different weeds with edible leaves found on Australian farms and roadsides and in gardens. In most Australian suburban yards there are a dozen or so such plants, including such typical morsels as dandelion, catsear, pigweed, wood-sorrel, chickweed, amaranth, swinecress, sowthistle, cobbler's pegs, yellow weed, plantain, peppercress and dock. These quick-growing opportunistic plants do not produce the tough toxin-laden leaves of shrubs and trees, and their tender succulent greens are eatable raw or lightly steamed.

Native plants do not fare well in the nutrient-enriched soils of gardens and

farms, and most weeds in Australia are plants from overseas. The seeds of sorrel, docks and the like probably came in on potting soil with imported fruit trees, perhaps as early as the First Fleet. Thanks to the rise of world trade over the last two centuries, Australia now has weeds from throughout the globe. Among these are traditional wild vegetables of European peasants, South American Indians and African and Asian villagers.

Like most culinary weeds, prickly lettuce (*Lactuca serriola*) should be harvested before flowers or seeds appear, while the leaves are still tender. Rich in vitamin A, they make a good soup ingredient but are too bitter for salads. Photographed in Brisbane.

The innocent victim of a smear campaign, glossy nightshade (*Solanum americanum*) not only does not have poisonous berries, but even its leaves can be cooked and eaten, as they are in many peasant communities around the world.

Top right: Look but don't touch! The leaves of scrub nettle (*Urtica incisa*) sting the skin severely but when boiled make a splendid vegetable. This herb thrives in rainforest clearings, as here at Lamington National Park in southern Queensland.

Dainty but dangerous, the small nettle (*Urtica urens*) has stinging leaves 1.5 to 5 centimetres long, distinguishing it from the larger scrub nettle, which has leaves usually twice this size. Photographed in inner-city Melbourne.

Glossy nightshade (*Solanum americanum*), for example, is used as a village vegetable in the lands to the north and east of Australia: by the Kanaks of New Caledonia, and by villagers in Timor and New Guinea. In colonial Australia the leaves were not used, but the shiny berries were cooked in jams (see Feral Fruits chapter).

In England, nettles are among the best-known of wild vegetables; the leaves were sold in markets centuries ago. Cooking disarms the sting from what are tender-tasting leaves. Australia has two kinds: the native scrub nettle (*Urtica incisa*) of creek beds and rainforest fringes, and introduced small nettle (*U. urens*), a weed of farms. Nettles were little used by Australian colonists, but the South Australian pioneer George Angas, in his 1847 best-seller *Savage Life and Scenes in Australia and New Zealand*, observed that "A species of stinging nettle grows abundantly amongst the reeds; and especially in times of scarcity, it is eaten by the natives, who bake it between heated stones".

Spiny emex (*Emex australis*) is an interesting plant that has come to us from South Africa. No other weed goes by so many colloquial names—double gee, prickly jack, bullhead, three-cornered jack, cat's head, goathead, Cape spinach. This last name is the most telling, for it lends credence to the old story that spiny emex was introduced to Australia in 1830 as a spinach substitute, by English migrants who had stopped over at Cape Town. The leaves afford an excellent substitute for spinach, and it is regrettable that the edible properties of this weed are largely forgotten.

Spiny emex is a trailing weed of roadsides, farms, and pavements in Sydney and other towns. Country people detest the seed pods, which tear the feet of dogs and children. To find them, search the undersides of rubber thongs.

There is a story that a couple of Australian entrepreneurs at Exmouth tried to sell American tourists spiny emex seedpods—cradled in cottonwool—as the eggs of mountain devil lizards. The price: $20 a pair.

Pigweed, also known as purslane (*Portulaca oleracea*), was a weed well known to colonists. The juicy leaves and stems were widely cooked as a vegetable, and sometimes still are. Pigweed is found worldwide, but unlike most weeds in Australia is considered a native plant. Colonial botanist F. M. Bailey proclaimed it "a splendid substitute for spinach". The Reverend William Woolls in 1867 said it was "formerly cultivated as a pot-herb [in Europe], the young shoots and leaves having been used in spring and autumn as ingredients in pickles and salads . . . It is highly important that the value of purslane should be made known, for, in many parts where the usual garden-vegetables cannot be procured, it might be employed with much advantage as an antiscorbutic [scurvy cure]."

Pigweed was cultivated in France as early as the sixteenth century, and various breeds were developed, some

Only weeks before their death, Burke and Wills ate an "abundance of Portulac", as Wills wrote in his diary, referring to pigweed (*Portulaca oleracea*). This herb probably extended their lives, along with the fish, nardoo and rats given to them by Aborigines. Photographed at Ayers Rock.

English legends say that lactating sows sought out the leaves of sowthistles (*Sonchus oleraceus*) to increase their flow of milk, an obvious allusion to the copious milky sap that flows from the cut stems.

with golden leaves. Yet one American gardener dismissed the plant as "a mischievous weed that Frenchmen and pigs eat when they can get nothing else. Both use it in salad, that is to say, raw." Explorers Burke and Wills and Leichhardt ate the leaves without complaint. Pigweed also has edible seeds, and was so important a food of Aborigines and settlers that it earns a place in the chapters on Wild Seeds and Colonial Greens.

Another widespread weed, the common sowthistle (*Sonchus oleraceus*), was little used by settlers, but was a favourite of Aborigines. Like pigweed, sowthistle grows throughout most of the world, and villagers eat it in Asia and

Africa. Botany texts in Australia without exception list it as introduced, but I am sure these books are wrong, for the first explorers often found "thistles" in remote valleys, and outback Aborigines were seen eating the leaves. E. Stephens, a settler near Adelaide, even witnessed a thistle feast: "[The Aborigines] saw about a quarter of an acre of luxuriant sow thistles on our land. Some of them asked if they might have them. I obtained the requisite permission, and told them that they could take the lot. In a moment they had climbed the fence, and this little plot was one seething mass of men, women and children. Ten minutes later the ground was bare of thistles, and the tribe passed on gratefully devouring the juicy weed." It is difficult to believe Aborigines would become so excited over a weed—unless it was also a traditional food.

Sowthistle is ubiquitous in gardens and farms in southern and eastern Australia, and grows as a native herb along creek and swamp margins. The raw leaves have a bitter edge and make an excellent substitute for endive in salads. (The two plants are closely related.) I eat them fresh with continental mustard on flatbread.

Related to common sowthistle are the dandelion (*Taraxacum officinale*) and catsears (*Hypochoeris radicata*), two lawn weeds from Europe that are often confused. The dinkum dandelion has smooth leaves with jagged margins, and flowers on hollow stems. Catsear has hairy leaves with straight or wavy margins, and flowers on wiry, usually branched stems. Dandelion leaves taste bitter unless they are first blanched yellow by covering them for a few days with old boards, lino, or other backyard junk. Catsear leaves make a good soup, and the roots of both plants make splendid coffee (see Wild Coffees chapter).

Tourists to central Australia and the Flinders Ranges often pause to photograph beautiful desert vistas of bright red "native hops". What few tourists realise, and what their bus drivers don't tell them, is that "native hops" is an introduced weed—known properly as ruby dock (*Rumex vesicarius*). The vast colonies of this plant represent, not the "desert in bloom", but degradation and environmental imbalance. Ruby dock hails from north Africa where bedouins eat the sour leaves.

Ruby dock is one of many close relatives of supermarket sorrel (*Rumex*

One of Australia's most versatile wild plants is curled dock (*Rumex crispus*). Mary Gilmore described the colonial use of such weeds: "But dock was used like horehound and nettles, for beer; sometimes it was wrapped round tough meat with the idea of making it tender."

acetosa) found wild in Australia. These include some highly useful vegetables. Sheep sorrel (*R. acetosella*), a common weed on sandy soils in southern Australia, was a popular green during the reign of Henry VIII. The acid leaves make exquisite sorrel soup (and a nasty drink called sorrelade). Although native to the Northern Hemisphere, sheep sorrel thrives in Australia, even on the very summit of Mount Kosciusko.

Larger of leaf than the sorrels are the damp-loving docks (*Rumex* species). These have sour leaves equal to the best silver beet (which is often sold as "spinach" in Australian stores). Docks are so freely available that I never buy supermarket silver beet, which is never as fresh anyway.

The most useful of the docks, and one of my favourite wild foods, is curled dock (*R. crispus*), a tall herb with enormous succulent leaves, the stout stems of which may be stewed as rhubarb. It is extraordinarily satisfying to gather an armful of the leaves and create a two-course meal (or three-course if some of the leaves are saved for soup). The diced stems simmered in a little sugar and water taste mildly of rhubarb, and many people prefer them to the real thing. Stewed with apples they make an excellent filling for tarts and pies.

Three other edible docks are worth knowing. Broad-leaf dock (*R. obtusifolius*) has crinkly leaves which make good greens. It is found around Melbourne and in the Dandenongs, but further north towards Sydney is common only in the Blue Mountains.

Swamp dock (*R. brownii*) is unique among the edible docks in being an Australian native. It is common in lawns in eastern Australia, especially in Brisbane. The hooked seed pods have even spread to England on sheep fleeces and this Aussie original is now a weed in England—a remarkable reversal of the usual trend. What makes this dock even more interesting is that forest-growing

A feast for a forager: this clump of delectable broad-leaf dock (*Rumex obtusifolius*), fresher than any shop-bought spinach, grows in a park above Ferntree Gully in Melbourne.

Australia's native swamp dock (*Rumex brownii*) is very similar to one of the Himalayan docks and may have recently evolved from seeds of that dock carried by migrating birds. All of Australia's native docks have bristly seed pods which cling to feathers.

plants are much smaller than their urban-growing kin. Their natural habitat is stream margins in forests, but plants in this habitat usually have tiny leaves less than a centimetre in width. The garden forms, growing in enriched soil, are three or four times this size. It's as if this species only achieved its full potential after the arrival of Europeans.

Another unusual dock is turkey rhubarb (*R. sagittatus*), or rambling dock, which grows as a vine. A soft-leaved creeper with papery pods, it was introduced from Africa, presumably as an ornamental, and now runs wild along fences and vacant allotments, especially in Sydney. The very sour leaves make an ideal substitute for true spinach.

Of all the weeds available in Australia as food, the one I recommend least is cobblers pegs (*Bidens pilosa*). The unpleasant taint of the cooked leaves cannot be disguised by any known spinach recipe. Nonetheless, cobblers pegs is an important village vegetable in Africa, where villagers even dry the leaves for future use.

Although most of the edible weeds in Australia came in a century or two ago, some are only just arriving. An estimated ten new plants turn feral in Australia

A newcomer among Australian weeds, thickhead (*Crassocephalum crepidioides*) is becoming widespread in Sydney, where it was unknown twenty years ago. In Brisbane's western suburbs, where this plant was photographed, it is now very common.

Turkey rhubarb (*Rumex sagittatus*) may be a misnomer, as the plant has no apparent connection with turkeys or rhubarb. This useful vegetable is abundant around Sydney and deserves to be more widely known.

Winter is salad time when chickweed (*Stellaria media*) is sprouting. The juicy leaves and stems go well with tomatoes and beans. Look in moist shady corners for a soft herb with tiny leaves and stems with a line of silky hairs along one side.

A peasant potherb all over the world, fat-hen (*Chenopodium album*) has been harvested in England, Scotland, Germany, Denmark, Russia, Canada, America, India and Africa. The seed spikes may be boiled as mush. Photographed on a footpath in Hawthorn, Melbourne.

each year, a figure of concern as some of these weeds become invaders of natural forests. South African thickhead (*Crassocephalum crepidioides*) is one of the more recent invaders. It arrived in South-East Asia in the 1920s and in Brisbane in the 1950s, and has now appeared in Sydney. In Asia the greens have become a popular rural vegetable, and I was fed the steamed leaves by Khmer villagers while camping in jungles in eastern Thailand in 1976. Thickhead leaves have a carroty taste and go well in tomato salads; they are too aromatic for spinach dishes.

If thickhead is one of Australia's newer edible weeds, chickweed (*Stellaria media*) is surely among the oldest. The seeds probably arrived in potting soil with the First Fleet. The juicy leaves are ideal in salads.

Left: The leaves of the weed called ox tongue (*Picris echioides*) have a rough surface, hence its curious name. Boiling softens the bristles and a tender vegetable results. Photographed at Millicent, South Australia.

Right: Anyone who has tried to grow vegetables will know yellow weed (*Galinsoga parviflora*), a pesky weed that sprouts among the cabbages and tomatoes.

Among the tastiest of spinach substitutes is fat-hen (*Chenopodium album*); its mealy leaves supply vitamins A and C. Fat-hen, like chickweed, is a common weed of vacant allotments in temperate Australia. It often grows alongside amaranths (*Amaranthus* species), and these also sprout nutritious leaves. Green amaranth (*Amaranthus viridis*) is featured in the Colonial Greens chapter.

Garden asparagus (*Asparagus officinalis*) has become a significant weed of irrigation channels and river flats in southern Australia, often forming dense stands. The wild shoots make a delicious vegetable.

The common farm and garden weed called yellow weed (*Galinsoga parviflora*) has soft bland leaves that furnish more bulk than flavour in spinach dishes. It grows alongside dozens of other edible

A noxious weed of farms in southern Australia, soursob (*Oxalis pes-caprae*) hails from South Africa, where it is also considered a weed. The sour lemony-tasting leaves make a good substitute for sorrel, to which it is unrelated.

garden weeds, but rather than continue listing them here I refer the reader to my book *Wild Herbs of Australia & New Zealand*, which identifies more than seventy such weeds, along with recipes.

Some tips for foragers: choose the younger leaves of fresh plants; old weeds, especially those in seed, may taste bitter.

Hot, dry weather also makes leaves bitter, and the best greens can always be gathered after rain. Beware of scrumptious-looking weeds growing close to sewage outlets, drains and factories. And especially beware of those men in overalls who squirt pavement weeds with smelly chemicals. Good picking!

MIXED PICKINGS

SEAWEEDS

Previous pages: The floral emblem of New South Wales, the waratah (*Telopea speciosissima*) was a food plant of Aborigines, who relished the sugary nectar. Of the other States' floral emblems, kangaroo paws have edible rootstocks and Sturt peas reportedly have edible seeds.

The story of how Aborigines harvested seaweeds can be but short in the telling, for there is very little to say. The colonial literature yields only two, very old accounts of Aborigines harvesting algae, both from Tasmania and both referring to bull kelp (*Durvillea potatorum*).

Bull kelp is the menacing weed that lurks in cold depths along the rugged coasts of southern Australia. From thick slimy stalks fastened to submarine rocks, it extends great leathery fronds up to three metres long, which slap about eerily in tidal pools.

That remarkable French botanist, Labillardière, exploring Tasmania's coast with D'Entrecasteaux in 1793, saw natives "broiling" and eating this rubbery wrack: " . . . when it is softened to a certain point, they tore it to pieces to eat it."

Dr Milligan, the sympathetic superintendent of Tasmania's last full-blood Aborigines, provides the other account, recorded by the Reverend Francis Nixon in 1857. According to Milligan, "the leaf of the larger kelp, whenever it could be obtained, was eagerly looked for and greedily eaten, after having undergone a process of roasting and maceration in fresh water, followed by a second roasting, when, though tough, and too much like sole leather, it is susceptible of mastication, and, no doubt, nutritious". Aborigines also fashioned kelp into buckets for carrying water.

Despite exhaustive searches through old journals, I can find no other suggestion that Australian Aborigines ate seaweeds of any kind. (The Tangenekald of the Coorong steamed their meats in seaweeds, but it is not stated that the weed was eaten.)

This is a little puzzling, for many of Australia's seaweeds are identical or closely related to those eaten overseas. Why weren't they used?

Among the flotsam found on beaches in southern Australia are strips of wave-tossed bull kelp (*Durvillea potatorum*), which present an eerie spectacle. Photographed at Beachport, South Australia.

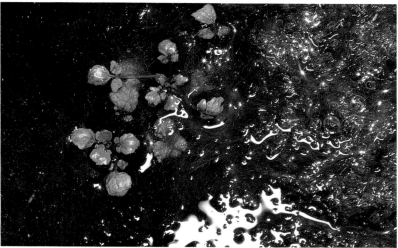

I have two suggestions. Firstly, Aborigines had no pots to boil or fry foods or prepare complex dishes. Their cooking style did not suit seaweeds, which are used overseas largely to flavour rice dishes. Only bull kelp, that most robust of the wracks, is bulky enough to be worth roasting in a fire. In any event, seaweeds are largely indigestible and low in calories. They serve mainly as a source of vitamins and minerals. Traditional coastal Aborigines, enjoying a rich diet of seafood and fruits, would not have needed the extra vitamins. Salty seaweeds would have been shunned in favour of tasty fish, yams and berries.

Even bull kelp itself is not immediately inviting. I once roasted a leathery frond and found it rubbery and rank. Other seaweeds are more suited to western palates.

Sea lettuce (*Ulva lactuca*), for example, is worth adding to salads and soups. It is the small weed of intertidal pools that looks like soggy lettuce. The lettuce "leaves" should be thoroughly scrubbed (in fresh water) and eaten raw in salads or boiled like spinach. They may be sun-dried for future use. Despite the delicate texture, the sheets are as tough as plastic bags.

Neptune's necklace (*Hormosira banksii*) is another common weed that is easy to recognise. The large knobbly "beads" dangle in thick strings around edges of shallow rocky pools. A pickle is made by boiling the beads in fresh water and covering them with spiced vinegar.

Brown kelp (*Ecklonia radiata*) can also be used as pickle. This weed has a greenish brown lobed blade with a largely corrugated surface, unlike bull kelp which is smooth. To pickle it, chop and boil the blades before adding vinegar.

Sea lettuce, Neptune's necklace and brown kelp are three of the most common seaweeds in temperate Australia, but there are many others that

Looking about as appetising as a knuckle sandwich, a colony of spirogyra (*Spirogyra* species) smothers a small watercress plant in a drain at Bondi. In Asia the spirogyra alga is used in soups.

Top left: On intertidal rock platforms around Sydney, sea lettuce (*Ulva lactuca*) is one of the most common seaweeds. It is easy to see how this alga got its name. Photographed just south of Bondi Beach.

A rock pool choked with edible seaweeds at Yuraygir National Park east of Grafton. The main weeds are Neptune's necklace (*Hormosira banksii*) and brown kelp (*Ecklonia radiata*). Both are suitable for pickling.

Seaweeds such as this Neptune's necklace are a rich source of iodine, iron, calcium, carotene and the B vitamins. Most seaweeds can be eaten raw. Photographed near Wollongong.

can serve as food. Indeed, it is thought that nearly all Australian algae are edible, save only those with a bitter, spicy or irritant taste.

Seaweeds of most kinds can be nibbled raw like vitamin pills while you stroll by the sea. Boiling softens the tissues and renders the flavours amenable to cooked dishes. Before cooking, weed should be washed and soaked to remove the taint of the sea. Scrub off sand and crustaceans, and soak in well-salted water. Seaweeds left in fresh water are apt to go slimy.

Speaking of fresh water, there is one kind of freshwater alga that can be eaten. Surprisingly, it is that bright green slime that coats rocks in shallow pools. *Spirogyra* comprises thousands of slimy

strands that look most unappetising. They can, however, be eaten raw, straight from the sludge, after flushing out the grit and detritus. In texture they lie halfway between alfalfa sprouts and cottonwool, with no discernible taste. In South-East Asia the dried strands have been sold as food. Aborigines apparently never used them.

As an afterthought, it is worth noting that although mainland Aborigines ate no seaweed, in north Queensland they did harvest a seagrass. At Cape Bedford the Koko-yimidir gathered on the mudflats at low tide to harvest the egg-sized pods of the seagrass *Enhalus acoroides*. These morsels were roasted and the seeds inside eaten.

WILD
MUSHROOMS

With so much known about Australia's edible fruits, roots, leaves and seeds, it comes as a shock to discover just how little we know about native mushrooms. Scarcely anything is known about the fungi eaten by Aborigines, and no-one can make a guess at the number of edible mushrooms in this country.

The fungi themselves are largely to blame for this shortfall. Furtive plants of little economic significance, they tend to shrivel beyond recognition when dried in museum collections. For these reasons they are largely ignored by botanists. Indeed, there is scarcely a handful of experts skilled at their identification, and many varieties cannot be assigned a genus, much less given a name.

With such ignorance about mushrooms today, it is not surprising that the anthropological record is meagre. Colonists often listed "various mushrooms" as foods of tribes they observed, but rarely provided names or descriptions.

Early settlers were wary of dabbling with mushrooms, no doubt because the Old World fungi include such dangerous plants. Death cap (*Amanita phalloides*) and panther (*A. pantherina*), Europe's main killers, are palatable fungi with no warning colour or taste. Australia's colonists could hardly be expected to experiment freely with the unfamiliar species growing here. Also, the country was colonised by the British, a culture renowned for its disinterest in gourmet foods like fungi.

Even so, it is possible to cobble together a list—obviously very incomplete—of Australian edible fungi. From accounts of Aboriginal diet at least five species can be identified. To these we can add a large number of European and Asian fungi that happen to grow in Australia. Whether these are also native

What are they? Probably *Agrocybe* species, a leading mushroom expert told me. The difficulties of identification and the shortage of experts make culinary experimentation with fungi a risky pastime. These mushrooms had a pleasant taste.

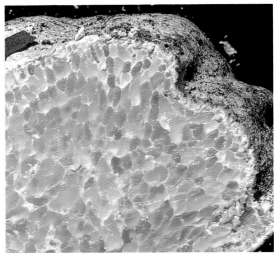

Aborigines doted on the underground "stone" of the mushroom called blackfellow's bread (*Polyporus mylittae*). This example, excavated near the Ada River in Victoria, is lying on its side with the broken "stone" at right.

Right: Quaker missionary James Backhouse said of the underground organ of native bread: "This species of tuber is often found in the Colony [of Tasmania], attaining to the size of a child's head: its taste somewhat resembles boiled rice." Photographed at Powelltown east of Melbourne.

to Australia is often a moot point: we may guess that some came in with potting soil from Europe, and that others are cosmopolitan, their spores spread worldwide by global air currents.

Of the fungi eaten by Aborigines, the best known is that colonial curio known as "native bread" (*Polyporus mylittae*). Nineteenth-century farmers ploughing new fields were sometimes startled to come across huge underground "stones", packed with what appeared to be compacted boiled rice. These "stones", weighing up to twenty kilograms, are the underground storage organs of a fungus that sprouts mushroom caps, not after rain like most fungi, but after bushfires. There are many old reports of Aborigines in Tasmania and Victoria feasting upon these windfalls.

The following account comes from the *Hobart Town Gazette* of September 1818, amongst items about missing convicts, murders and stolen arms: "On Saturday afternoon as some labourers were employed in ploughing a small allotment of ground in Argyle street, the plough unexpectedly came in contact with a large root of a fungous nature. Several natives being on the spot, eagerly ran after one of the men, who from motives of curiosity was anxious to know what he had found, exclaiming 'Bringally', (for bread-root); they quickly devoured large pieces of it. The owner of the ground

(William Ashton in Liverpool-street) has some of this extraordinary production of nature in his possession, where it has been viewed and tasted by several persons, who esteem it very palatable."

Quaker missionary James Backhouse in 1843 described the "tuber" as "attaining to the size of a child's head: its taste somewhat resembles boiled rice. Like the heart of the Tree-fern, and the root of the Native Potato [potato orchid], cookery produces little change in its character. On asking the Aborigines how they found the Native-bread, they universally replied, 'A Rotten Tree.' On the dry, open hills about Bothwell, it is to be detected in the early part of summer, by the ground bursting upwards as if with something swelling under it, which is this fungus."

The related stone-maker fungus (*P. tumulosus*) has an even bigger and harder "stone", sometimes so heavy a man cannot lift it. Aborigines reportedly ate the mushrooms of this species, but not the stone.

In the deserts of central Australia three fungi have been recorded as foods of Aborigines. The desert truffle (*Elderia arenivaga*) was both a delicacy and a source of water in the trackless deserts of the Northern Territory. An excellent account of this curious plant is given by botanist Peter Latz, who grew up among Aborigines:

"This truffle is white and juicy when young, becoming yellowish and wrinkled with maturity. Size and shape are variable but they are generally about as big as an apricot . . .

"This was an important and much sought after food throughout its range. Difficult to find, it required an intimate knowledge of its particular habitat requirements and skill in finding the small hairline cracks in the soil which indicated its presence. Nevertheless, in the right season, quite large quantities of this delicacy were gathered.

"This fungus could be eaten raw but was usually roasted in hot sand before being eaten. Gathered when fresh, a considerable amount of drinkable water could be wrung from them. Truly a remarkable plant, providing both food and water!

"During my childhood at Hermannsburg we often gathered this food in considerable quantities. In recent years, however, this truffle has become quite rare. It is probably that heavy predation by rabbits and changes in burning practices could explain its decline."

Another mushroom used in the desert was the aptly named horse-dropping fungus (*Pisolithus tinctorius*). This brown lumpy fungus was eaten by the desert Pintupi and Anmatjirra. An unidentified bolete (*Boletus* species) was eaten at Ooldea in South Australia. Latz notes that gilled mushrooms were shunned by desert tribes, the Aranda considering them to be malignant fallen stars.

I can find no suggestion that Aborigines in northern or eastern Australia used fungi, and only one other account describing specific fungi. This comes from the pen of Dr Milligan, who in the mid-nineteenth century had the melancholy task of caring for the last full-blood Tasmanian Aborigines. His priceless notes record that the Aborigines ate "various epiphytic fungi, of which one of the most important is that which grows on the Eucalypti, and is known, when dry, under the name of Punk, and is used as a tinder in the Colony. Punk, when young, is nearly snow-white, soft, and, to the taste, insipid, with a distant flavour of mushroom; in this stage they eat it freely, either raw or softly roasted."

Dr Milligan's "punk" is evidently one of the bracket fungi of genus *Piptoporus*. One member of this group, the curry

Tasmania's beech fungus (*Cyttaria gunnii*) drew strong praise from Quaker missionary James Backhouse: ". . . it is produced in clusters, from swollen portions of the branches, and varies from the size of a marble to that of a walnut . . . Its taste, in this state, is like cold cow-heel . . . It may be considered the best native esculent in V. D. Land."

The forest mushroom (*Agaricus langei*) looks much like the common field mushroom, except the young gills of the forest mushroom are paler pink and are separated from the stalk by a gutter, and the ring around the stalk is a distinctive papery skirt. Both species make excellent eating.

punk (*P. australiensis*), actually smells like curry, but is not thought to be edible.

Milligan also cites the harvest of native bread, of "several mushrooms", and of the beech fungus (*Cyttaria gunnii*), "a great favourite" found growing on Antarctic beech trees.

The fungi cited here are obviously only a few of the many that Aborigines must have used. The gaps in our knowledge are enormous. I can find no precise records from Western Australia, even though explorer George Grey referred to this State when he asserted that "different kinds of fungus are very good. In certain seasons of the year they are abundant, and the natives eat them greedily." I cannot even guess the species Grey refers to, except to say they probably included none of those described here.

I can also find very little about fungi eaten by settlers. The field mushroom (*Agaricus campestris*) was probably the one most used. It earns a place in Mrs Lance Rawson's *Enquiry Book* of 1894, with recipes for broiling, stewing, baking and preserving the caps.

Eating the green-spored parasol mushroom (*Chlorophyllum molybdites*) makes many people ill. It has distinctive scales on the large cap (not yet opened on this youngster), a tough ring on the stem, and grey to greenish-brown gills.

The field mushroom sprouts in suburban lawns, horse paddocks and other artificial habitats, but seems never to grow in native forests, feeding the suspicion that it is not an Australian native. A dainty mushroom with silky white caps when young, its gills start out pink, and become a dark chocolate brown. The field mushroom resembles some poisonous fungi, but the latter always bruise colourfully, have yellow or white gills, carry shingles on the cap, or smell strange. The yellow stainer (*A. xanthodermus*), for example, has thimble-shaped caps when young, bruises yellow when squeezed, and smells like disinfectant, especially when kept in a bag. The white-spored parasol mushroom (*Macrolepiota dolichaula*) has white gills, and the green-spored parasol mushroom (*Chlorophyllum molybdites*), grey or greenish brown gills. Most people fall ill after trying these fungi, but some can eat them without complaint. The field mushroom has several native relatives in forests in south-eastern Australia, and these are thought to be edible, although little is known about them.

There are many other edible fungi in Australia, but only a few that are particularly easy to identify. The curious ink caps (*Coprinus* species) are among the most distinctive. These delicacies are so named because their caps decompose into a black fluid which can be used as ink. Ink caps were favourites of the great

mushroom writer Miron Elisha Hard, who attested that "A weak stomach can digest any of the Coprini when almost any other food will give it trouble. I am always pleased to give a dish of any Coprini to an invalid."

The shaggy mane ink cap (C. comatus) looks like a hairy goose egg when young, developing a slender bell shape as the margin of the cap rots away. This fungus is found worldwide, and sells in markets in France.

Young caps of the glistening ink cap (C. micaceus) sparkle as if sprinkled with flecks of mica (hence micaceus). These mushrooms are one of urban Australia's best-kept secrets, for they sprout prolifically in gardens and lawns around the bases of dead trees and ailing shrubs, providing an abundant supply of gourmet food which almost no-one knows about. I used to gather bowlfuls after rain from around a dead mandarin tree in my yard.

Miron Elisha Hard rates them as "without doubt the best mushroom that grows".

The flavour is delicate (some say bland) and put to best effect in salads. The mushrooms keep poorly and should be used on the day of picking; they autodigest very quickly, even when refrigerated. Even so, this is a mushroom worth getting to know.

The other common urban mushrooms are the puffballs. These are the small white blobs of putty (Lycoperdon species) found on lawns after rain. While still firm, these can be picked for salads and stews. Avoid them when they turn rubbery—they become floury and tasteless.

In fields and paddocks there grow very large puffballs, the grandfather of which is the giant puffball (Langermannia gigantea), allegedly growing up to a metre wide. From afar these have been

Delicious: a cluster of glistening ink caps (Coprinus micaceus) sprouting at the base of a dead mango tree. Note the furrowed tan-coloured caps, and the silky-white fibrous stalks two to five millimetres thick.

Not one of the gourmet mushrooms, the small puffballs (*Lycoperdon* species) of suburban lawns are edible nonetheless. They should be picked while still firm and eaten raw in salads or added to stews.

mistaken for sheep in a paddock. The huge growths are sliced into "steaks" before eating. The smaller puffballs (including *Calvatia* species) are known to confuse golfers. Any puffball with firm white flesh and a white centre may be eaten raw or cooked. They are not the tastiest of fungi.

Boletes and morels remain poorly known in Australia, despite their fame in Europe, where they sell in markets in France. Boletes resemble ordinary mushrooms but instead of gills have small round pores or tubes through which the spores are shed. Morels (*Morchella*) are distinctive fungi with honeycombed caps. They are rare in Australia and little known as foods.

That French delicacy, the underground truffle (*Tuber* species), is also rare here. (The so-called desert truffle of Aborigines is not closely related.) Before the Age of Science, European scholars explained away these mysterious growths as soil calluses, oak galls, or nodules created by semen from rutting deer. One of the overseas truffles has found its way to Australia, where it grows beneath introduced trees, but it has little culinary merit.

The mushrooms considered thus far are forms well known and much liked in Europe (and North America). Australia is also home to a couple of fungi that are popular foods in the Orient, in China and Japan. Hairy jew's ear (*Auricularia polytricha*) was even exported from north Queensland to China.

Jew's ear is a rubbery ear-like fungus found on rainforest logs after rain. Chinese farmers cultivate it on oak

Once a food exported to China, the hairy jew's ear (*Auricularia polytricha*) is nowadays a little-known fungus of dead rainforest branches. Note the velvety purplish upper surface. Photographed at Cunninghams Gap near Warwick.

boughs. Although lacking a strong taste, it absorbs the flavour of other foods and provides delicate texture in Chinese and Japanese dishes.

The white jelly fungus (*Tremella fuciformis*) is another Chinese delicacy found in Australian forests. Like the jew's ear, it must be considered native here, unlike the many fungi restricted to human habitats.

White jelly fungus is one of several edible gelatinous fungi found growing on damp rotten wood. (I once found a tiny jelly fungus growing on an old chair on my patio—it tasted delicious, and I nibbled it off before sitting.)

Jelly fungi are usually orange, yellow, white or brown, often resembling brains or other organs, sometimes sprouting branches like antlers or stalactites. Little is known about identification of these fungi, but they appear to be inoffensive, having a pleasant slippery jelly taste. Similar to these are the coral fungi

It looks revolting, but this yellow jelly fungus (*Tremella* species), which was growing on a rainforest tree after rain, had a pleasantly bland gelatinous taste.

(*Ramaria* species) which are branched fleshy fungi, orange or pink in hue, resembling corals or cauliflowers. It appears that some but not others of these are edible, which shows yet again how little we know about Australia's fungi.

FLOWERS

Sugary foods are scarce in the bush, and Aborigines placed a high premium on the sweet fragrant nectars of native flowers. Especially popular were banksias, grevilleas and other members of that typically Australian family, the Proteaceae. These large blossoms carry copious nectar to sate the appetites of their pollinating birds, mainly honeyeaters and lorikeets. Insect-pollinated flowers hold very little nectar and were little used.

The blossoms of banksias (*Banksia* species) sometimes overflow with nectar. I remember camping on Moreton Island one night and watching the nectar drip onto my provisions. The leaves beneath the blossoms were sticky. Aborigines gleefully sucked the honey straight from the flowers or soaked the banksia cones in bark troughs to make drinks. Banksias are most prolific in Western Australia, where fifty-eight of the seventy-three

species grow, and there are many old accounts of Aborigines there using them as food. Colonist G. F. Moore talked in 1884 of the "honeysuckle" tree, producing an "abundance of honey, which the natives are fond of regaling upon, either by sucking or soaking the flowers in water". One writer extolled the "delicious juice resembling a mixture of honey and dew", and another claimed the "natives" lived five or six weeks at a time on the generous honey.

According to ethnogapher Walter Roth, in his "Notes of savage life in the early days of West Australian Settlement", an alcoholic brew was prepared by soaking the blossoms in bark vats. Mead was made from grasstree flowers (*Xanthorrhoea* species) in much the same way.

Elsewhere in Australia the nectars of grevilleas, eucalypts, hakeas, grasstrees, waratahs (*Telopea speciosissima*) and

So laden with nectar are the flowers of the coast banksia (*Banksia integrifolia*) that the leaves beneath them become sticky. Bushmen used to smear the old flower cones with fat and burn them as candles. Photographed in heathlands on Moreton Island.

Now very popular in horticulture, the heath banksia (*Banksia ericifolia*) was once a food plant of Aborigines, who sucked the sweet floral nectar. Photographed in the Budawangs south-west of Sydney.

mountain devils (*Lambertia formosa*) were sucked as treats. In the outback, the white flowers of doubah (*Leichhardtia australis*) were eaten (as were the pods, leaves, roots, shoots and seeds of this most versatile plant). In northern Australia explorer Ludwig Leichhardt observed the harvest of tea-tree blossoms (*Melaleuca* species) and followed suit: "We gathered some blossoms of the drooping tea-tree, which were full of honey, and, when soaked, imparted a very agreeable sweetness to the water. We frequently observed great quantities of washed blossoms of this tree in the deserted camps of the natives; showing that they were as fond of the honey in the blossoms of the tea-tree, as the

The sweet nectar of this desert grevillea (*Grevillea* species) is still a favourite among outback Aborigines. Honeyeaters and other birds pollinate the flowers.

The mountain devil (*Lambertia formosa*) has exceptionally attractive flowers from which Aborigines reportedly sucked the nectar. Lambertias, like banksias and grevilleas, are members of the remarkable Proteaceae family. Photographed in the Royal National Park.

natives of the east coast are of that of the several species of Banksia."

Leichhardt was not above "purchasing" such drinks from Aboriginal camps. Near the Lynd River he admitted to finding three stringybark coolamons "full of honey water, from one of which I took a hearty draught, and left a brass button for payment".

Such drinks can be made by laboriously steeping dozens of blossoms in a bowl of water, until a tangy brew is achieved. The common paperbark tea-tree (*M. quinquenervia*) makes a tasty brew.

Sometimes whole flowers were eaten. In Victoria Aborigines nibbled the tiny green flowers of "honey pots" (*Acrotriche serrulata*) for their sweetness. The green fruits of this heath are also edible. Another of the heaths, also called honey pots, or jam tarts, (*Melichrus procumbens*) has saucer flowers brimming with nectar; these are carried close to the ground and face downward, an odd arrangement that may attract lizards as pollinators.

Tiny green fruits looking and tasting like apples (though smaller than peas) ripen in the wake of the flowers of honey pots (*Acrotriche serrulata*). Photographed at Westlake near Melbourne.

Top left: The small nectar saucer of honey pots (*Melichrus procumbens*) faces downwards, presumably to attract a ground-dwelling pollinator. Photographed in Girraween National Park in Queensland's Granite Belt.

Below: An elderly Aboriginal woman who lived at Coranderrk Mission near Healesville remembered the Aborigines eating the tiny green flowers of honey pots (*Acrotriche serrulata*). Photographed in the Grampians.

Jam can be made from the buds of the native rosella (*Hibiscus heterophyllus*). This plant is growing beside the Brisbane River in Sherwood.

Right: The purpose of the spines adorning the flower spike of the mat-rush (*Lomandra longifolia*) is probably to deter wallabies from chewing the tiny sweet blooms. Photographed at Wollongong.

Aborigines in Victoria ate the tiny creamy flowers of mat-rushes (*Lomandra* species). Those of the long-leaf mat-rush (*L. longifolia*), although sweet to taste, are guarded by pungent spines. Beetles pollinate the flowers.

The native rosella (*Hibiscus heterophyllus*) has buds that country people made into rosella jam. The big yellow or white flowers, slimy in taste, can be eaten raw or mixed in salads. A true hibiscus and a close relative of the cultivated rosella, this shrub or small tree is found in damp forests in eastern Australia. Because of its showy flowers, one early writer thought it looked "at a distance as if a flock of white birds had alighted upon it".

Aborigines just north of Sydney ate the flower stalks of the flame lily, or gymea lily (*Doryanthes excelsa*). These are probably the biggest flower stalks of an Australian plant, growing to more than four metres, although Aborigines ate them when only a metre or so tall. The hefty stems, thicker than a man's arm, were roasted before eating.

Among garden plants there are many with flowers that can be eaten. Elderberry flower clusters (*Sambucus nigra*) may be fried in fritters, and day lily petals (*Hemerocallis* species) can be chewed. Rosewater is made from rose petals, and a gentle tea is brewed by steeping flower heads of clovers (*Trifolium repens* and *T. pratense*).

The most unusual flowers in Western diet are the glamour vegetables called globe artichokes. These are the giant buds of the artichoke plant (*Cynara cardunculus*), which is a cultivated form of artichoke thistle (*C. scolymus*), a prickly weed of farms and pastures in Europe. The cultivated artichoke plant

has lost its spines and the buds are slightly larger, but the two plants are very similar and it is not exaggerating to call artichokes thistle heads. In southern Australia this thistle became a weed last century, and European migrants now gather the buds as artichokes. They are steamed or boiled and the spines removed to expose the delectable heart at the base of each bud.

Anyone who lives in Melbourne, Adelaide or nearby farming districts should try wild artichokes. The thistles

are prolific pests (and declared noxious weeds) in cow paddocks on black-soil plains, and grow on wasteland in inner-city Melbourne and along railway lines near Adelaide.

Look for a ferocious thistle with silvery foliage and enormous purple flower heads. The large, frond-like leaves bear golden spines and furry undersides. The plants grow about a metre tall and should be harvested in spring before the flowers open. The steamed buds taste delicious.

In Europe, both the very young leaves and the young roots of this thistle have been used as food. Actually, this is only one of several kinds of thistle with edible buds (and roots). Another is the variegated thistle (*Silybum marianum*), distinguished by its smaller flower heads

Thistles were once cultivated in English gardens as spectacular feature plants, and looking at this artichoke thistle (*Cynara cardunculus*) growing in a field in western Victoria, it is not difficult to see why.

Top left: Giant flower stalks of the gymea lily (*Doryanthes excelsa*), noted James Backhouse, were "roasted and eaten by the Aborigines, who cut them for this purpose, when they are about a foot and a half high, and thicker than a man's arm". Photographed at Waterfall near Sydney.

Below left: Bees dote on the nectar of the flowers of white clover (*Trifolium repens*). Photographed in Sydney.

The flowers of five corners (*Styphelia viridis*) are followed by sweet green fruits, which are partly enclosed by five leafy bracts, hence the name "five corners". Photographed on Moreton Island.

Birds pollinate the flowers of five corners, which contain enough nectar to be sucked from the floral tube. Five corners is a typical shrub of coastal heathlands, as here at Cooloola on the mainland adjacent to Fraser Island.

and shiny dark-green leaves with pale mottlings. In Europe its buds were used as artichokes and the boiled roots and seedling leaves eaten. I met a middle-aged man who told me his Greek parents used to harvest the buds near Warwick.

Another spiky weed in southern Australia, the shrub called gorse or furze (*Ulex europaeus*), has small buds that were pickled in England. A noxious pest, gorse can be recognised by its yellow pea flowers and spiny stems.

Australian settlers made little use of wild nectars, but there is one record of their harvesting the flowers of the heath called five corners (*Styphelia* species). G. C. Mundy, an early antipodean traveller much given to florid prose (he once described a mistletoe clump as a "huge oval chandelier of bronze"), wrote so quaintly of five corners that I can think of no better way to close this chapter. Writing in *Our Antipodes* in 1855 he said: "We found two kinds of natural bush-fruit growing in great plenty

on the uplands,—namely, the 'five corners,' produced by a beautiful species of fuchsia after the fall of the blossom, and the geebung, a native plum very woolly and tasteless. With regard to the former flower, the children of Mr. Suttor taught me to find at the bottom of each calyx a single drop of the richest honey-water; and we sipped together some hundreds of these fairy cups of hydromel.'

WILD
HERBS AND SPICES

Among the least-known of Australian native foods are the herbs and spices. Few people realise that our flora includes a swag of fragrant mints, gingers, basils and lemon grasses. A few of these plants were gathered as colonial medicines, but their culinary merits remain largely unexplored. Our seven lemon grasses, for example, appear never to have been used to spice food.

Apart from these native herbs and spices, many overseas herbs grow wild in Australia. Fennel has become a weed in suburban Sydney. Tansy, yarrow and parsley run wild in the south. Two of our common street trees yield an excellent substitute for pepper, and along drains there grows a weedy alternative to chilli.

Herbs and spices take their flavours from essential oils in their tissues. ("Essential" here means "essence-forming", not "indispensable".) These special oils, known also as volatile oils or aromatic oils, are volatile—that is, they evaporate quickly and are thus easy to smell—unlike the fixed oils used to fry and lubricate. Essential oils serve as chemical defence, making plants distasteful to herbivores, and repelling toxic fungi and bacteria.

As a general guide, herbs are fragrant plants from western Asia or the Mediterranean and have aromatic leaves, while spice plants come from the South-East Asian rainforests and have pungent roots, bark, buds or seeds. (Botanists have a different definition of "herb", meaning a plant without a woody stem, and this is the meaning I use in other chapters.) The culinary herbs of Europe fall mainly into two remarkable families—the mint family (Lamiaceae, once called Labiatae), and the carrot family (Apiaceae, originally

Umbelliferae). In Australia we are lucky to have native herbs in both these families.

Representing the mint family are several native (and introduced) mints, and three wild basils. The exact number of mints is unknown, as these plants are difficult to identify, perhaps in part because they hybridise in the wild. I once took a sprig of mint from the Dandenongs to the Melbourne Herbarium and paraded it before a clutch of botanists, none of whom could put a name to it or even say if it was native.

The native mints (*Mentha* species) are creeping herbs of forests and woodlands, usually found near streams or soaks. They have soft fragrant leaves smelling of spearmint, peppermint or pennyroyal. Less aromatic than the European mints, they appear to have been little used by pioneering cooks. Colonial botanist Frederick Bailey remarked that river mint (*Mentha australis*) yielded peppermint oil, and was "excellent for making a wholesome drink, for which it was used by the South Australian pioneers". Other native mints were used as medicines.

In amongst fallen gum leaves on the dark forest floor, the native forest mint (*Mentha laxiflora*) spreads its dainty leaves. Although smelling of spearmint, the leaves have been little used for flavouring. Photographed in the Grampians.

What mint is this? Melbourne botanists were unable to identify sprigs of this mint, which is probably a native species, found growing in the foothills of the Dandenongs. Plants are often identified by their flowers, creating problems when no flowers are present.

The toothpaste-flavouring herb, spearmint (*Mentha spicata*), thrives in Ferntree Gully behind Melbourne, where it has replaced native herbs and should be considered a pest. The leaves are very aromatic.

Right: A strong clove-like smell characterises sacred basil (*Ocimum tenuiflorum*), which has eugenol in its leaves, the aromatic oil found in cloves. This dainty herb is deemed sacred in India. Photographed west of Blackall, central Queensland.

sacred balm and holy basil (*Ocimum tenuiflorum*), is found widely in tropical Asia, but its native range extends into northern Australia. Closely related to the common kitchen basil (*O. basilicum*), it is likewise used in Asian villages as a flavouring and medicine. Sacred basil is probably the "marjoram" used by Ludwig Leichhardt: "We collected a considerable quantity of the marjoram, and added it to our tea, with the double intention, of improving its flavour, and of saving our stock; we also used it frequently as a condiment in our soup." In Queensland, early settlers made a bush tea of the dried leaves, and Aborigines drank a basil brew to cure fevers.

A second basil found in northern Australia, hairy basil (*O. americanum*), is possibly an introduced weed from Asia. Like sacred basil, it is used there to flavour curries and fish dishes. The seeds are soaked to make drinks.

The third species, musk basil (*Basilicum polystachyon*), is also found in Asia, with a natural distribution reaching

These native species have been joined in Australia by several of their European kin. Peppermint (M. *piperita*), spearmint (M. *spicata*) and apple mint (M. *rotundifolia*) have escaped from gardens in southern Australia to become feral plants. Spearmint thrives in Ferntree Gully behind Melbourne, and clumps of European pennyroyal grow along billabongs and banks of the Murray River in outback New South Wales.

Mints prefer a cool climate; the basils are tropical. Sacred basil, known also as into Australia as far as southern Queensland. This scrawny herb has no culinary use, but was used medicinally both by Javanese and by Aborigines. Basils are all soft herbs with aromatic paired leaves, and tiny white or purplish, four-lobed flowers in spikes.

One other member of the mint family deserves mention. Native coleus (*Plectranthus graveolens*) is a pretty shrub with fleshy crinkled leaves, velvety to touch, and small violet flowers. It sprouts in tiny pockets of soil and leaf litter on rock outcrops in eastern Australia. I have heard it called "five spice" because of its delicate, almost fruity fragrance. But the aroma is too ephemeral for cookery, and sprigs of "five spice" sprinked into the evening casserole impart no flavour at all.

The carrot family in Australia includes several plants of culinary interest. There are three native celeries (see the Colonial Greens chapter), a few edible tubers and, in the Australian Alps, a range of small herbs akin to caraway and aniseed.

Along the Snowy River, settlers once collected the seeds of slender seseli (*Gingidia harveyana*) as a caraway substitute. The herb was known as "anise plant" for its aniseed scent. Another mountain dweller, Australian caraway (*Oreomyrrhis eriopoda*), has a delicate caraway aroma, and may have potential as a herb, although there are no actual accounts of its use. Related species are aromatic, but grow only in alpine meadows, and little is known about them. Worth investigating is bog caraway (*O. ciliata*), of which one field guide states: ". . . it has a very penetrating sickly-sweet odour which often persists long after specimens have been pressed and dried."

These plants aside, the carrot family in Australia is a disappointment. Our aromatic species are all mountain-top relicts, survivors from long ago when Australia was cold. We lack the variety of European and Asian umbellifers, among which can be counted parsley,

fennel, dill, coriander, cumin, aniseed, caraway, chervil and lovage. As compensation of sorts, two of these herbs have become common weeds in Australia.

Fennel (*Foeniculum vulgare*) is a prolific weed of roadsides and waste ground in temperate Australia. It has a special affinity for railway lines, and thrives along rail embankments in New South Wales, even in inner Sydney. The filamentous leaves smell of aniseed, and

The native coleus (*Plectranthus graveolens*), which smells like sage, is too weakly aromatic to serve as a kitchen herb. The plant is well known to bushwalkers, who often sniff its leaves along the trail.

Below: Australian caraway (*Oreomyrrhis eriopoda*) sports a thick taproot that can be eaten like parsnip, and leaves and seeds almost aromatic enough to flavour food. Largely restricted to alpine meadows, this interesting herb has been little used as food.

A patch of fennel (*Foeniculum vulgare*) brightens a farmer's paddock on the Tenterfield–Goondiwindi road. Fennel is a major weed in temperate Australia, declared noxious by the governments of Victoria, Tasmania and South Australia.

Right: A honeybee feeds at a fennel flower in a Brisbane garden. The unusual floral structure of fennel is called an umbel; each minute yellow spot is a single flower.

Scorned by farmers as a mere weed, slender celery (*Ciclospermum leptophyllum*) deserves praise for its virtues as a salad garnish and flavouring herb. A native of South America, it has leaves and seeds smelling slightly of parsley.

the big yellow flower heads sprout on stake-like stalks. Fennel seeds are strewn on breads and pies and the leaves flavour dishes of fish. I often chew wild seeds as a breath freshener.

The other feral herb is European parsley (*Petroselinum crispum*), found on the coasts of Tasmania, Victoria and South Australia, especially on dunes and beaches close to towns. At Port Fairy, west of Melbourne, it infests the coastal vegetation. In old suburbs of Sydney it grows in pavement cracks and unkempt gardens. The wild plants carry the flat shiny leaves of Italian parsley, the ancestral form of this species, and look nothing like the curled parsley of gardeners. The flavour is comparable, but with a bitter edge.

Another member of the carrot family, slender celery (*Ciclospermum leptophyllum*), is one of suburban Australia's best-kept secrets. The filamentous leaves, tasting of parsley–celery, provide an excellent garnish in salads and sandwiches. This weed grows in gardens all over Australia, yet hardly anyone knows it can be used as food.

Completely lacking in Australia are any native equivalents to garlic (*Allium sativum*). We have nothing to compare to the Northern Hemisphere *Allium* which includes the onion, garlic, chives, shallots and leeks, all plants with pungent sulphur-based aromas. As a mixed blessing, it is worth noting that a number of foreign *Allium* species with edible bulbs are established in Australia, where they thrive as weeds.

Most useful among these is three-cornered garlic (*A. triquetrum*). During spring most of Melbourne's rail cuttings and many of the city's road verges are flush with the pretty white flowers of this dainty herb. It flourishes also in the Adelaide Hills, in Tasmania, and along the cliff paths south of Bondi Beach. The mild bulbs are ideal for salads, sandwiches and curries. This very useful herb can be recognised by its white flowers with six petals, by its garlic smell, and especially

by its stems, triangular in cross-section. The plant bears its soft leaves in winter, flowers in spring, and dies away each summer, leaving behind plump white cloves that can be scratched from the soil by the hundreds. Strangely, I can find no mention in books of this garlic being used as food, but I can vouch from long experience that it can. It was evidently introduced to Australia as a garden ornament for its showy white flowers. Wild colonies growing in Morialta Conservation Park near Adelaide probably date back to garden plantings early this century.

Crow garlic (A. vineale) is a major weed of wheat farms in Victoria, declared noxious by legislation (as is three-cornered garlic). It bears big mild bulbs of excellent flavour. Identifying features are the hollow cylindrical leaves and stems, and pink or white flower heads topped by a sharp green spike.

In the farmlands of western Victoria and south-eastern South Australia there grow other wild garlics which make excellent herbs. Wild leek (A. ampeloprasum) is one. It is an impressive herb with big purple flower heads on towering stalks. I once dug a clump of these "leeks" at Millicent in South Australia and was rewarded with sixteen big bulbs—a half-year's supply of garlic. Other garlics found wild include Naples onion (A. neapolitanum) and sand leek (A. scorodoprasum). None of these wild

Along Melbourne rail embankments, three-cornered garlic (Allium triquetrum) sprouts showy flowers and lush leaves from white tear-shaped cloves. Photographed at Hawthorn in spring.

Clusters of three-cornered garlic adorn the cliffs just south of Bondi Beach, where they grow alongside watercress, New Zealand spinach, sow-thistle and many other potherbs.

Close kin of turmeric, the Cape York lily (*Curcuma australasica*) has a gingery underground stem, and egg-shaped watery tubers that Aborigines in north Queensland once boiled in bailer shells. Photographed at Cape York.

Right: This wild lemon grass (*Cymbopogon* species) growing in central Australia is used as a medicine by the Pitjantjatjara. The whole plant has a distinctive lemony smell, identifying the presence of therapeutic aromatic oils.

(*Rosmarinus officinalis*), a weed around Adelaide.

Before turning to the Australian spices, the native lemon grasses (*Cymbopogon* species) merit a mention. Technically, these qualify as herbs, but are usually used in curries alongside spices. There are seven native species, all aromatic to some degree. Most are confined to central and northern Australia, beyond reach of epicures, and little is known about them. Botanical texts refer to their lemon or ginger aromas. Two species grow near cities. Barbwire grass (*C. refractus*) has seed heads resembling barbed wire. It is common on hills behind Brisbane and Sydney but is too weakly aromatic to serve as a herb. Silky heads (*C. obtectus*) has fluffy seed heads and grows west of the Dividing Range. It is stronger smelling and a weak lemon tea can be brewed from the leaves. The outback and tropical lemon grasses are more aromatic and probably suitable for curries.

Australia lies close to the fabled Spice Islands (eastern Indonesia) and it is not surprising that our rainforest flora,

herbs has the pungency of the kitchen garlic.

Wild garlics can sometimes be found in grasslands alongside yarrow (*Achillea millefolium*), another of Europe's familiar herbs. Yarrow even earns an undignified mention in the book *Weeds in Australia* by Lamp and Collet, alongside fennel, the wild forms of carrot and artichoke, and wild garlics. Other feral herbs found in Australia include various weedy substitutes for mustard (see Cresses and Mustards chapter); tansy (*Tanacetum vulgare*), found (rarely) along roads in southern Australia; and rosemary

closely allied to that of Asia, includes many relatives of the spices. Our lilly pillies (*Syzygium* species), for example, important fruits of the rainforest, lie in the same genus as the clove tree (*S. aromaticum*), the dried buds of which constitute cloves (and the fruit of which is a red edible "lilly pilly"). Likewise, we have jungle plants in the same genera as nutmeg, pepper, turmeric, ginger and curry leaves.

Our native cinnamons, tall rainforest trees, all have aromatic bark, but apparently none smells of cinnamon. The camphor laurel (*Cinnamomum camphora*), that dreadful weed of bushland in New South Wales, is a species of cinnamon, although its bark smells of camphor.

The north Queensland nutmeg tree (*Myristica insipida*), a common rainforest tree, produces a nutmeg seed of sorts. I have never seen it, but colonial botanist Frederick Bailey described it as a "nutmeg, but of weak flavour". The "mace" of this seed is a favourite food of nutmeg pigeons.

Turmeric has one close relative in Australia, the Cape York lily (*Curcuma australasica*), a beautiful herb with yellow flowers framed by pink bracts. The underground stems of this lily smell gingery but cannot be used as spice. Deep in the soil this lily carries bunches of watery tubers which Kakadu Aborigines dug as famine fare.

Pepper, that favourite spice of Australians, comes from an Indonesian vine with five close relatives in Australian jungles. The native pepper (*Piper novae-hollandiae*) carries bunches of small reddish fruits, the seeds of which can be ground as pepper. The other native peppers have not been tried; they are obscure vines of the northern rainforests.

In the uplands of south-eastern Australia early colonists found they could make pepper from the ground fruits of the mountain pepper tree (*Tasmannia lanceolata*), a plant unrelated to true

Sighted for the first time this century, Australian ginger (*Zingiber officinale*) sprouts in the gloom of Lockerbie Scrub. I am the first naturalist in Australia to find this plant, known only from a piece of ginger handed last century to colonial botanist F. M. Bailey.

Australian ginger is as spicy as its cultivated counterpart, although the rhizomes are smaller and more fibrous. Is this plant native to Australia, or was it brought over by early seafarers from Indonesia or New Guinea?

pepper. Colonial historian Daniel Mann noted in 1811 that this "spice tree" was "a very strong aromatic, and possesses a more pungent quality than pepper". The whole plant has a sharp spicy smell and bushmen can identify a tree merely by sniffing a crushed leaf.

The other spice represented in Australia is ginger (*Zingiber officinale*). In Lockerbie Scrub at the very top of Cape York Peninsula, clumps of ginger grow deep inside the monsoon rainforest. These plants are not a unique Australian species but are identical to the ginger of commerce. They were first brought to scientific attention in 1900 in a paper published by Queensland colonial botanist Frederick Bailey. While visiting Frank Jardine's Somerset Station, just south of Cape York, Bailey was handed pieces of ginger by Jardine's son, "which that gentleman assured me was indigenous". Back in Brisbane, Bailey planted the ginger, and described the subsequent plant as a new variety of common ginger—*Zingiber officinale* variety *cholmondeleyi*. The specimen was preserved at the Queensland Herbarium, and wild ginger was not seen again for ninety years. In 1988 I visited Cape York, and after much tramping in the rainforest found a clump of this mystery ginger. I was thrilled to be the first person this century to see Australian ginger growing wild, and the first ever to take photos. Botanists now consider this ginger to be indistinguishable from Asian ginger, and the varietal name *cholmondeleyi* has been abandoned. The

big question is, was this ginger brought in by early travellers to Australia or is it indigenous? I suspect it to be an introduction of Indonesian seafarers, although this is impossible to prove. In any event, the ginger borne on the wild plants is hot and spicy, and makes a fine substitute for the shop-bought article.

A second species of ginger also grows wild at Lockerbie. This is zerumbet ginger (*Z. zerumbet*), the underground stems of which are a mild substitute for the real thing. Zerumbet ginger may also have been introduced by voyagers, for it is widely used in Asia and the Pacific as a spice and medicine. It is prolific at Cape York, and also grows on Hammond Island in Torres Strait. Other kinds of ginger inhabit rainforests in Queensland and New South Wales but are only weakly spicy.

The hot chilli, a Latin American spice, has no relatives in Australia, although a handy substitute can be found in the

Native or introduced? The large colonies of zerumbet ginger (*Zingiber zerumbet*) in the Lockerbie Scrub may be the progeny of early introductions by Indonesians or Melanesians. The rhizome has an inferior gingery taste.

weed called smartweed or water pepper (*Polygonum hydropiper*). Children wading through creeks often complain of smarting legs after brushing against this plant—hence "smartweed". Hold a leaf to the light and you will see hundreds of tiny glands containing a peppery oil that stings legs, repels plant eaters, and is used in Asia to flavour food. This oil is so potent that Aborigines used to throw the crushed plant into waterholes to poison fish, which could then be eaten. The leaves can be used very effectively to spice curries. The herb called "Vietnamese mint" (*P. odoratum*) is closely related.

Among cultivated trees, an interesting substitute for pepper can be found in the pepper tree (*Schinus molle*). This native of South America has been planted throughout inland Australia as a shade tree around homesteads, hotels and old coach stops. With lazy drooping branches and shaggy green foliage, it is one of the characteristic sights of the outback.

Crush a leaf of the pepper tree and you will be surprised by the acrid peppery smell. The pale red berries are even spicier, and these "peppercorns" have been ground to make an effective pepper. They are, however, very oily, and often clog the peppergrinder.

The broad-leaf pepper tree (*S. terebinthifolia*), often planted in Queensland parks, can be used the same way.

Traditional Aborigines sometimes used aromatic leaves to flavour their foods, although the flavours were unlike our herbs and spices. On Groote Eylandt the leaves of wattle-flowered paperbark (*Melaleuca acacioides*) are strewn over hot rocks to flavour cockles. In Arnhem Land, two herbs (*Corynotheca lateriflora* and *Gardenia fucata*) are cooked with kangaroo meat in underground ovens. In South Australia meats were flavoured with seaweeds and cresses.

But Aborigines had no taste for European spices, nor for the unhealthy

In Mexico pepper tree fruits (*Schinus molle*) are ground as pepper and fermented into liquor. The leaves are chewed to harden the gums, the bark is used to tan hides and the gum to treat venereal diseases.

Below: While walking alongside a stream, stinging legs can be blamed on the smartweed (*Polygonum hydropiper*), the leaves of which carry spicy irritating oils. Aborigines poisoned fish by hurling the foliage into streams.

habit of smothering food in salt, as explorer George Grey noted in 1841: "Although the natives could in many districts procure native salt, and most certainly from its abundance cannot be unacquainted with it, they never use it, until they have seen Europeans do so, and even then do not at first like it."

GUMS, MANNA AND LERP

At the edge of Betoota billabong in far western Queensland stands this fine bauhinia tree (*Lysiphyllum gilvum*). Like their cultivated relatives, the native bauhinias have leaves folded like butterflies. Aborigines ate the gum and sucked nectar from the flowers.

Alice Duncan-Kemp, who settled west of Windorah in 1906, provided a description of one of outback Australia's more unusual bush foods: "When rains draw near, the old gins about the homestead wander up and down the creeks scoring or cutting the bark [of the bauhinia tree] with a tomahawk. After rain they visit the scored trees and gather the *minni*, a thick sweet sap which exudes from the cuts like jellied honey-coloured gum; a great delicacy among the blacks, who eat it straight from the tree.

"White children consider *minni* an excellent substitute for sweets, when cooked in a baking-dish with a little sugar and water for a couple of hours, and sprinkled with roasted nuts or Mungaroo from the roots of nut-grass."

In Western Australia, Aboriginal women collected sticky edible gums oozing from the trunks of wattles (probably *Acacia microbotrya*). Pioneer Ethel Hassell, who doted on the treat, said the gum was rolled into balls as big as children's heads, and stored for future need.

Colonial botanist Joseph Maiden commented that acacia gum "must possess some nutritive value, as instances are on record of the lives of children and others who have been lost in the bush having been sustained by it. Boys sometimes soak it in water to make a thick jelly and sweeten it; thus a toothsome confection is made."

In western Victoria, Aboriginal men owned the best gum-bearing wattle trees, and notches were cut to facilitate the flow. Wattle gum later became scarce after settlers felled the trees to obtain tanbark for tanning hides.

Northern Aborigines harvested the gum of kurrajongs (*Brachychiton* species) and terminalia trees (*Terminalia* species). The Bardi of Dampier Land get gum from the northern kurrajong (*B. diversifolius*), which is cooked in ashes until brown, then crushed to a powder and drunk with water and sugar. Explorer Ludwig Leichhardt gathered terminalia gum near the Gulf of Carpentaria: "We collected a great quantity of Terminalia gum, and prepared it in different ways to render it more palatable. The natives, whose tracks we saw everywhere in the scrub, with frequent marks where they had collected gum—seemed to roast it. It dissolved with difficulty in water: added to gelatine soup, it was a great improvement."

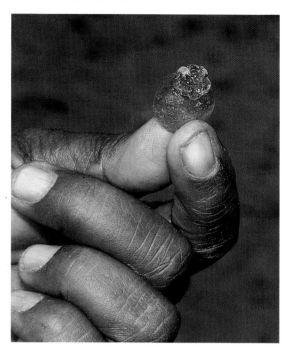

The gum that oozes from mulga trunks (*Acacia aneura*) has a brittle toffee exterior and sticky honey interior. Foods such as this are highly valued in desert areas.

Treat from a trunk: the gum from the wild bauhinia tree is still gathered as a sweet by Aborigines in some outback towns. This fine specimen at Betoota is as big as a plum.

Tiny white "limpets" of sugar, starch and wax, the lerps of *Glycaspis* bugs are often to be seen on eucalypt leaves in cities. In forested areas the lerps are preyed upon by pardalotes and honeyeaters.

Right: Eucalypt leaves under insect attack provide a sweet treat for the forager. These leaves are covered in *Glycaspis* lerps and associated honey-like secretions.

Lennie Duncan of Cherbourg near Kingaroy collects wattle gum (*Acacia bancroftii*) to chew as a snack. The gum has a hard toffee texture but not a strong taste.

At Cherbourg Aboriginal settlement near Kingaroy, gums from two kinds of wattles are still gathered by older people. Lennie Duncan took me into a forest and showed me the trees. "An old mate of mine, he's got a car. When we come out here we never drive past this," he said, pointing to the honey-coloured gum. "It's something to chew on." He said it could be soaked in a mug or basin with water and sugar, and put in the fridge to make jelly.

Gums flow from tree trunks where borers or axe blows have damaged the wood. Only a few kinds of gums, of a pale colour, taste sweet; most are dark and astringent and highly unpalatable. Sometimes a similar but more sugary substance—called manna—oozes from injured bark or leaves. This also was a treasured food of Aborigines and colonists.

Lieutenant-Colonel Mundy described a nineteenth-century manna outing near Bathurst: "It sounds strange to English ears,—a party of ladies and gentlemen strolling out in a summer's afternoon to gather manna in the wilderness: yet more than once I was so employed in Australia. This substance is found in small pieces on the ground under the trees at certain seasons, or in hardened drops on the surface of the leaves; it is snowy white when fresh, but turns brown when kept like the chemist's drug

Whole families of desert Aborigines were sometimes sustained by sugary red lerps (*Austrochardia acaciae*) found on outback mulga trees. These lerps look much like some kinds of scale insects found on suburban shrubs, but the latter are not edible.

so called, is sweeter than the sweetest sugar, and softer than Gunter's softest ice-cream."

Another colonist, Mrs Charles Meredith, describes it as "snow-white flakes, sometimes soft, and often nearly as hard as sugar-plum, with a sweet and rather pleasant flavour".

In Victoria, manna was sometimes so prolific that Aborigines could live largely upon it. One writer claimed that forty to fifty pounds (18 to 23 kilograms) could be gathered by an Aborigine in a day.

Another sweet substance sometimes found on foliage is lerp. Lerps are tiny shields made by sap-sucking bugs from sugars and starches excreted from the sap. European colonists made little use of this substance, but Aborigines liked to suck the shields from the leaves. A variety of lerps can be found on eucalypt foliage, especially in our cities, where the trees are stressed. Eucalypt lerps are white and waxy, but in desert areas a shiny red lerp (*Austrochardia acaciae*) on

Looking like anything but food, *Eucalyptolyma* lerps disfigure the leaves of a eucalypt. These lerps have a sweet crumbly taste.

mulga stems was important to inland tribes. In 1957 anthropologist Norman B. Tindale met a family of desert Aborigines who had been living for a week almost solely on this food. Their lips were sore and bleeding from running the rough mulga twigs through their mouths. Some lerps contain up to ninety per cent starch.

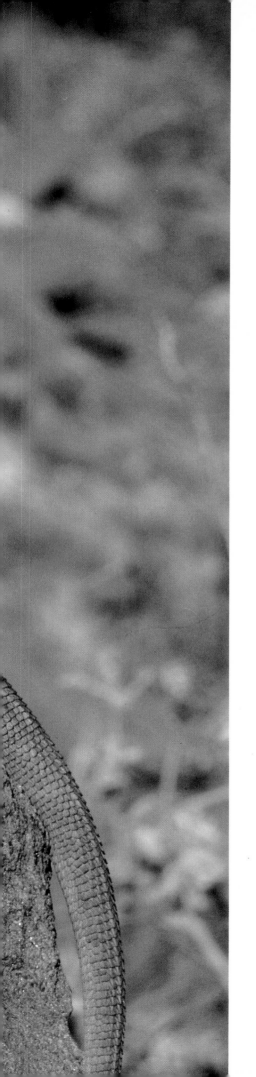

ANIMAL FOODS

ABORIGINAL GAME

Previous pages:
Probably the most colourful of Australian dragons, the red-barred dragon (*Ctenophorus vadnappa*) is noted for the spectacular pattern on the body of the breeding male. Such lizards were important tucker for inland Aborigines. Photographed at Arkaroola in the Flinders Ranges.

The wallaroo, known in the outback as the euro, was an important food of traditional Aborigines, yielding about forty kilograms of lean meat.

Traditional Aborigines ate many more kinds of meats than city Australians do today. The Anbarra of Arnhem Land, for instance, still eat sixty kinds of fish, thirty different shellfish, six crustaceans, and various birds, mammals, and reptiles. By comparison, the average meat-eating white Australian eats about six species of fish, three mammals, two birds, one shellfish, and not much else.

Aborigines ate prodigious amounts of meat when it was available. Kangaroos, possums, lizards, fish and shellfish were major staple foods. Coastal and riverine tribes ate more meat than their desert kin, who depended largely upon small animals such as dragon lizards, grasshoppers, and even hairy caterpillars.

Men were very adept at hunting game. A man's prestige rested partly on his skill at securing kangaroos and other large prey. In some tribes a youth's passsage into manhood required him to take a large kangaroo.

Kangaroos were hunted in many ways, all requiring extraordinary skill. They might be stalked individually, speared from hiding-places, surrounded in groups, driven into nets or pitfall traps, or trapped by flames.

Sometimes kangaroos were chased relentlessly until they dropped. The explorer George Grey in 1841 described this most extraordinary mode of hunting: "But the mode of tracking a kangaroo until it is wearied out, is the one which beyond all others, excites the admiration of the natives; this calls out every qualification prized by savages, skill in tracking, endurance of hunger and thirst, unwearied bodily exertion, and lasting perseverence. To perform this feat a native starts upon the tracks of a kangaroo, which he follows until he sights it, when it flees timidly before him; again he pursues the track, and again the animal bounds from him; and this is repeated until night-fall, when the native lights his fire and sleeps upon the track; with the first light of day the hunt is resumed, and towards the close of the second day, or in the course of the third, the kangaroo falls a victim to its pursuer. None but a skilful huntsman, in the pride of youth and strength, can perform this feat, and one who has frequently practised it, always enjoys great renown amongst his fellows."

Mary Bundock, a settler in northern New South Wales, tells a similar story: "I have heard on one occasion [an Aborigine] came to an uncle of mine and asked him for matches, as he had lost his firestick while following a big old man kangaroo. My uncle asked him 'What do you want matches for?'

"The black man replied, 'To cook my kangaroo.' 'Have you killed him then?' asked my uncle.

" 'No' was the answer 'he is up there' pointing to a mountain about 2 miles away, 'very tired and I go back there and kill and eat him.' Which he accordingly did!"

A different kind of kangaroo chase was noted by anthropologist Norman B.

Tindale in outback South Australia: "Sighting a kangaroo one [youth] would chase after it and relying on the curved course taken by such animals the second youth would take up the heavy running in the heat and over the heavy ground. Alternation of chasers would run the animal to a standstill when it would be despatched with a stick. After such an activity youths spent several days in recuperation."

It is difficult for us to imagine the skill required to track a kangaroo for many kilometres through forest. By similar skills of observation, Aborigines could locate possums in trees and echidnas in logs. A possum could be detected by a column of mosquitoes hovering about a hollow in a tree, or by discreet scratch marks on the trunk. Where claw marks were very faint, the hunter might breathe on the bark to better discern adhering hairs or grains of sand.

The stone axe was a valued tool for extracting game from tree hollows and logs. K. Langloh Parker described in 1905 how in western New South Wales echidnas ("piggiebillahs") were taken: "[The] track was followed to a hollow

The Aboriginal predilection for burning forests would have benefited the whiptail wallaby, which feeds on grasses and other herbs. Photographed at Carnarvon Gorge, Queensland.

Aborigines caught brushtail possums by moonlight in southern Australia, as witnessed by George Grey: ". . . the dusky forms of the natives moving about in the gloomy woods, and gazing up into the trees to detect an animal feeding, whilst in the distance natives with fire-sticks come creeping after them, is a picturesque sight."

Scratch marks show that this tree is regularly used by a brushtail possum. To find prey, Aboriginal hunters made much use of scratches and other signs, usually more subtle than these.

log; then came the difficulty, how to get it out, for porcupines cling tightly with their sharp claws, and all a dog can do where a piggiebillah is concerned is to bark, their spines are too much to tackle at close quarters. But the old gins are equal to the occasion: a tomahawk to chop the log, and a yam-stick to dislodge the porcupine, who takes a good deal of killing before he is vanquished.

"They say a fully initiated man can sing a charm which will make a piggiebillah relax his grip and be taken captive without any trouble."

To obtain a possum, steps were cut into the tree and a hole chopped into the hollow where the possum slept. Old eucalypts bearing such axe wounds can still be found in remote forests throughout Australia.

In many districts dingoes, and especially their puppies, were eaten. Explorer George Grey explained that in Western Australia "A dog is baked whole in the same manner as a kangaroo;—it is laid on its back in the hole in the heated sand, and its nose, fore-paws and hind-paws are left sticking out of the ashes which are scraped over it, so that it bears rather a ludicrous appearance." According to Grey, "puppies are of course the greatest delicacy, and are often feasted upon".

In southern Australia wombats were taken as food. William Buckley, who lived many years with Victorian Aborigines last century, described them as good eating: "The natives take these creatures by sending a boy or girl into their burrows, which they enter feet first, creeping in backwards until they touch the animal. Having discovered the lair, they call out as loud as they can, beating the ground overhead, whilst those above are carefully listening, their ears being pressed close to the earth. By this plan of operations they are enabled to tell with great precision where they are. A perpendicular hole is then made, so as to strike the extremity of the burrow; and

having done this, they dig away with sharp sticks, lifting the mould out in baskets. The poor things are easily killed, for they make no resistance to these intrusions on their haunts."

Along the coasts of southern Australia whales and seals were especially important foods. A beached whale was occasion for great feasting, even when the meat was mouldy and putrid. Grey speaks evocatively of the pre-eminence whale meat held to southern tribes: "A whale is the greatest delicacy that a native can partake of, and whilst standing beside the giant frame of one of these monsters of the deep, he can only be compared to a mouse standing before a huge plum-cake; in either case the mass of the food compared to that of the consumer is enormous . . . In general the natives are very particular about not eating meat that is fly-blown or tainted, but when a whale is in question, this nicety of appetite vanishes . . . they remain by the carcase for many days,

The etiquette for eating dingoes varied from place to place. Some tribes ate both adults and puppies, some ate only the pups, and still others eschewed dingo meat altogether. Photographed near Injune in Queensland.

To southern Aborigines nothing was more exciting than finding a beached whale. George Grey described how the delighted Aborigine "rubs himself all over with the blubber, then anoints his favourite wives, and thus prepared, cuts his way through the blubber into the flesh or beef . . . of this he selects the nicest morsels, and either broils them on the fire, or cooks them as kabobs".

The pursuit of seals was "an exciting species of hunting", according to George Grey. These are Australian sea lions on Kangaroo Island. Sea lion bones have been found in ancient Aboriginal middens on Bass Strait islands, where this seal was exterminated by early sealers.

rubbed from head to foot with stinking blubber, gorged to repletion with putrid meat,—out of temper from indigestion, and therefore engaged in constant frays,—suffering from a cutaneous disorder by high feeding, and altogether a disgusting spectacle. There is no sight in the world more revolting than to see a young and gracefully formed native girl stepping out of the carcase of a putrid whale."

In western Victoria Aborigines sometimes buried whale meat until it was rotten. In South Australia the great ribs served as beams in huts.

Seals were crept upon while resting upon rocks or in the surf. Again, Grey provides a compelling description: "Killing seals is, from the habits of these animals, necessarily an exciting species of hunting in the southern and western portions of the continent. It is only enjoyed by the natives when they can surprise a seal upon the beach or in the surf . . . they are themselves fond of this sport, and the clambering about the wild rocks of their native shore,—at one time leaping from rock to rock, spearing fish that lie in the quiet pools,—in the next

moment dashing into the boisterous surf, to spear a large fish, to battle with a seal, or to turn a turtle, cannot but be an exhilarating occupation; and when to this we add that their steps are followed by a wife and children, as dear to them as ours are to us, who are witnesses of their agility and prowess, and who, when the game is killed, will help to light the fire in which it is to be cooked, and drag it to the resting-place, where the father romps with the little ones until the meal is prepared,—and that all this takes place in a climate so mild and genial, that a house is not necessary, we shall perhaps the less wonder that it should be so difficult to induce a savage to embrace the customs of civilized life."

Aborigines hunted nearly all other kinds of mammals. Quolls, bandicoots, platypuses, gliders, bats, water rats, even tiny marsupial moles and native mice, were all valued items of food. When rabbits and cats spread into the deserts these too were hunted, and many tribes consider them to be traditional foods. In the Northern Territory water buffalo are sometimes hunted, and the meat is highly esteemed, but these are difficult

prey to take, even using modern weapons.

The birds hunted by Aborigines were as varied as the mammals. The colonist James Dawson provides an extensive list: "The aborigines eat eagles and birds of prey, the emu, turkey bustard, gigantic crane, herons, and swan; geese and ducks in great variety, cormorants, ibis, curlew, coot, water-hen, lapwings, cockatoos, parrots, pigeons, crows, quails, snipes, and a great many kinds of sea fowls. The pelican and its eggs are considered too fishy to eat."

Here again, Aborigines employed great ingenuity. Ducks in lagoons were grabbed by hand by a hunter swimming underwater, breathing through a reed. Flying birds were struck with clubs or boomerangs, or guided into nets strung between trees. Smaller birds were taken from perches smeared with sticky fig sap, or from tangles of sticky herbs strewn about the edges of pools. Crows and hawks were caught by hand by a hunter lying stretched upon a rock in the sunshine, pretending to be asleep, holding a piece of fish or meat as bait.

Reptiles were important in the diet of Aborigines, especially in the deserts, where small dragons, goannas and bluetongue lizards were important foods. Women grabbed these among the spinifex or dug them from burrows. Snakes were roasted whole, and if eggs

Sugar gliders were flushed from their holes and captured in flight. According to Constance Petrie, "When a native climbed up the tree, the squirrel would hear him coming, and, running out of his hole, would fly down to the base of another tree. If the blacks on the ground did not succeed in knocking him down before he got beyond their reach they would climb the second tree . . . and so on, till in the end the poor thing was captured."

Top left: Almost any kind of bird was eaten by Aborigines, and white-necked herons were not excluded, nor were their chicks and eggs.

Below right: Before eating an intermediate egret, Aborigines singed and plucked the feathers, then baked the bird in an oven of heated stones, or roasted it over a fire.

Captain Cook watched Queensland Aborigines using wooden barbs to harpoon turtles like this loggerhead (*Caretta caretta*), resting in a pool on Low Island at the southern end of the Great Barrier Reef. Turtle eggs were also eaten.

Below left: Goannas were much loved by Aborigines for their chicken-flavoured flesh, and for the soothing oil extracted from their bodies, which was widely used in medicine. This is a freckled monitor (*Varanus tristis*) on Magnetic Island near Townsville.

Below right: From its habit of waving its arms, Gilbert's dragon (*Gemmatophora gilberti*) is also called the ta-ta or bye-bye lizard. Aborigines ate such dragon lizards and their eggs, including unlaid eggs. Photographed at Mount Isa.

were found inside, these were also eaten. Venomous snakes such as brown snakes and death adders were sometimes eaten, but not if the cause of their death was unknown: Aborigines widely believed that snakes could bite themselves to render their flesh toxic. Sometimes pythons were located by listening to the alarm calls of birds.

Along rivers and creeks, freshwater tortoises and their eggs were much relished. Tortoises were baked whole and

A saw-shelled tortoise (*Elseya latisternum*) rests upon a rock in Carnarvon Gorge, central Queensland. This tortoise is so named because the shells of the young have toothed edges.

Left: Muddy-flavoured Krefft's tortoises (*Emydura krefftii*) were caught by hand or snared in nets. By diving into pools and flailing their limbs about, Aborigines would grope for and then grab swimming tortoises. Photographed near Injune, Queensland.

the "gravy" was drunk from their shells. Along the coasts, sea turtles were harpooned, dived upon from canoes, or caught ingeniously with remora (sucker) fish. Walter E. Roth in 1901 described how remoras were used near the Tully River: "Then, going out to sea, the native ties a fine twine round the Remora's tail, and as soon as he sights any big fish, turtle or dugong, advances his canoe as far as possible, and drops the sucker-fish overboard. In all probability the sucker will go straight for the object and attach itself: it acts only as a guide, and tells the hunter the next move of his prey." By carefully playing out the line, the hunter was able to paddle within spearing distance.

In northern Australia crocodiles were

speared and eaten. Explorer Ludwig Leichhardt often found their remains at Aboriginal camps. Roth notes that "As a rule the larger-sized ones can only be caught when stranded in the smaller water-holes after flood by letting fly dozens of spears into them."

Frogs were widely eaten, especially in the deserts, where water-holding frogs (*Cyclorana platycephalus*), dug from dry claypans, served also as a source of emergency water. In Western Australia the desert Gugadja still eat eight kinds of frogs. A. R. Peile provides a present-day account: "On Sundays when the children go on a picnic, they spend much of their time digging for frogs. The hind legs are first dislocated with a quick flick of the wrist to prevent them from jumping away. No preparation for cooking is necessary, other than brushing off any sand. The frogs are then thrown on the coals and after a few sizzling moments are joyfully eaten, legs, body, head and all, and the grease-like coating on them after cooking is quite delicious."

An enormous variety of fish were eaten by Aborigines. As noted previously, sixty kinds of fish are eaten by the Northern Territory Anbarra alone. Fish

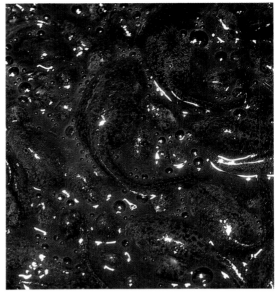

The name of the water-holding frog (*Cyclorana platycephalus*) bespeaks its importance to desert Aborigines, a unique distinction for an Australian amphibian. The sour water is held in the frog's bladder. Photographed at Meeberrie Homestead in Western Australia.

Top right: Raw tadpoles were eaten by desert Aborigines, as witnessed by Alice Duncan-Kemp: "Older children were busy cupping tadpoles between their hands as they ran up and down the shallows. They swallowed the wriggling mess raw. The children and the gins laughed at my disgust, and said it was 'good fella tucker all right'."

were netted, speared, or caught on lines with hooks. In Moreton Bay semi-tame dolphins steered schools of tailor towards spearmen waiting in the surf. Along the eastern seaboard hooks and lines were used in two separate areas—along central New South Wales (including Sydney Harbour), and in north Queensland—but not in the area in between, for reasons unexplained. Enormous tidal rock traps were made by arranging stones on shallow rock platforms. These survive as archaeological relics along our eastern and northern shores.

Shellfish in great numbers were eaten by Aborigines. More than a hundred species were harvested in north Queensland alone. Remains of Aboriginal shellfish feasts, known as middens, can be found on sand dunes around the entire coastline, even close to major cities (at La Perouse in Sydney, for example). Along eastern shores the pipi or ugari (*Plebidonax deltoides*) of sandy beaches was especially popular. In northern Australia Aborigines piled old shells onto mounds that eventually became large enough to accommodate huts and

Fishermen carry home a haul of catfish from the Mary River in the Northern Territory in 1921. The tree in the background is a pandanus, the leaves of which were woven into bags and cloaks.

fireplaces. One mound at Milingimbi Island in Arnhem Land is six metres high and almost thirty metres wide, and dates back to the fifth century BC.

Insects were very important foods to Aborigines. (White Australians often infer from this that the Aboriginal diet was meagre and that Aborigines lived poorly. In fact, insects are very tasty and nutritious, and it is more to be wondered that European cultures make so little use of them. I have eaten a variety of moths, grasshoppers, grubs, ants and the like, and find them excellent foods.)

The most famous insect food of Aborigines is the witchetty grub. Nowadays there is a tendency to call any white grub a witchetty, but the term properly applies to wood-boring caterpillars of cossid moths (Cossidae). These are large, nutty-tasting from their wood diet, and, like most insects, extremely rich in protein and fat. They can be eaten raw but are especially delicious when roasted over a fire.

The largest of all witchetty grubs are the larvae of the giant wood moth (*Xyleutes boisduvali*), which happens to be the world's heaviest moth. The grub is extracted with a hook from gum tree roots, where it lives for several years. Aborigines also feasted on the adult moths, which are so greasy with fat that they stain insect cabinets when pinned out by entomologists.

In the Australian Alps, where millions of bogong moths (*Agrotis infusa*) congregate in rock caverns each summer, huge concourses of Aborigines came to

An old fish trap on Stephens Island in Torres Strait traps fish behind the stone wall as the tide recedes. Old traps of this kind can still be seen around Australia's coasts, wherever the sea shelf is shallow and the surf gentle.

Below: Several early settlers witnessed Aborigines in Moreton Bay hunting with bottle-nosed dolphins. Tom Petrie recounted how the dolphins would appear, driving before them schools of tailor fish: "When they came near, the blacks would run out into the surf, and with their spears would job down here and there at the fish, at times even getting two on one spear . . . The porpoises would actually be swimming in and out amongst all this, apparently quite unafraid of the darkies. Indeed, they all seemed rather to be on good terms . . ."

Although some moths have broader wings, none has a larger body than the giant wood moth (*Xyleutes boisduvali*) of eastern Australia. The larvae were eaten as witchetty grubs, and adult moths were cooked and eaten.

Right: Lennie Duncan of Cherbourg fells a eucalypt sapling to harvest a witchetty grub, detected by a swelling on the trunk and a scatter of sawdust below. Witchetties are still very popular among outback Aborigines, and a few white stockmen eat them as well.

Below left: The witchetty grub extracted by Lennie was very small, despite the swelling it had produced in its host tree. After several years' growth a grub can reach the size of a small banana.

feast upon the dainty morsels. White observers reported that returning Aborigines looked sleek and fat.

In north Queensland, green tree ants (*Oecophylla smaragdina*) and their larvae were eaten, and in central Australia the sweet honeypot ants (*Melophorus* species) were important foods. Around Sydney ants were eaten with bland fern starch to furnish flavour. In north Queensland wasp nests were smoked and the fatty larvae eaten.

The honey of stingless native bees (*Trigona* species) was considered a treat by Aborigines everywhere, and to many tribes was the supreme delicacy. A small white feather might be glued to a bee so that its path through the forest to the nest could be easily followed. The honey and bee bread were hacked out with an axe. Native bee honey can be very sweet, or sour and watery.

Along the sea-coasts delicious-tasting worms called cobras were cut from mangrove trees and old logs. Aborigines in Moreton Bay "farmed" these worms by dragging piles of casuarina saplings onto muddy river banks and returning a year later to harvest the worms and replenish the logs. The long white worms were swallowed raw.

Most white Australians are repelled by the idea of eating live mangrove worms, ant grubs, snakes, rotten whales, and a great many other of the Aboriginal foods described here. But in doing so they betray their own cultural prohibitions, and create a barrier between black and white Australians of their own making. They could learn from a story told by

Constance Petrie in 1904, about her father, Tom, who like many colonial lads learned from the Aborigines to eat grubs: "Once, when a boy, he was out in the scrub where Toowong now is, with a couple of natives, and the latter came across some grubs and took them to where several sawyers were at work, to roast them. A man named Jack was awfully disgusted, and said he felt ill at the mere thought of eating such things! However, when the white boy took one, he followed suit after some persuasion, and liked the morsel so well that he ate more. In the end that man grew so fond of grubs that he would give the blackfellows tobacco to find him some."

Refuse from an ancient feast: a line of moon turban shells (*Subninella undulata*) has been exposed on the eroded face of a sand dune at Beachport, South Australia. Old shell middens can be found right around the Australian coastline.

Below: Hawkmoth caterpillars (*Hyles lineata livornicoides*) munching on tar vines were snacked upon by desert Aborigines, who starved the grubs for a day or two before roasting them. The cooked grubs have a pleasant savoury taste and can be stored for long spells. Photographed near Windorah.

COLONIAL GAME

Colonial hunter Horace Wheelwright sometimes ate koalas but found them "extremely difficult to shoot, on account of the thick hide; and it is cruelty to shoot at them with shot, if they are any height up a tree; but a bullet brings them down 'by the run.'" Photographed in the Grampians.

Today's Australians are very conservative in their choice of meats, so it comes as a surprise to discover that our pioneering ancestors were adventurous carnivores. Kangaroos, possums, bandicoots, echidnas and even platypuses were served at table, as well as all manner of birds, including honeyeaters and lorikeets. Colonial cuisine even extended to snakes, lizards and turtle eggs.

The best account of colonial use of game is probably Horace Wheelwright's *Bush Wanderings of a Naturalist*, published in London in 1861. Wheelwright was a failed English attorney who migrated to Australia in 1852, "dropping out" and becoming a rough-living game shooter in the forests and swamps around Melbourne. Wheelwright's account is a treasure trove of anecdotes about colonial use of native fauna. He talks of eating, for example, parrots, honeyeaters, black snake, possum and koala ("not unlike . . . the northern bear in taste").

Wheelwright appears to have lived largely on kangaroo meat. He provides a fascinating insight into its importance in the bushman's diet: "We used to make a good soup of the heads whenever we could get vegetables, which are not always at hand in the bush . . . Perhaps at times we might have preferred a beef-steak; but as we got the kangaroo for nothing, we just used it and made no invidious comparisons. 'Spare the damper but pitch into the kangaroo, lads!' used to be our bush motto when flour was scarce. The young bucks and flying does are the best eating; the old men are tough and stringy."

In Melbourne, kangaroo hams were

worth eight to ten shillings apiece, according to quality. The tails were served as the famous soup called "kangaroo steamer". Wheelwright provides a recipe for curing kangaroo hams, which he says were "first rate": "15 lbs. of salt, 2 lbs. of treacle, 3 lbs. of coarse sugar, 3 oz. of saltpetre, 1/4 lb. of carbonate of soda, mixed cold in a tub, the brine strong enough to float a potato: don't boil the brine. The above quantity is sufficient for fifty hams."

The great English naturalist John Gould also recorded much about the eating properties of Australian fauna, in his classic *The Mammals of Australia* (1845–1863). According to Gould, echidna is "similar to a sucking-pig", ringtail possum is "delicate, juicy and well-tasted", but wombat is "tough, with a musky flavour, and not altogether agreeable".

Gould welcomed the day when future generations of civilised Australians would dine upon our marsupial fauna. He exclaimed of the black-striped wallaby: "Its flesh is excellent, and when the vast continent of Australia becomes more thickly inhabited, it will doubtless be justly esteemed."

During Gould's time some members of the kangaroo tribe were heavily culled for the table. Of the popular red-necked wallaby he wrote that "the localities it affects afford it a retreat, so secure as to preclude all chance of its extermination, although many thousands are killed annually for the sale of its flesh, which is very generally eaten and highly esteemed, being delicate, juicy and well flavoured".

Less widely eaten than kangaroo and wallaby was the flesh of the echidna. The naturalist Daniel Bunce, out botanising in Tasmania in the 1840s, watched while a sportsman "made a grab at what he considered to be a prostrate oppossum, but quickly withdrew his hand, at finding that his digits had alighted upon nothing

Possums such as this ringtail were staple foods of early colonists. Pioneer Dame Mary Gilmore recalled that "many a time a child grew strong on well-sucked possum bones". Ringtail meat was compared to rabbit. Photographed at Taringa, Brisbane.

Hunters and their prey: a photo taken, probably in north-west Queensland, early in the century. Kangaroo meat was considered superior to possum, which often had a eucalyptus taint. Both meats were very lean.

Fatty on a diet of ants and termites, echidna meat was an early food of pioneers. A book published in 1818 recorded that "A species of ant-eater is found an addition to the luxuries of the table". Photographed on Black Mountain, Canberra.

less than the quills upon a fretful porcupine". The animal was dispatched and baked in clay and tasted "most delicious".

A century later during World War II Italian prisoners of war on Australian farms hunted the local "porcupines", for in southern Italy real porcupines are a traditional food. My friend Geoff Monteith recalls Italian soldiers on his father's farm during an adventurous childhood in the Burnett Valley. From curiosity his father once cooked up an echidna, first dunking it in hot water and extracting the quills with pliers. "The meat was dark and stringy with layers of fat," Geoff recalled. "I didn't like it much. Bandicoots are nicer."

Mammal expert Ellis Troughton had similar thoughts after trying scones fried in echidna fat. A pervasive flavour of ants convinced Troughton that this was

"probably the most bilious and trying experience to which an enquiring mammologist can be subjected by an experimenting camp cook".

Another unusual item of diet was the Tasmanian devil. According to a Mr Harris, writing to the Linnean Society last century, "These animals were very common on our first settling at Hobart Town, and were particularly destructive to poultry, &c. They, however, furnished the convicts with a fresh meal, and the flesh was said to be not unlike veal."

Wombat meat was little appreciated by English colonists, although it was said to taste like pork. It was highly esteemed by the Chinese (often called celestials), if an old report in the *Ovens and Murray Advertiser* is to be believed: " A NOVELTY.—We happened a few days ago to walk through one of the Chinese camps, and were attracted by a crowd of mixed people standing outside the shop of a Celestial butcher who lives in Joss-house-street, main encampment. Taking a place among the assemblage, we beheld, tethered to the door-frame, a full-grown Wombat, which was ever and anon turned and hauled about by some one of the bystanders. One Chinaman, more curious than the rest of his fellows, put the animal through its 'facings;' and after spending some time in stroking down its back, examining its hair and pinching its sides, he lifted the round plump body of the Wombat on its fore legs, and viewed

it all over. The act was received by his countrymen as a capital joke, setting them all laughing, accompanied by a sing-song sonorous 'yabber' that we did not understand. When it had subsided, we moved out of the heterogeneous group, and observed on an adjoining table pieces of strange-looking meat. We made inquiry, and learned that the flesh was pieces of Wombat offered for sale by the Chinese victualler."

In the tropics, the more adventurous cooks served fruit bats, also known as flying foxes. Mrs Lance Rawson, of colonial cookery book fame, developed the following sumptuous recipe: "Cut the wings off—the part that smells—and burn them. Skin the fox, cut it up and having scooped out a pumpkin, fill it with the cut up pieces and bake the pumpkin in the ashes for two or three hours. I am sure no-one could have had a nicer dish." Mrs Rawson also dined upon carpet snake, bandicoot, ibis, curlew, goanna, and even cured "bacon" from dugong meat.

From the accounts of early settlers, it appears that most kinds of bird were assigned to the pot at one time or another. Bustards, ducks and pigeons were especially popular. Victorian journalist Donald Macdonald in 1887 ranked young curlew, snipe, quail, squatter pigeon and bronzewing as the best game birds. He also observed: "An old swan is literally a rank failure at table, but the young bird, just before the pin feathers sprout, is 'a dainty dish to set before a king'."

Horace Wheelwright, the attorney turned hunter, was an especially zealous shooter of native birds. In his book he proclaimed his love of ornithology as "perhaps the only one of the innocent pleasures of youth which follows a man into maturer years, and upon which he can look back, in the decline of life, with feelings of pure and unalloyed joy". Yet, regrettably, much of Wheelwright's "innocent pleasure" consisted of shooting (and often eating) the birds. In a typical ornithological note, describing

Game-shooting colonists ate a great variety of curlews, plovers and other seabirds, including no doubt the beach thick-knee, or beach stone curlew. This shore-dwelling bird is found on our eastern and northern coasts. Photographed on Moreton Island.

Left: Flying foxes are a gourmet food in Noumea, but white Australians no longer eat them. Colonial cook Mrs Lance Rawson lauded the meat as "excellent eating during the fruit season". Illustrated is a grey-headed flying fox, or fruit bat.

John Gould said of the common bronzewing: "It is a plump, heavy bird weighing when in good condition fully a pound; and is constantly eaten by every class of person in Australia."

the "pretty flycatcher", he says: "It was a rare and solitary bird, and I generally used to kill single examples in the thick scrub."

Wheelwright provides an extraordinary record of the eating properties of Victorian birds, a surprising number of which he was able to sell in the markets of Melbourne as game. Here are some examples of his assessments:

Of the black swan: "The swan is hardly worth shooting here for the

market, as they only fetch 5s. each, and they are a heavy bird to carry about."

White cockatoo: "They are excellent eating, and when stuffed and roasted in the same way, can hardly be known from a duck. I recollect we used to cook wood-pigeons at home so, and, when eaten with the fenman's duck sauce, a little port wine, cayenne pepper, and a slice of lemon, we could not tell them from widgeon."

Musk duck: "It is rank and fishy to the taste, and, except as a curiosity, hardly worth shooting."

Satin bowerbird: "The flesh is rather bitter, like that of the starling at home, and they are not much fancied for the table of the epicure, but often found their way into our bush larder."

Rainbow lorikeet and other small parrots: "They are capital eating, and, as they come in good flocks, are much sought after 'for the pot'."

Teal: "Teal fetch about three shillings per couple in the market, are considered the finest-eating birds of the whole lot, and a teal supper at ten shillings per head

Black swan, grey teal and black duck were sold in the game markets of Melbourne and other cities. Horace Wheelwright in 1861 noted that black duck was worth seven shillings, and the swan, a much larger bird but poorer eating, only five. Photographed near Injune, Queensland.

used to be the general evening's finish for the 'men about town' in Melbourne."

Other birds sold at market by Wheelwright included spur-winged plovers, magpie geese, wattlebirds and quail. Wheelwright concludes, "Parrots can also at times be sold, when game is scarce; and let me say that a parrot pie is no bad dish."

The large honeyeaters called wattlebirds were especially esteemed, appearing for sale at markets in Sydney, Melbourne and Hobart. Gould said of the yellow wattlebird that "hundreds are annually sent to the markets of Hobart Town for the purposes of the table. It is highly prized as an article of food, and in winter becomes excessively fat."

In Victoria, short-tailed shearwaters were enormously popular, and they are known to this day as "muttonbirds". Nestlings and eggs were brought by the boatload from Bass Strait islands to Melbourne markets, and a quota of squabs are still sold in Melbourne delicatessens to this day.

Colonial Australians even ate the flesh of reptiles. Turtle soup was a delicacy served by the best restaurants,

In January 1845 Ludwig Leichhardt recorded in his journal: "A sleeping lizard with a blunt tail and knobby scales, fell into our hands, and was of course greedily eaten." The lizard, of course, was a shingleback (*Tiliqua rugosus*), that sluggish lizard of outback plains. Photographed at Nyngan, New South Wales.

and turtle steaks were sold as novelties in Cairns fish shops as late as the 1950s. Bushmen ate snakes and goannas, and the tail of the latter was considered a treat. Hungry explorer Ludwig Leichhardt even ate a shingleback (*Tiliqua rugosa*): "A sleeping lizard with a blunt tail and knobby scales, fell into our hands, and was of course greedily eaten."

Colonial writer J. Bonwick, noting the propensity of Australians to eat huge amounts of meat, thought it was all due to the weather: "Meat is largely eaten . . . by Europeans in this country; for, though the climate is hot, the air is dry and salubrious."

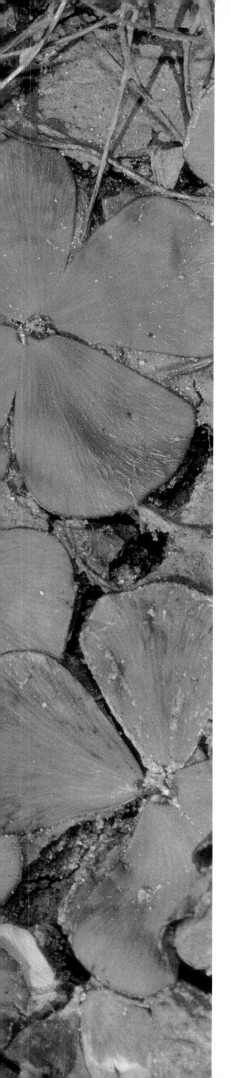

EPILOGUE

CONSERVATION

212

CONSERVATION

Previous pages: Fossil-like, a nardoo plant (*Marsilea drummondii*) grows flush with the mud, where it has been left by an evaporating pool of water. Nardoo benefits from land degradation, growing readily in roadside ditches and in pools formed after rain on parched desert pastures. Photographed at Caccory Ruins north of Birdsville.

Right: An abandoned bilby burrow in the desert north of Birdsville bears silent witness to human abuse of the land. In western Queensland cattle graze over all the country inhabited by bilbies, reducing the vegetation that supplies their food.

John Gould, the great nineteenth-century naturalist, thought highly of the desert bandicoot known as the bilby. " . . . its flesh is sweet and delicate," he declared in *The Mammals of Australia*. "When boiled it resembles that of the rabbit; prejudice would therefore be the only obstacle to its general adoption as an article of food, and this surely might easily be combated. I trust from what I have said, that a sufficient hint has been thrown out to induce those who have the opportunity to import it into Europe."

Gould's hint was never taken up, much to our regret. For what was last century a common outback bandicoot, found south as far as Adelaide, is now an endangered species, lingering precariously in a few northern deserts. Introduced foxes, cattle grazing and changing fire patterns threaten its survival.

Gould's book is a treasure house of information about the culinary attributes of Australian marsupials—and a chilling testimony to how much we have lost. Gould described the aromatic meat of the banded hare-wallaby, now extinct on the mainland, and spoke enthusiastically of the barred bandicoot—"delicate and excellent food"—another marsupial endangered by human impact. Of the rare bridled nailtail wallaby he proclaimed: ". . . its flesh, like that of the other small Kangaroos, is excellent, and

The desert-dwelling bilby has become a symbol of Australia's endangered animals, and it is difficult to believe this beautiful bandicoot was once eaten by colonists. In the deserts around Birdsville, where this bilby was photographed, their numbers are still declining.

when procurable was eaten by me in preference to other meat." Gould dined on this wallaby in south-eastern Australia, where it lives no longer, having vanished throughout its range except for one vulnerable colony in central Queensland. Disturbance to its habitat has rendered it rare.

Native birds have also suffered the European onslaught. In the 1850s, magpie geese, considered "capital eating", were sold in Melbourne markets for twelve to fifteen shillings a pair. Professional hunters shot the geese in swamps around Melbourne, where they roosted in tea-tree scrubs. Nowadays magpie geese do not breed south of Rockhampton, 1400 kilometres to the north. They have not been seen near Melbourne since 1911, and their nesting colonies in Victoria, South Australia and New South Wales have long vanished.

The memoirs of the nineteenth-century Victorian hunter Horace Wheelwright help explain why. He described a good day's shoot in December 1852, when he and a companion shot forty quail, twenty-two snipe, six pigeons, eight ducks, three night herons, two black cockatoos, eight parrots, three coot, two moorhen and a rail. Wheelwright lamented that game was rapidly disappearing from all settled districts and that "in a few years the shooter's occupation in Victoria will be gone".

Magpie geese are still common in northern Australia; other birds have not been so lucky. The dwarf emus of Kangaroo and King Islands, miniature species just over a metre high, were completely exterminated for their meat. The same fate befell the Lord Howe Island pigeon. Not even a skin of this

Visitors to Kakadu from southern States are usually impressed by the sight of magpie geese and do not realise that these handsome birds once bred in swamps as far south as Melbourne. Photographed at Yellow Waters, Kakadu National Park.

An elegant wildflower, the twining fringed lily (*Thysanotus patersonii*), is a common component of lily fields in southern woodlands. The clearing of forests and hungry cattle, sheep and rabbits have converted most lily fields to paddocks of weeds.

Especially vulnerable to introduced grazing animals are soft-leaved forest lilies, such as this rarely seen fringed lily (*Thysanotus fractiflexus*) found only on Kangaroo Island.

bird survives, and we know what it looked like only from a single nineteenth-century painting.

Food plants have been affected too. Tuberous lilies and orchids have vanished from grazed fields in southern Australia. In the outback, hungry camels have taken their toll on quandong trees, and rabbits have decimated the doubah and the desert truffle. In Victoria, pigfaces have almost gone from the inland plains. The early settler E. M. Curr described a plain in Victoria, thirty miles (50 kilometres) across, covered in ripe pigface fruit, but noted in 1883 that "The plant is now nearly, if not quite, extinct in that locality".

Of the vanishing food plants, especially

significant to Aborigines was murnong. In Victoria the sweet tubers were a staple food, gathered in vast numbers. Early colonists spoke of seeing "millions of murnong or yam, all over the plain", and noted that "the wheels of our dray used to turn them up by the bushel".

But as soon as sheep were turned onto the plains the murnong disappeared. Curr noted that "several thousand sheep not only learnt to root up these vegetables with their noses, but they for the most part lived on them for the first year, after which the root began gradually to get scarce". Witnesses to a committee of inquiry into the Aborigines in Victoria testified that murnong and other staples (like lilies) had become exceedingly scarce. Murning is now all but extinct on Victoria's grassy plains.

The Australian bush is in a sorry state. The destruction wrought by sheep, cattle and other introduced animals, by weeds, clearing, logging and changing fire patterns, has damaged every habitat, over the length and breadth of the continent.

Australia has proved especially vulnerable to introduced mammals because our own mammal fauna is so distinctive. Ours is the only continent originally without hard-hoofed animals, native rabbits, cats, foxes and pigs. These introduced pests have devastated the native fauna by preying upon it, by competing for food, and by compacting soil and destroying undergrowth. Their impact, combined with massive habitat disturbance, has triggered extinctions on a scale unprecedented in recorded history. No other continent has lost so many animals in so short a time.

If that were the end of the matter it would be bad enough. But Australians continue to degrade their fragile land. Forests are still being felled and river systems destroyed by dams. Massive, environmentally untenable tourist developments threaten the remaining wetlands of the east coast. Governments no longer allow exotic animals to be brought in, yet new ornamental plants flow in without restriction, some of them destined to become tomorrow's bushland weeds.

For thousands of years a staple food of Victoria's Aborigines, murnong (*Microseris scapigera*) is now uncommon in that State. One colonist lamented that the Aborigines' "murnong and other valuable roots are eaten by the white man's sheep, and their deprivation, abuses and miseries are daily increasing".

A lonely murnong seed head in the Mount Lofty Ranges awaits a passing breeze to cast aloft its seeds. In many disturbed forests the seed heads of introduced flatweeds are more in evidence.

Nature writers often contrast the devastation wrought by white Australians with the care for the land shown by Aborigines. Australia's original inhabitants lived harmoniously with the wilderness, they say. But it can be argued that traditional Aborigines, within the limits of their technology, were as destructive as we have been. Rather than cherishing a concept of wilderness, a uniquely modern idea, the Aborigines transformed the continent by regular use of fire. They seasonally burnt out undergrowth, destroying small plants and animals, changing vegetation structure, and singeing back areas of rainforest. Nearly all the explorers spoke of Aborigines "burning, burning, ever burning", as Ernest Giles put it in 1889. Fire was the Aborigines' most powerful tool, and they employed it to the greatest effect.

Aborigines acted in other ways that were not environmentally harmonious. In the deserts they sometimes overharvested plant foods, leading to local extinctions of desert kurrajongs, desert palms and shrubs harbouring witchetty grubs. They introduced Australia's first feral animal, the dingo, thereby committing to extinction the mainland populations of the so-called Tasmanian wolf and Tasmanian devil. Their spears may have exterminated the diprotodon and other giant lumbering mammals.

It made good sense for Aborigines to burn the land. Fires swept away undergrowth, making walking and hunting easier, creating new feed for prey, and encouraging the growth of food plants. Fire was a dramatic form of disturbance that released nutrients locked up in the forests, rendering them available to the plants and animals on which the Aborigines fed.

Aborigines everywhere and in all flammable habitats lit fires. That burning could increase food supplies in every habitat across Australia says much about the niche occupied by Aborigines—that of opportunistic foragers, benefiting from disturbance, this being largely of their own making.

It is significant that a large share of Aboriginal food plants are opportunists— plants adapted to growing along habitat fringes and in soils disturbed, not only by fires, but by storms, floods and tree falls. Yams, edible herbs, many rainforest fruits, and most fruits of seashores and deserts are plants of this kind. Examples include the cresses, pigweed, pigfaces, coast beard heath, nitre bush, wild tomatoes, raspberries, candlenut, long yam and cunjevoi. These plants have largely benefited from European disturbance, and some are more common today than two hundred years ago. They are all quick-growing nutritious plants that grab the nutrients released when stable forest systems are disturbed.

Most of the foods of Europeans also hail from disturbed habitats. Our vegetables are descended from quick-

growing herbs of forest clearings; domesticated cattle, pigs and chickens are bred from animals that fed in those clearings. Our farms mimic the conditions found in nature where environments are disturbed.

Indeed, it seems the human niche is largely that of an opportunistic omnivore, a predator on the plants and animals that thrive on disturbance. There is nothing unusual in this: many animals do the same. But what sets us apart from other opportunists, and bodes ill for the future, is that we actively create our own disturbances. Aborigines scorched the land and we now clear and despoil it. This appears to be the way of the human species—it is our nature to disrupt. By so doing we increase the productivity of the land, which is then able to support more people, leading to more degradation. For those who care about such things as wilderness and bilbies, this is an ugly equation. Whether we can change our ways remains to be seen.

A beneficiary of land misuse, nitre bush (*Nitraria billardieri*) thrives on degraded pastures, in old wheat fields, and along roadsides in farming districts. This spiky fruit-bearing shrub is almost certainly increasing in frequency in southern Australia's agricultural belt.

WILD FOOD NUTRIENTS

In the 1980s Australia's wild foods attracted international attention when a sample of Northern Territory green plums (*Terminalia ferdinandiana*) scored world record amounts of vitamin C. With up to sixty times the ascorbic acid of oranges, the fruits may prove a viable commercial source of this vitamin.

Analyses of Australian bush foods began in earnest only in the 1980s, when testing was begun by the Human Nutrition Unit at the University of Sydney and the Food Science Section of the Department of Defence Support in Tasmania. The latter were testing tropical bush foods likely to be encountered by Australian soldiers repelling an Asian invasion, and Major Les Hiddens was their supplier. The following tables present some of the results of both teams, supplemented by earlier tests by P. Maggiore of the Western Australian Institute of Technology in behalf of Nicolas Peterson, and more recent tests for Peter Latz.

The figures show that Australia's wild foods are nutritionally comparable to cultivated foods. Some foods are exceptionally rich in ascorbic acid and thiamine, but others are very low in these and other nutrients. A large number of bush foods are rich in minerals, scoring high levels of iron, potassium, calcium and zinc.

The figures in these tables represent single plant or animal samples, not averaged figures. Great variations between samples can be expected. For example, the two analyses of wild tomatoes (*Solanum chippendalei*) by Peterson show very different vitamin C levels of 58.74 and 12.16 mg respectively per 100 grams. Some of the nutritional figures quoted in the text of this book are taken from tests other than those recorded here, and, accordingly, are slightly different.

Where necessary, kilocalories have been converted to kilojoules as follows: 1 kcal = 4.184 kj.

Page opposite: An artichoke thistle bud (*Cynara cardunculus*).

PLANT	PLANT PART	ENERGY (kj)	WATER (g)	PROTEIN (g)	FAT (g)	CARBOHYDRATE (g)
Mulga (*Acacia aneura*)	Seed	–	9.1	27.6	5.8	53.8
Wattle (*Acacia dictyophleba*)	Seed	1513	11.2	26.8	6.3	49.0
Candlenut (*Aleurites moluccana*)	Seed	2426	24.4	7.8	49.9	–
Bunya pine (*Araucaria bidwillii*)	Seed	906	42.7	9.1	1.9	42.6
Kurrajong (*Brachychiton populneus*)	Seed	1455	5.6	18.1	24.7	14.6
Bulbine lily (*Bulbine bulbosa*)	Tuber	177	83.5	29.0	0.2	7.5
Moreton Bay chestnut (*Castanospermum australe*)	Seed	873	59.9	3.8	2.9	–
Bush cucumber (*Cucumis melo*)	Fruit	140	88.9	1.4	1.2	4.5
Cycad (*Cycas media*)	Seed	537	73.6	4.1	3.2	–
Nalgoo (*Cyperus bulbosus*)	Tuber	1134	31.5	2.9	1.0	62.5
Chocolate lily (*Dichopogon strictus*)	Tuber	233	84.0	1.8	0.1	12.4
Tree fern (*Dicksonia antarctica*)	Stem core	255	–	1.6	0.6	12.3
Round yam (*Dioscorea bulbifera*)	Tuber	163	67.9	2.4	0.2	7.2
Spike rush (*Eleocharis dulcis*)	Tuber	648	45.4	2.6	0.8	35.9
Woollybutt grass (*Eragrostis eriopoda*)	Seed	1499	8.8	17.3	0.6	70.7
Rock fig (*Ficus platypoda*)	Fruit	–	8.2	3.8	2.5	81.5
Red bopple nut (*Hicksbeachia pinnatifolia*)	Seed	639	60.0	3.6	3.0	29.2
Desert peppercress (*Lepidium* species)	Leaf, stem	624	51.5	8.63	1.11	25.1
Burrawang cycad (*Macrozamia communis*)	Seed	362	57.2	7.3	0.2	14.4
Waterlily (*Nymphaea* species)	Tuber	867	46.8	3.1	0.3	–
Wild panicum (*Panicum decompositum*)	Seed	–	9.3	12.5	3.8	65.2
Stinking passionfruit (*Passiflora foetida*)	Fruit	650	59.8	6.5	0.7	–
Burdekin plum (*Pleiogynium timorense*)	Fruit	376	75.9	1.0	2.6	–
Pigweed (*Portulaca oleracea*)	Leaf, stem, seed	136	89.0	2.09	0.37	4.9
Pigweed (*Portulaca oleracea*)	Seed	–	10.0	19.8	10.4	55.4
Wild raspberry (*Rubus fraxinifolius?*)	Fruit	–	78.4	–	tr	–
Desert quandong (*Santalum acuminatum*)	Fruit	345	76.7	1.7	0.2	19.3
Sandalwood (*Santalum lanceolatum*)	Fruit	646	62.9	4.8	4.4	24.4
Bush raisin (*Solanum centrale*)	Fruit (dried)	1252	28.82	8.44	5.53	53.92
Wild tomato (*Solanum chippendalei*)	Fruit	355	77.81	2.47	0.33	18.01
Wild tomato (*Solanum chippendalei*)	Fruit	30	81.7	1.38	0.54	15.54
Tamarind (*Tamarindus indica*)	Fruit	1211	19.3	3.7	–	–
Green plum (*Terminalia ferdinandiana*)	Fruit	432	72.0	1.1	0.1	25.6
Bulrush (*Typha* species)	Rhizome	277	69.9	2.8	0.1	14.1
Maloga bean (*Vigna lanceolata*)	Root	361	76.0	2.82	0.31	17.5
Grass tree (*Xanthorrhoea australis*)	Stem core	759	–	3.5	0.3	41.3

ANIMAL	ANIMAL PART	ENERGY (kj)	WATER (g)	PROTEIN (g)	FAT (g)	CARBOHYDRATE (g)
Bogong moth (*Agrotis infusa*)	whole moth	1260	49.2	26.8	19.8	1.5
Magpie goose (*Anseranas semipalmata*)	egg	807	70.2	11.9	14.6	3.1
Flatback turtle (*Chelonia depressa*)	flesh	468	71.2	25.4	1.5	0.4
Gall (*Cystococcus* species)	larva	523	77	4.9	1.1	–
Lerp	scale (plus larva?)	1269	25	0.7	0.7	73.3
Honeypot ants (*Melophorus* species)	abdomen	1104	32.5	1.7	0.9	–
Green tree ants (*Oecophylla smaragdina*)	larva	450	71.6	15.6	0.8	–
Native bee (*Trigona* species)	honey	1790	13.2	5.8	7.7	–
Sand goanna (*Varanus* species)	tail	736	61.8	29.2	5.7	1.8
Mussel (*Vecesumio angati*)	flesh	–	79	11.6	–	–
Witchetty grub (*Xyleutes* species?)	whole grub	1730	40.7	8.7	34.9	16

FIBRE (g)	SODIUM (mg)	POTASSIUM (mg)	MAGNESIUM (mg)	CALCIUM (mg)	IRON (mg)	VITAMIN C (mg)	SOURCE
–	117.1	316.6	–	78.0	–	–	Latz (1982)
–	83.6	220.8	–	88.3	–	–	Peterson (1978)
–	–	–	–	–	–	tr	James (1983)
2.6	9.0	194.0	62	7.0	4.0	–	Brand, Cherikoff & Truswell (1985)
33.5	8.0	567.0	288	110.0	2.1	–	Brand, Cherikoff & Truswell (1985)
4.6	8.0	130.0	18	275.0	8.1	–	Brand & Cherikoff (1985)
–	–	–	–	–	–	0	James (1983)
3.0	7.0	378.0	27	24.0	1.7	1.4	Brand & Cherikoff (1985)
–	–	–	–	–	–	tr	James (1983)
–	85.6	380.6	–	63.1	–	–	Peterson (1978)
1.2	4.0	106.0	18	10.0	3.3	–	Brand & Cherikoff (1985)
–	–	–	–	–	–	–	Cane, Stockton & Vallance (1979)
21.4	6.0	207.0	23	12.0	1.5	–	Brand & Cherikoff (1985)
12.9	29.0	250.0	20	–	–	–	Brand et al. (1983)
–	36.1	144.5	–	40.1	–	–	Peterson (1978)
–	40.2	437.3	–	65.2	–	–	Latz (1982)
3.2	8.0	237.0	45	259.0	2.7	–	Brand, Cherikoff & Truswell (1985)
–	–	1665.0	–	455.0	–	–	Dadswell (1934)
19.7	5.0	291.0	60	4.0	5.6	–	Brand, Cherikoff & Truswell (1985)
–	–	–	–	–	–	tr	James (1983)
–	53.7	140.0	–	87.5	–	–	Latz (1982)
–	–	–	–	–	–	5.0	James (1983)
–	–	–	–	–	–	5.0	James (1983)
–	–	709.0	–	112.0	–	5.0	Dadswell (1934)
–	157.6	221.8	–	391.1	–	–	Latz (1982)
–	–	–	–	–	–	tr	James (1983)
–	51.0	659.0	40	42.0	tr	–	Brand et al. (1983)
2.5	–	–	–	–	–	16.4	Brand et al. (1983)
–	119.0	195.0	–	46.0	–	–	Peterson (1977)
–	19.31	564.67	–	80.94	–	58.74	Peterson (1977)
–	36.16	418.72	–	66.61	–	12.16	Peterson (1977)
–	–	–	–	–	–	0	James (1983)
–	18.0	52.0	53	43.0	11.5	3150.0	Brand et al. (1983)
12.2	–	–	–	–	–	–	Brand & Cherikoff (1985)
–	–	774.0	–	177.0	–	–	Dadswell (1934)
–	–	–	–	–	–	–	Cane, Stockton & Vallance (1979)

SODIUM (mg)	POTASSIUM (mg)	MAGNESIUM (mg)	CALCIUM (mg)	IRON (mg)	THIAMINE (mg)	SOURCE
22	281	132	219	12	–	Cherikoff, Brand & Truswell (1985)
110	89	9	27	3.8	0.14	Cherikoff, Brand & Truswell (1985)
54	303	18	4	1	0.04	Cherikoff, Brand & Truswell (1985)
–	–	–	–	–	455	James (1983)
69.6	75.6	–	16.5	–	–	Peterson (1978)
–	–	–	–	–	302	James (1983)
–	–	–	–	–	238	James (1983)
–	–	–	–	–	38	James (1983)
9	324	21	119	2.9	0.04	Cherikoff, Brand & Truswell (1985)
36	27	19	324	6	tr	Cherikoff, Brand & Truswell (1985)
5	201	27	9	11.7	–	Cherikoff, Brand & Truswell (1985)

BIBLIOGRAPHY

Altman, J. C. The dietary utilisation of flora and fauna by contemporary hunter–gatherers at Momega Outstation, north-central Arnhem Land. *Australian Aboriginal Studies* (1), 1984: 35–46.

Angas, G. F. *Savage Life and Scenes in Australia and New Zealand.* Smith, Elder, London, 1847.

Backhouse, J. *A Narrative of a Visit to the Australian Colonies.* Hamilton Adams, London, 1843.

Bailey, F. M. *The Queensland Flora,* vols 1–6. H. J. Diddams & Co., Brisbane, 1899–1902.

Beaglehole, J. C. (ed.) *The Endeavour Journal of Joseph Banks 1768-1771.* Angus & Robertson, Sydney, 1962.

Bradley, W. *A Voyage to New South Wales . . . 1786-1792.* Ure Smith, Sydney, 1969.

Brand, J. C. & Cherikoff, V. Australian Aboriginal bushfoods: The nutritional composition of plants from arid and semi-arid areas. *Australian Aboriginal Studies* (2), 1985: 38–46.

Brand, J. C., Cherikoff, V. & Truswell, A. S. The nutritional composition of Australian Aboriginal bushfoods. 3. Seeds and nuts. *Food Technology in Australia* **37**, 1985: 275–279.

Brand, J. C., Rae, C., McDonnell, J., Lee, A., Cherikoff, V., & Truswell, A. S. The nutritional composition of Australian Aboriginal bushfoods 1. *Food Technology in Australia* **35**, 1983: 293–298.

Breton, R. N. *Excursions in New South Wales, Western Australia, and Van Dieman's Land . . .* Bentley, London, 1833.

Bunce, D. *Travels with Dr Leichhardt.* Oxford, Melbourne, 1979.

Cane, S., Stockton, J. and Vallance, A. A note on the diet of Tasmanian Aborigines. *Australian Archaeology* **9**, 1979: 77–81.

Cherikoff, V., Brand, J. C. & Truswell, A. S. The nutritional composition of Australian Aboriginal bushfoods. 2. Animal foods. *Food Technology in Australia* **37** (5), 1985: 208–211.

Cleland, J.B. The ecology of the Aboriginal in South and central Australia, *in* B. C. Cotton (ed.), *Aboriginal Man in South and Central Australia,* part 1. Government Printer, Adelaide, 1966.

Collins, D. *An Account of the English Colony in New South Wales.* Cadell & Davies, London, 1798.

Crawford, I. M. *Traditional Aboriginal Plant Resources in the Kalumburu Area.* Western Australian Museum, Perth, 1982.

Cribb, A. B. & Cribb, J. W. *Wild Food in Australia.* Collins, Sydney, 1974.

Cunningham, P. *Two Years in New South Wales.* H. Colburn, London, 1827.

Curr, E. M. *The Australian Race.* Government Printer, Melbourne, 1886.

Dadswell, I. W. The chemical composition of some plants used by Australian Aborigines as food. *Australian Journal of Experimental Biology and Medical Science* **12**, 1934: 13–18.

Dawson, J. *Australian Aborigines.* George Robertson, Melbourne, 1881.

Duncan-Kemp, A. *Our Sandhill Country.* Angus & Robertson, Sydney, 1933.

Everist, S. L. *Poisonous Plants of Australia.* Angus & Robertson, Sydney, 1974.

Eyre, E. J. *Journals of Expeditions of Discovery into Central Australia, and Overland from Adelaide to King George's Sound, in the Years 1840-1,* 2 vols. T. & W. Boone, London, 1845.

Gott, B. Ecology of root use by Aborigines of southern Australia. *Archaeology in Oceania* **17**, 1982: 59–67.

Gott, B. Murnong—*Microseris scapigera*: A study of a staple food of Victorian Aborigines. *Australian Aboriginal Studies* (2), 1983: 2–18.

Gould, J. *The Mammals of Australia.* Macmillan, Melbourne, 1983.

Grey, G. *Journals of Two Expeditions of Discovery in North-west and Western Australia during the years 1837, 38, and 39,* 2 vols. T. & W. Boone, London, 1841.

Hynes, R. A. and Chase, A. K. Plants, sites and domiculture: Aboriginal influence upon plant communities in Cape York Peninsula. *Archaeology in Oceania* **17** (1), 1982: 38–50.

Isaacs, J. *Bush Food.* Weldon Publishing, Sydney, 1987.

James, K. W. Analysis of indigenous Australian foods. *Food Technology in Australia* **35**, 1983: 342–343.

Labillardière, J. *Voyage in Search of La Pérouse.* Stockdale, London, 1800.

Lamp, C. & Collet, F. *Weeds in Australia.* Inkata Press, Melbourne, 1976.

Latz, P. K. Bushfires and bushtucker: Aborigines and plants in central Australia. M.A. thesis, University of New England, 1982.

Leichhardt, L. *Journal of an Overland Expedition in Australia, from Moreton Bay to Port Essington, a Distance of Upwards of 3000 miles, during the Years 1844–1845.* T. & W. Boone, London, 1847.

Leigh, J., Boden, R. & Briggs, J. *Extinct and Endangered Plants of Australia.* Macmillan, Melbourne, 1984.

Levitt, D. *Plants and People: Aboriginal Uses of Plants on Groote Eylandt.* Australian Institute of Aboriginal Studies, Canberra, 1981.

Low, T. *Wild Herbs of Australia & New Zealand.* Angus & Robertson, Sydney, 1985.

Low, T. Explorers and poisonous plants, in J. Covacevich, P. Davie and J. Pearn (eds), *Toxic Plants & Animals: A Guide for Australia.* Queensland Museum, Brisbane, 1987.

Low, T. *Wild Food Plants of Australia.* Angus & Robertson, Sydney, 1988.

Mann, D. D. *The Present Picture of New South Wales.* Booth, London, 1811.

Maiden, J. H. *The Useful Native Plants of Australia, (including Tasmania).* Trubner & Co., London, 1889.

Maiden, J. H. Some plant-foods of the Aborigines. *Agricultural Gazette of New South Wales* **9** (4), 1898: 349–354.

Maiden, J. H. Native food plants. *Agricultural Gazette of New South Wales,* 1900: **10** (2): 115–130; **10** (4): 279–290; **10** (7): 618–629; **10** (8): 730–740.

Meagher, S. J. The food resources of the Aborigines of the south-west of Western Australia. *Records of the Western Australian Museum* **3**, 1974: 14–65.

Meredith, Mrs C. *Notes and Sketches of New South Wales.* Ure Smith, Sydney, 1973.

Mitchell, T. L. *Three Expeditions into the Interior of Eastern Australia, with Descriptions of the Recently Explored Region of Australia Felix, and of the Present Colony of New South Wales.* Boone, London, 1839.

Mitchell, T. L. *Journal of an Expedition into the Interior of Tropical Australia, in Search of a Route from Sydney to the Gulf of Carpentaria.* Longman, Brown, Green & Longmans, London, 1848.

Mueller, F. von. *Introduction to Botanic Teachings at the Schools of Victoria.* Government Printer, Melbourne, 1877.

Mueller, F. von. *Select Extra-tropical Plants.* Government Printer, Sydney, 1881.

Mundy, G. C. *Our Antipodes.* Bentley, London, 1855.

Nixon, F. R. *The Cruise of the Beacon.* Bell & Daldy, London, 1857.

O'Connell, J. F., Latz, P. K., & Barnett, P. Traditional and modern plant use among the Alyawara of central Australia. *Economic Botany* **37**, 1983: 80–109.

Parker, K. L. *The Euahlayi Tribe.* Archibald Constable, London, 1905.

Peile, A. R. Gugadja Aborigines and frogs. *Herpetofauna* **10** (1), 1978: 9–14.

Peterson, N. The traditional pattern of subsistence to 1975, *in* B. S. Hetzel & H. J. Frith (eds), *The Nutrition of Aborigines in Relation to the Ecosystem of Central Australia.* CSIRO, Melbourne, 1978.

Peterson, N. Aboriginal uses of Australian Solanaceae, *in* J. G. Hawkes, R. N. Lester & A. D. Skelding (eds), *The Biology and Taxonomy of the Solanaceae.* Linnean Society Symposium, Series 7. Academic Press, London, 1979.

Petrie, C. C. *Tom Petrie's Reminiscences of Early Queensland.* Watson, Ferguson & Co., Brisbane, 1904.

Phillip, A. *The Voyage of Governor Phillip to Botany Bay.* Stockdale, London, 1789.

Pratt, A. *The Flowering Plants, Grasses, Sedges, and Ferns, of Great Britain . . .* Warne, London, 1891.

Rawson, Mrs L. *Australian Enquiry Book.* Kangaroo Press, Sydney, 1984.

Roth, W. E. Food: Its search, capture and preparation. *North Queensland Ethnography* **3**, 1901: 1–31.

Roth, W. E. Notes of savage life in the early days of West Australian settlement. *Proceedings of the Royal Society of Queensland* **17**, 1903: 45–69.

Schurmann, C. W. The Port Lincoln Tribe, *in The Native Tribes of South Australia.* E. S. Wigg & Son, Adelaide, 1879.

Smyth, R. B. *Aborigines of Victoria.* Government Printer, Melbourne, 1878.

Stephens, E. The Aborigines of Australia. *Journal of the Royal Society of New South Wales* **23**, 1889: 476–502.

Tench, W. *Sydney's First Four Years.* Angus & Robertson, Sydney, 1961.

Thomson, D. F. The Bindibu expedition: Exploration among the desert Aborigines of Western Australia. *Geographical Journal* **128**, 1962: 1–14.

Wheelwright, H. W. *Bush Wanderings of a Naturalist.* Routledge, Warne & Routledge, London, 1861.

White, J. *Journal of a Voyage to New South Wales.* Debrett, London, 1790.

Woolls, W. *A Contribution to the Flora of Australia.* F. White, Sydney, 1867.

Worgan, G. B. *Journal of a First Fleet Surgeon.* Library Council of New South Wales, Sydney, 1978.

INDEXES

INDEX OF SCIENTIFIC NAMES

INDEX OF COMMON NAMES

PHOTOGRAPHIC CREDITS
(Numbers refer to pages)
All photographs were taken by the author, apart from the following:
Bruce Cowell 38–9, 65 (top), 80–1, 126–7
Richard Daintree 24–5, 104, 139 (below)
Thomas Dick 82
Glen Fergus 171 (top) 176 (below)
Owen Foley 5, 6 (top), 91 (below), 107 (below), 193, 199 (right), back flap photo of author
Bruce Fuhrer 164 (both), 165
Tom & Pam Gardner 213
Trevor Hawkeswood 42 (top left)
Trevor Hawkeswood & Tim Low 89, 185 (below), 188 (top right)
Chris & Sandra Pollitt 131 (top), 192, 195 (top), 197 (top right), 198 (top), 199 (left), 205, 207 (right), 208 (both)
Queensland Herbarium 68 (top)
Queensland Museum 194 (top), 195 (below), 201 (below), 207 (left), 212 (below)
Peter Slater 9 (top)
Raoul Slater 197 (top left), 197 (below)
Steve Wilson 200 (top left), 209 (top)
Anon. 200 (below), 206 (top)